Disability Human Rights Law

Special Issue Editor
Anna Arstein-Kerslake

MDPI

Special Issue Editor
Anna Arstein-Kerslake
Melbourne Law School,
University of Melbourne
Australia

Editorial Office
MDPI AG
St. Alban-Anlage 66
Basel, Switzerland

This edition is a reprint of the Special Issue published online in the open access journal *Laws* (ISSN 2075-471X) in 2016 (available at: http://www.mdpi.com/journal/laws/special_issues/Disability_Human_Rights_Law).

For citation purposes, cite each article independently as indicated on the article page online and as indicated below:

Author 1; Author 2; Author 3 etc. Article title. *Journal Name*. **Year**. Article number/page range.

ISBN 978-3-03842-389-8 (Pbk)
ISBN 978-3-03842-388-1 (PDF)

Table of Contents

About the Guest Editor

Anna Arstein-Kerslake is an academic at Melbourne Law School and the Convenor of the Hallmark Disability Research Initiative (DRI) at the University of Melbourne. She is the founder of the Disability Human Rights Clinic (DHRC) at Melbourne Law School. She holds a Ph.D. in Law from the National University of Ireland, Galway (NUIG), a J.D. from the City University of New York (CUNY) School of Law and a B.A. in Sociology from San Diego State University (SDSU). Prior to joining Melbourne University, she held a Marie Curie Research Fellowship at the Centre for Disability Law and Policy (CDLP) at (NUIG). She has participated widely in consultation with governments and other bodies, including the United Nations Committee on the Rights of Persons with Disabilities, the United Kingdom Ministry of Justice, Amnesty Ireland, Interights, the Mental Disability Advocacy Center, among others. Anna has worked as a human rights advocate on a number of different projects, including legislative drafting, strategic litigation, policy development, scholarly work, and others.

Preface to "Disability Human Rights Law"

Human rights law has traditionally been siloed into individual rights and community rights. Historical politics have forced civil and political rights to be conceived separately from social, economic, and cultural rights. This has caused an unnecessary tension between these groups of rights and has convoluted the implementation and realization of human rights. The Convention on the Rights of Persons with Disabilities (CRPD) has broken down the distinction between individual and community rights–between civil and political and social, economic, and cultural rights. It has ushered in a new era of human rights law and instigated a new field of study: disability human rights law.

This new field is an interdisciplinary amalgamation of human rights law, disability studies, and disability rights law. It views rights in a novel way, opening a new line of scholarly inquiry. It sees rights as they apply to the individual, with regard to the individual's particular abilities, needs, and circumstances. The traditional, and often archaic, rights boundaries are broken down. Civil and political rights exist entwined with social, economic, and cultural rights. The rights of the community and the rights of the individual are often indistinguishable and dependent upon one another. It is the epicenter of a new wave of rights protection.

This book focuses on this new field. The aim of the book is to begin to explore the potential of Disability Human Rights Law to transform modern human rights law. The first chapter, written by Professor Theresia Degener, Vice Chair of the United Nations Committee on the Rights of Persons with Disabilities, lays out the foundations of this new rights landscape. She explores the history of the disability rights movement and the move from a medical model to a social model of disability. She argues for the adoption of a human rights model of disability and highlights the benefit of such a model for providing actual guidelines on how best to realize the rights of people with disability–which previous models were lacking. The next 10 chapters cover different areas of human rights law where the CRPD has provided new guidance and interpretation.

Anna Arstein-Kerslake
Guest Editor

laws

MDPI

Article

Disability in a Human Rights Context

Theresia Degener

Department of Social Work, Education and Diaconia, Protestant University of Applied Sciences, Bochum 44803, Germany; degener@evh-bochum.de; Tel.: +49-234-3690-1172

Academic Editor: Anna Arstein-Kerslake
Received: 23 May 2016; Accepted: 12 July 2016; Published: 25 August 2016

Abstract: The Convention on the Rights of Persons with Disabilities (CRPD) is a modern human rights treaty with innovative components. It impacts on disability studies as well as human rights law. Two innovations are scrutinized in this article: the model of disability and the equality and discrimination concepts of the CRPD. It is argued that the CRPD manifests a shift from the medical model to the human rights model of disability. Six propositions are offered why and how the human rights model differs from the social model of disability. It is further maintained that the CRPD introduces a new definition of discrimination into international public law. The underlying equality concept can be categorized as transformative equality with both individual and group oriented components. The applied methodology of this research is legal doctrinal analysis and disability studies model analysis. The main finding is that the human rights model of disability improves the social model of disability. Three different models of disability can be attributed to different concepts of equality. The medical model corresponds with formal equality, while the social model with substantive equality and the human rights model can be linked with transformative equality.

Keywords: disability law; human rights; models of disability; discrimination; reasonable accommodation; accessibility; models of equality; human rights model of disability; substantive equality; transformative equality

1. Introduction

The United Nations Convention on the Rights of Persons with Disabilities (CRPD) [1] of 2006 has had profound impact on disability law and human rights law globally. With 162 State Parties the Convention has reached more than 80% universal ratification for its 10th anniversary. Most State Parties have reviewed and revised domestic disability law and have established National Monitoring Mechanisms as prescribed by the Convention. The CRPD seeks to bring about a paradigm shift in disability policy that is based on a new understanding of disabled persons as right holders and human rights subjects. The theoretical background for this change is a modern model of disability as developed in disability studies and recent group oriented approaches in modern human rights law. According to Article 1 the purpose of the CRPD "to promote, protect and ensure the full and equal enjoyment of all human rights and fundamental freedoms by all persons with disabilities, and to promote respect for their inherent dignity." It is the first human rights instrument which acknowledges that all disabled persons are right holders and that impairment may not be used as a justification for denial or restrictions of human rights. Such an approach recognizes that disability is a social construct which is created when impairment interacts with societal barriers. It is based on a new thinking about disability which is usually described as a paradigm shift from the medical to the social model of disability. The theoretical background is disability studies, a multidisciplinary research school that has emerged from disability rights movements in the UK and USA some 30 years ago. The debate about medical versus social model of disability has been the central focus during the first two decades and several scholars have emphasized that disability studies have moved on to new, less dichotomist models such as the political/relational approach of Alison Kafer ([2], p. 7). While it is true that the dichotomy between medical and social model of disability is an outdated subject for disability studies discourse, it has gained new attention within legal discourse. During the negotiations of the CRPD the medical and social model played a pivotal role. During the first decade of its existence the CRPD has been the catalyst for many law and policy reforms, which relate to the shift from, medical to the social model of disability. It is important to understand the new model of disability, which is supposed to be the foundation of modern disability law. Hence it is necessary to address the issue of disability model again. During the negotiations, reference was usually made to the social model of disability, which should replace the medical model of disability. While the latter reduces disability to a medical phenomenon of impairment, the first takes a social-contextual approach to disability. Persons with disabilities are described as "those who have long-term physical, mental, intellectual or sensory impairments which in interaction with various barriers may hinder their full and effective participation in society on an equal basis with others."([1], art. 1). Disability as a social construct is the main feature of the social model of disability. However, it is opined that the CRPD is based on the human rights model of disability, which moves beyond the social model.

The CRPD also significantly impacts on international human rights law and its system. The CRPD Committee, established in 2009, consists of 18 independent experts of whom all but one, are disabled persons. No other treaty body has had such a high number of experts with impairments. As a consequence accessibility of UN buildings and information and communication systems became an issue. A Secretariat-Wide Inter-Departmental Task Force on Accessibility has been established and several resolutions on making the United Nations more accessible and inclusive for persons with disabilities have been adopted [3]. The CRPD is a modern human rights treaty with many innovative provisions. For example, State Parties have to establish a national human rights mechanism, the Convention allowed the EU to become a member as a regional integration organization, it has two standalone development provisions, but most significantly it modernizes international equality law ([1], art. 11, 32, 33, 42). As Andrea Broderick has analyzed recently: "From a theoretical and comparative perspective, it can be said with certainty that the CRPD goes further in its approach to equality than previous international human rights instruments" ([4], p. 149).

The purpose of this article is twofold. First, my goal is to show that the CRPD is based on the human rights model of disability which builds on the social model but develops it further. Secondly, I wish to demonstrate that the Convention introduces a new equality concept into international human rights law, which can be categorized as transformative equality.

2. The Disability Model of the CRPD[1]

Since the 1960s, there have been many different models of disability in scientific literature. The medical (bio)-model, the social model, the economic model, the minority group model, the universalist model, the Nordic relational model, the capabilities model and others. All these models attempt to understand and occasionally explain or define disability.[2]

The most important models of disability in the English-speaking world have been the medical and the social model of disability. Both models were developed by scholars of disability studies during the 1970s and 1980s in the UK and the USA. With the adoption of the United Nations Convention on the Rights of Persons with Disability (CRPD), a new model emerged which is the human rights model of disability.

The medical model of disability, which the CRPD tries to overcome, regards disability as an impairment that needs to be treated, cured, fixed or at least rehabilitated. Disability is seen as a deviation from the normal health status. Exclusion of disabled persons from society is regarded as an

---

[1] Part 2 and 3 of this article are an updated version of an earlier publication, see [5]. I thank Maria Bergh, Michele Friedner, Piers Gooding, Susan Schweik, Tom Shakespeare and Gerard Quinn for helpful comments on this earlier version.

[2] For an overview of these and other models see ([6], pp. 61–181; [7]; [8], pp. 15–28).

individual problem and the reasons for exclusion are seen in the impairment. Disability according to the medical model remains the exclusive realm of helping and medical disciplines: doctors, nurses, special education teachers, and rehabilitation experts. Michael Oliver, one of the founding fathers of the social model of disability, has called this the ideological construction of disability through individualism and medicalization, the politics of disablement [9]. Another feature of the medical model of disability is that it is based on two assumptions that have a dangerous impact on human rights: (1) disabled persons need to have shelter and welfare; and (2) impairment can foreclose legal capacity. The first assumption legitimizes segregated facilities for disabled persons, such as special schools, living institutions or, sheltered workshops. The second assumption has led to the creation of mental health and guardianship laws that take an incapacity approach to disability [10,11]. During the negotiations of the CRPD, the medical model served as a determent. While there was often no consensus among stakeholders which way to go in terms of drafting the text of the convention, there was overall agreement that the medical model of disability definitely was not the right path [12,13]. Rather the social model of disability was supposed to be the philosophical basis for the treaty. The paradigm shift from the medical to the social model has often been stated as the main achievement of the CRPD. However, while it is true that the social model of disability has been the prevalent reference paradigm during the negotiation process, my understanding of the CRPD is that it goes beyond the social model of disability and codifies the human rights model of disability.

The social model of disability explains disability as a social construct through discrimination and oppression. Its focus is on society rather than on the individual. Disability is regarded as a mere difference within the continuum of human variations. The social model differentiates between impairment and disability. While the first relates to a condition of the body or the mind, the second is the result of the way environment and society respond to that impairment. Exclusion of disabled persons from society is politically analyzed as the result of barriers and discrimination.

3. The Difference between the Social and the Human Rights Model

While I do not claim ownership of the terminology, the human rights model of disability appeared in an article on international and comparative disability law reform that I wrote together with Gerard Quinn 1999/2000 and in the background study to the CRPD that we edited in 2001. In a chapter called "Moral Authority for Change", we wrote:

> Human dignity is the anchor norm of human rights. Each individual is deemed to be of inestimable value and nobody is insignificant. People are to be valued not just because they are economically or otherwise useful but because of their inherent self-worth...The human rights model focuses on the inherent dignity of the human being and subsequently, but only if necessary, on the person's medical characteristics. It places the individual center stage in all decisions affecting him/her and, most importantly, locates the main "problem" outside the person and in society [14].

In this background study to the CRPD, we did not discuss whether there is a difference between the social and the human rights model of disability. I think there is and I have six propositions in this regard.

3.1. Proposition 1: Disability Is a Social Construct but Human Rights Do Not Require a Certain Health or Body Status

First, whereas the social model merely explains disability, the human rights model encompasses the values for disability policy that acknowledges the human dignity of disabled persons. Only the human rights model can explain why human rights do not require absence of impairment.

The social model of disability was created as one explanation[3] of exclusion of disabled people from society. It has been developed as a powerful tool to analyze discriminatory and oppressive structures of society. To use Michael Oliver's words:

> Hence, disability according to the social model, is all the things that impose restrictions on disabled people; ranging from individual prejudice to institutional discrimination, from inaccessible public buildings to unusable transport systems, from segregated education to excluding work arrangements, and so on. Further, the consequences of this failure do not simply and randomly fall on individuals but systematically upon disabled people as a group who experience this failure to discrimination institutionalised throughout society [16].

This sociological explanation of disability may lay the foundation for a social theory of disability. However, the social model does not seek to provide moral principles or values as a foundation of disability policy. The CRPD, however, seeks exactly that. According to article 1 CRPD the purpose of the treaty is "to promote, protect and ensure the full and equal enjoyment of all human rights and fundamental freedoms by all persons with disabilities, and to promote respect for their inherent dignity." In order to achieve this purpose, eight guiding principles of the treaty are laid down in article 3 CRPD and the following articles tailor the existing human rights catalogue of the International Bill of Human Rights[4] to the context of disability. Human rights are fundamental rights. They cannot be gained or taken away from an individual or a group. They are acquired qua birth and are universal, i.e., every human being is a human rights subject. Neither social status, nor identity category, nor national origin or any other status can prevent a person from being a human rights subject. Therefore, human rights can be called unconditional rights. It does not mean that they cannot be restricted but it means that they do not require a certain health status or a condition of functioning. Thus, human rights do not require the absence of impairment. The CRPD reflects this message in its preamble and in the language of its articles. For example, when the universality of all human rights for all disabled persons is reaffirmed ([1], preamble para. c), or when it is recognized that the human rights of all disabled persons, including those with more intensive supports needs, have to be protected ([1], preamble para. j). The article on the rights to equal recognition as a person before the law with equal legal capacity ([1], art. 12, para. 1 and para. 2) is of course another example of this assumption.

Thus, the human rights model of disability defies the presumption that impairment may hinder human rights capacity. The social model of disability also acknowledges the importance of rights ([16], p. 63) and has often been associated with the rights based approach to disability as opposed to needs based or welfare approach to disability policy [17–20]. However, non-legal scholars of disability studies have emphasized that the social model of disability is foremost not a rights-based approach to disability but extends beyond rights to social relations in society, to the system of inequality ([21]; [22], p. 23). They do, however, concede that social model advocates have supported struggles for civil rights and anti-discrimination legislation ([16], pp. 152–56; [22], p. 23).

3.2. Proposition 2: Human Rights Are More Than Anti-Discrimination

Secondly, while the social model supports anti-discrimination policy civil rights reforms, the human rights model of disability is more comprehensive in that it encompasses both sets of human rights, civil and political as well as economic, social and cultural rights.

The social model of disability served as a stepping-stone in struggles for civil rights reform and anti-discrimination laws in many countries ([18], p. 6; [23], pp. 10–13; [24]). Meanwhile, the social model of disability has become officially recognized by the European Union as the basis for its disability

---

[3] Other models are e.g., the normalization principle, the minority model, or the Nordic relational model [15].
[4] Consisting of three human rights instruments: Universal Declaration of Human Rights, International Covenant on Civil and Political Rights and International Covenant on Economic, Social and Cultural Rights.

policy [25]. Within disability studies, this rights based approach in disability was characterized as a tool for stipulating citizenship and equality [16]. To demand anti-discrimination legislation was a logical consequence of analyzing disability as the product of inequality and discrimination. In the US, where the social model of disability was conceptualized as the minority group model [26], the fight for civil rights was similarly seen as a way to disclose the true situation of disabled persons as members of an oppressed minority. The focus on rights was perceived as an alternative to needs based social policy that portrayed disabled persons as dependent welfare recipients. The ideology of dependency was coined by Michael Oliver as an essential tool of social construction of disability ([16], p. 83). Thus, anti-discrimination legislation was seen as a remedy to a welfare approach to disability. Disabled persons could thus be described as citizens with equal rights. Architectural barriers could be defined as a form of discrimination. Segregated schools could be described as apartheid. The shift from welfare legislation to civil rights legislation in disability policy became the focus of disability movements in many countries [18,20,27]. "We want rights not charity" was and still is a slogan to be heard around the world from disability rights activists.

However, anti-discrimination law can only be seen as a partial solution to the problem. Even in a society without barriers and other forms of discrimination, people need social, economic and cultural rights. People need shelter, education, employment or cultural participation. This is true for all human beings, and thus for disabled persons. However, because impairment often leads to needs for assistance, it is especially true that disabled persons need more than civil and political rights. While welfare policies and laws in the past have failed to acknowledge and empower disabled persons as citizens [28], laws on personal assistance services or personal budgets proofed that even classical social laws can give choice and control to disabled persons ([29], pp. 15–20; [30,31]). It is thus illustrative that the global independent living movement has always phrased their demands in terms of broader human rights, rather than in terms of pure anti-discrimination rights. The human rights model of disability includes both sets of human rights: political, and civil and economic, and cultural rights. These two baskets of human rights, which have been adopted as distinct categories of human rights during the cold war area for political reasons,[5] are fully incorporated in the CRPD as they are in the Universal Declaration of Human Rights (UDHR) of 1948 [33]. The legal hierarchy of civil and political rights over economic, social and cultural rights is slowly but steadily decreasing through international jurisprudence and the strengthening of monitoring and implementation of the International Covenant on Economic, Social and Cultural Rights (ICESCR) [34].

A major milestone was the coming into force of an individual complaints procedure for economic, social and cultural rights in 2012 enabling the United Nations "to come full circle on the normative architecture envisaged by the Universal Declaration of Human Rights."[6] The universality, indivisibility and interdependence of all human rights were firmly established as a principle of international human rights law on the World Conference of Human Rights two decades earlier in Vienna [36]. The CRPD is a good example of the indivisibility and interdependence of both sets of human rights. It not only contains both sets of human rights, the text itself is evidence of the interdependence and interrelatedness of these rights. Some provisions on rights cannot be clearly allocated to one category only. For instance, the right to be regarded as a person before the law ([1], art. 12) is a right commonly regarded as a civil right ([33], art. 6; [37], art. 16). However, article 12 (3) CRPD speaks of support measures disabled persons might need to exercise their legal capacity. Are these support measures realized by social services which fall into the economic, social and cultural rights sphere? Another example would be the right to independent living ([1], art. 19). It is one of the few rights of the CRPD which has no clear equivalent in binding pre-treaty law. The right to independent living and being included in the community is an answer to human rights violations against disabled persons

---

[5]   For an illustrative account of the political history of human rights, see [32].
[6]   Statement by Mr. Ivan Simonovic, Assistant Secretary-General, see [35].

through institutionalization and other methods of exclusion, such as hiding in the home or colonizing at distant places. The concepts of independent living and community living do not root in mainstream human rights philosophy, which is why the terms cannot be found in the International Bill of Human Rights but in international soft law related to disability that preceded the CRPD. The concept derives from the disability rights movement and other social movements such as the deinstitutionalization movement[7], which came into being in the 1960s and 1970s in the United States, Scandinavia, Italy and many other countries [38–40]. The common catalogue of human rights of the UDHR does not contain a right to independent or community living. If at all, the right to independent living can be traced back to the freedom to choose one's residence, which in other treaties is usually linked to the freedom of movement and designed as a pure civil right.[8] However, independent living requires—among others—personal assistance services, which are measures to realize social rights. Thus, the CESCR Committee has interpreted the right to an adequate standard of living ([34], art. 11) to include a right to independent living for disabled persons. However, it has also linked the issue to anti-discrimination measures. Its General Comment No.5 interprets article 11 ICESCR as a right to "accessible housing" and to "support services including assistive devices" which enable disabled persons "to increase their level of independence in their daily living and to exercise their rights." ([44], para. 33). During the last 15 years, there has been an influx of publications on deinstitutionalization, the right to independent and community living and the member state obligations under article 19 CRPD [31,39,40,45,46]. Most legal publications characterized this article as a social right with strong freedom and autonomy components. In the words of the Council of Europe Commissioner of Human Rights, Thomas Hammarberg who has published an issue paper on article 19:

> The core of the right...is about neutralising the devastating isolation and loss of control over one's life, brought on people with disabilities because of their need for support against the background of an inaccessible society. "Neutralising" is understood as both removing the barriers to community access in housing and other domains, and providing access to individualized disability-related supports on which enjoyment of the right depends for many individuals ([47], p. 11).

The CRPD Committee has not qualified the right to independent living yet as either civil or social human right. While the CRPD contains the progressive realization clause usually applied to state responsibility regarding social, economic and cultural rights, it also includes a reminder that even economic, social and cultural rights are immediately applicable under some circumstances in public international law.[9] The upcoming General Comment on article 19 CRPD will probably address this issue.

3.3. Proposition 3: Impairment Is to Be Recognized as Human Variation

As a third argument, I would state: Whereas the social model of disability neglects the fact that disabled persons might have to deal with pain, deterioration of quality of life and early death due to impairment, and dependency, the human rights model of disability acknowledges these life circumstances and demands them to be considered when social justice theories are developed.

The social model of disability has been criticized for neglecting the experience of impairment and pain for disabled people and how it affects their knowledge and their identity. Both the dichotomy of impairment and disability as well as the materialist focus of the social model have been criticized,

---

[7] Which in some countries was part of the disability rights movement, in other countries it was not.

[8] Art. 13(1) UDHR: "Everyone has the right to freedom of movement and residence within the border of each State." [41]. See also Art. 12(1) ICCPR, Art. 5(d), (i) CERD, Art. 15(4) CEDAW [37,42,43].

[9] Art. 4(2) CRPD reads: "With regard to economic, social and cultural rights, each State Party undertakes to take measures to the maximum of its available resources and, where needed, within the framework of international cooperation, with a view to achieving progressively the full realization of these rights, without prejudice to those obligations contained in the present Convention that are immediately applicable according to international law." [1].

especially by feminist disabled writers such as Jenny Morris. In her famous book *Pride against Prejudice*, she claims:

> However, there is a tendency within the social model of disability to deny the experience of our own bodies, insisting that our physical differences and restrictions are *entirely* socially created. While environmental barriers and social attitudes are a crucial part of our experience of disability—and do indeed disable us—to suggest that this is all there is to it is to deny the personal experience of physical or intellectual restrictions, of illness, of the fear of dying. A feminist perspective can help to redress this, and in so doing give voice to the experience of both disabled men and disabled women ([48], p. 10).

In a later publication, she writes:

> If we clearly separate out disability and impairment, then we campaign against the disabling barriers and attitudes which so influence our lives and the opportunities which we have. This does not justify, however, ignoring the experience of our bodies, even though the pressures to do this are considerable because of the way that our bodies have been considered as abnormal, as pitiful, as the cause of our lives not being worth living...In the face of this prejudice it is very important to assert that autonomy is not destiny and that it is instead the disabling barriers "out there" which determine the quality of lives. However, in doing this, we have sometimes colluded with the idea that the "typical" disabled person is a young man in a wheelchair who is fit, never ill, and whose only needs concern a physically accessible environment ([49], p. 9).

Other writers followed this path of criticism. Marian Corker and Sally French who brought discourse analysis to disability studies added that besides neglecting the importance of impairment, the social model fails to "conceptualize a mutually constitutive relationship between impairment and disability which is both materially and discursively (socially) produced."([50], p. 6). Many other disability studies scholars have shared this critique. Bill Hughes and Kevin Paterson proposed to develop a sociology of impairment based on post-structuralism and phenomenology as a response to this dilemma of impairment/disability dichotomy [51]. Tom Shakespeare has challenged the dichotomy on the basis that both are socially constructed and inextricable interconnected ([52], pp. 72–91). The founders and advocates of the social model have emphasized that the social model of disability was never meant to ignore impairment. Michael Oliver states: "This denial of the pain of impairment has not, in reality, been a denial at all. Rather it has been a pragmatic attempt to identify and address issues that can be changed through collective action rather than professional and medical treatment." ([16], p. 38).

However, he also contends that the social model is not a social theory of disability which when developed should contain a theory of impairment ([16], p. 42).

The human rights model of disability has not been brought into this debate yet. The CRPD does not make any statement regarding impairment as a potential negative impact on the quality of life of disabled persons because the drafters were very determined not to make any negative judgment on impairment. However, persons with higher support needs are mentioned in the preamble ([1], preamble para. (j)) as a reminder that they must not be left behind and that the CRPD is meant to protect all disabled persons not only those who are "fit" for mainstreaming. Impairment as an important life factor is also recognized in two of the principles of the treaty, though both principles do not mention impairment explicitly. Article 3 (a) introduces "respect for the inherent dignity...of persons" and paragraph (d) refers to "respect for difference and acceptance of persons with disabilities as part of human diversity and humanity." Respect for human dignity is one of the cornerstones of international human rights and domestic constitutional law today. It was introduced in many human rights catalogues after World War II as a response to the atrocities of the Nazi Regime and today is recognized as a core value of the United Nations [53]. However, it needs to be recognized that the CRPD relates to the concept of human dignity more often than other human rights treaties. Respect for the human dignity of disabled persons is the purpose and one of the eight guiding principles of the treaty ([1], art. (1), (3)(a)). In addition, it is referred to five times in such various contexts such as discrimination ([1], Preamble para. h)), awareness raising ([1], art. 8(1)(a)), recovery from violence ([1], art. 16(4)), inclusive education ([1], art. 24(1)(a)) and care delivery by health professionals ([1], art. 25(d)). Further, recognition of the "inherent dignity and worth and the equal and inalienable rights of all members of the human family" are regarded as the "foundation of freedom, justice and peace in the world." ([1], preamble para. (a)).

The diversity principle of article 3 CRPD is a valuable contribution to human rights theory in that it clarifies that impairment is not to be regarded as a deficit or as a factor that can be detrimental to human dignity. Thus, the CRPD is not only build on the premise that disability is a social construct, but it also values impairment as part of human diversity and human dignity. At this point, I think the human rights model goes beyond the social model of disability. This recognition is important as a fundamental premise for answering ethical questions that are triggered by the way society treats impairment, such as euthanasia, prenatal diagnosis, or medical normalization treatment. As we have stated in our background study:

> The human rights model focuses on the inherent dignity of the human being and subsequently, but only if necessary, on the person's medical characteristics. It places the individual centre stage in all decisions affecting him/her and, most importantly, locates the main "problem" outside the person and in society. The "problem" of disability under this model stems from a lack of responsiveness by the State and civil society to the difference that disability represents. It follows that the State has a responsibility to tackle socially created obstacles in order to ensure full respect for the dignity and equal rights of all persons ([14], p. 14).

Another important aspect of the principle of human dignity is that it reaffirms that all human beings are right-bearers. As Lee Ann Basser has pointed out, this is particularly important for disabled people who have long been denied this status. She refers to Dworkin's conceptualization of rights as special entitlements as "trumps" [54], and says if rights are trumps "then dignity is the key that turns the lock and allows entry into society and require that each person be treated with equal concern and respect in that society." ([55], p. 21). The international disability rights movement has fought for the CRPD for more than two decades. I think the long time struggle for a human rights treaty was not only a fight of DPOs for political change but also an individual struggle of disabled people for recognition and respect in the sense of Axel Honneth's recognition theory [56]. According to Honneth, political struggles of social movements always have a collective and an individual dimension. The individual dimension relates to the struggle as a process of identity formation, which needs to be facilitated by self-respect, self-confidence and self-esteem. The struggle for human rights of disabled persons is thus a struggle for the global collective of disabled people but also a fight for respect and recognition of the disabled individual by society. The human rights model of disability clarifies that impairment does not derogate human dignity nor does it encroach upon the disabled person's status as rights-bearer. Therefore, I think, the human rights model of disability is more appropriate than the social model to encompass the experience of impairment, which might not always be bad but certainly can be. It also allows us to analyze politics of disablement as the denial of social and cultural recognition, which is an aspect of the critique of the social model of disability [57,58]. The human rights model of disability demands that impairment is recognized in theories of justice. Whether these are social contract theories, take a capability approach or take an ethics of care as their basis is another matter.[10]

---

[10] For a combination of capabilities and other approaches see [59].

4. Proposition 4: Multiple Discrimination and Layers of Identity Are to Be Acknowledged

Fourthly, the social model of disability neglects identity politics as a valuable component of disability policy whereas the human rights model offers room for minority and cultural identification.

The social model also has been criticized for neglecting identity politics as a valuable component of emancipation. Identity politics can be defined as politics which values and cares for differences among human beings and allows persons to identify positively with features that are disrespected in society. Gay pride, black pride, feminism, or disability culture are manifestations of these identity politics. The social model of disability does not provide much room for these issues because its focus is not on personal emancipation but on social power relations. Identity politics in the context of disability can have several meanings. The term might relate to impairment categories or impairment causes. Deaf people have created their own culture and deaf studies have become an important strand of disability studies in which deaf identity plays an important role [60,61]. Like deaf or hard of hearing persons, blind and deafblind people were among the first groups who created their own organizations who are still operative today [62,63] and so are many other impairment-related organizations.

Another identity factor in the context of disability might be the difference between acquired and congenital impairment. To be born blind or deaf or physically or intellectually impaired is very different from becoming disabled through illness, accident, violence or poverty. Further, some impairments or "disorders" may come along with unique experiences of exclusion and identity. For example, Peter Beresford, who identifies as a mental health user, argued for a social model of madness, way before the CRPD came into being [64]. Finally, identity may be shaped by more than impairment, but also by gender, "race", sexual orientation and identity, age or religion. Disabled women were among the first to criticize the disability rights movement (and the women's movement) for neglecting other identity features [48,65–67]. Disabled people of color followed [68] and authors like Ayesha Vernon raised the issue of intersectional discrimination and multi-dimensional oppression [69].

Impairment related identity policy has been seen with suspicion by social model proponents because these organizations were either seen as apolitical self-help groups or as another example of the medicalization of disability. Anita Silvers found identity politics unsuitable for disabled persons because of the heterogeneous constituency of the disability community or because other identity constructs such as women's roles as caretakers or child-bearers are commonly denied to disabled individuals [70]. Tom Shakespeare has offered a helpful summary of further criticism against identity politics and the harm it might do to disability politics ([52], pp. 92–110).

Other systems of oppression such as sexism and racism have been acknowledged as an important factor in constructing identity and social status from the beginning of the social model of disability ([16], pp. 70–78), but it has been admitted that the social model of disability was not intended to cover all different experiences of oppression ([16], p. 39).

Human rights instruments are at least partly the political response to collective experiences of injustice. The history of human rights law as it developed after World War II shows that identity based social movements were strong players in the making of international law [71,72]. The current core human rights treaties are a manifestation of this process. The International Convention on the Elimination of All Forms of Racial Discrimination (CERD) of 1965 as well as the International Convention on the Protection of the Rights of All Migrant Workers and Members of Their Families (CRMW) of 1990 are responses to colonization and racism, the Convention on the Elimination of All Forms of Discrimination Against Women (CEDAW) of 1979 is the response to sexism, the Convention on the Rights of the Child (CRC) of 1989 is the answer to adultism and the CRPD is the answer to ableism. The development of these thematic human rights treaties have been called the personification [73] and the pluralization ([74], p. 77) of human rights. These treaties were adopted because human rights politics and theory as developed on the basis of the International Bill of Human Rights were based predominantly on the experiences of western, white, male, nondisabled adults and ignored the experiences of other individuals. This ignorance was and is a reflection of different systems of subordination that run alongside axes of inequality such as "race", gender, sexuality, body and mind functioning. The emergence of social movements that opposed these systems of subordination brought with it the birth of critical studies such as gender studies, critical race studies and disability studies. Human rights law as moral law and as ideology is not only a reflection of political conflict among states or a reflection of global and domestic power relations, it is also a tool for social transformation. Whether successfully or not, may be debated, but it is important to acknowledge these different functions of human rights law. The current human rights treaties may be the outcome of World War II and cold war conflicts, but they also reflect emancipation and democratic gains of social movements. Feminism for example did have a major impact on international public law in theory and practice during the last decades. The artificial distinction between private and public spheres of life and the assumption that states only hold responsibility for violations in the public sphere were successfully challenged by feminist international lawyers. The public/private distinction in international law is the result of the hegemony of male experiences of human rights violations. Human rights violence taking place in the private sphere, such as domestic violence, where ignored within the first four decades of international human rights law. Feminist legal scholars such as Hilary Charlesworth, Christine Chinkin [75] and Catherine MacKinnon [76] have successfully argued that this artificial distinction not only ignores women's experiences but that it also serves to hide state complicity with the perpetrators and that this legal doctrine stabilizes patriarchal subordination. Feminist critical race lawyers such as Mari Matsuda [77] and Angela Harris [78] have taken feminist legal theory a step further by introducing anti-essentialist approaches to civil rights law. Thus, I would argue that current human rights law is rather the result of human rights law becoming truly universal than seeing these group specific human rights instruments as testimony "that there is something specific about these groups...which...*cannot* be taken adequately into account by human rights instruments that have the ambition to covering the whole human genre."([79], p. 497, emphasis in the original).

The human rights model of disability as based on the existing canon of core human rights treaties gives consideration to different layers of identity. It acknowledges that disabled persons may be male or female, non-whites, disabled, children or migrants. It is clear that there are more layers of identity to be considered in international human rights law and that the issue of intersectionality of discrimination has yet to be solved [80,81].

In addition to human rights law in general, the CRPD also acknowledges different layers of identity within the context of disability and human rights. For instance, disabled children and disabled women have their own stand-alone articles. ([1], art. 6 and art. 7) The women's article even acknowledges "that women and girls with disabilities are subject to multiple discrimination" which is the first binding intersectionality clause in a human rights treaty. Further recognition of gender and age can be found throughout the treaty.[11] Other grounds, such as "race", color, language, religion, political or other opinion, national, ethnic, indigenous or social origin, property, or birth and age are, however, only recognized in the preamble ([1], preamble para. (p)). For these and other layers of identity—such as age or sexual orientation—lobbying was not strong enough during the negotiations.

A few impairment-related groups are recognized though. These are deaf, blind and deafblind persons. Article 30 CRPD on cultural participation demands that states recognize and support their "specific culture and cultural identity, including sign languages and deaf culture." ([1], art. 30(4)). The other context in which deaf, blind and deafblind persons are specifically mentioned is the right to education. Article 24 CRPD demands that persons who belong to these impairment groups are provided with the tools to education that are adequate to their identity, such as Braille and sign language ([1], art. 24(3)(a) and (b)), that they are provided with role models and qualified teachers and the most disputed paragraph reads:

---

[11] Women and girls with disabilities are mentions in the following provisions: Preamble para. (p), (q), (r), (s); Art. 3(g), (h); Art. 4(3); Art. 8(2)(b); Art. 13; Art. 16(2), (3), (5); Art. 18; Art. 23(1)(b), (c), (3), (5); Art. 25 (b), Art. 28; Art. 29; Art. 34 CRPD [1].

(1)...States Parties shall ensure an inclusive education system at all levels and lifelong learning directed to:

...

(c) Ensuring that the education of persons, and in particular children, who are blind, deaf or deafblind, is delivered in the most appropriate languages and modes and means of communication for the individual, and in environments which maximize academic and social development.

...

I remember very well the long nights we fought over the wording of this paragraph in the Ad Hoc Committee. The World Blind Union, the World Federation of the Deaf and the World Federation of the Deafblind were all represented with superb experts. We had long debates about whether or not there should be a human right to special education or at least a right to choose between mainstream and special education. The opinions oscillated between "segregation is always and inherently unequal" and "mainstream education means assimilation which means for many bad education." These debates were loaded with identity issues and it showed us that it was important to make room for it.

The final text is a true compromise and in my opinion a masterpiece. The credit for it goes to a large extent to Rosemary Kayess, an eminent international lawyer and disability rights activist from Australia, who acted as a facilitator to the article on the right to education.

4.1. Proposition 5: Prevention Policy Can Be Human Rights Sensitive

My fifth argument is that while the social model of disability is critical of prevention policy, the human rights model offers a basis for assessment when prevention policy can be claimed as human rights protection for disabled persons.

Prevention of impairment is an element of public health policy which has long been criticized by disability rights activists as being stigmatizing or discriminatory. The object of critique can be the mode of implementation of public health policy or the goals. While prevention of traffic accidents or polio is not seen as problematic, the ways these policies are proclaimed can be stigmatizing towards disabled persons. For instance, if advertisement for safe driving is accompanied by a poster of a quadriplegic person titled: "Being crippled for the rest of your life is worse than death", disabled persons are abused as determent. Another example are vaccination campaigns against polio which utilize slogans such as "Oral vaccination is sweet, polio is cruel!" Public health campaigns like these led to fierce protest from the disability rights movement in the 1970s and 1980s in several countries. The goals of medical prevention programs can be the target of protest if it has to do with life or death issues such as selective abortion or assisted suicide. The message that some see conveyed with these programs is that a life with a disability is not worth living. What is claimed as prevention of impairment policy is in fact a policy that aims at eliminating disabled persons. Michael Oliver has characterized these programs as the core of ideological construction of disability [16]. Feminist disability studies scholars have written widely on the conflicts between women's right to reproductive autonomy and disabled people's right to non-discrimination [81–84]. This particular difficult subject also came up during the negotiations of the CRPD but was dropped due to time pressure and the unlikelihood to achieve a compromise on this matter with pro-life advocates[12] and many feminists in the room.

Unlike the UN World Programme of Action Concerning Disabled Persons (WPA) of 1982 [85] and the UN Standard Rules on the Equalization of Opportunities for Persons with Disabilities of 1993 (StRE) [86], the CRPD does not refer to impairment prevention as a matter of disability policy. These two declarations are the most important human rights instruments preceding the CRPD. At the time of their adoption, they marked a milestone in the eventual recognition of human rights of disabled persons because they added a human rights component to traditional disability policy. The latter

---

[12] The Vatican is a UN member state and the delegation took a very active role in this matter.

consisted of a three-tiered approach to disability: definition, prevention and rehabilitation. The WPA and the StRE added a fourth element to disability policy: equality of opportunities. However, both instruments refer to prevention of impairment as an element of disability policy and include prenatal care as an important measure ([85], para. 13 and 52–56; [86], para. 22). Especially the WPA has been influenced not only by an upcoming international disability rights movement ([87], pp. 97–99), but also by health professionals. This is revealed by the fact that the Leeds Castle Declaration on the Prevention of Disablement of 12 November 1981 is cited almost in full length in the WPA text ([85], para. 54). This declaration which was written by a group of scientists, doctors, health administrators and politicians praises biomedical research as "revolutionary new tools which should greatly strengthen all interventions." ([85], para. 54). The WPA even includes a paragraph on the cost effectiveness of prevention programs: "It is becoming increasingly recognized that programmes to prevent impairment or to ensure that impairments do not escalate into more limiting disabilities are less costly to society in the long run than having to care later for disabled persons."[13]

The WPA has been criticized for perpetuating the medical model of disability ([88], p. 278; [89]). While the WPA and StRE are both referenced in the preamble of the CRPD ([1], preamble para. f)), prevention does not appear prominently in the text of the treaty. This was a deliberate decision taken during and before the negotiations ([13], p. 120). The purpose of the CRPD is to promote and to protect the rights of persons who have a disability. It was argued that it was incoherent to deal with prevention of disability in the same instrument. Thus, with the adoption of the CRPD, it was made clear that primary prevention of impairment might be an important aspect of the right to health ([34], art. 12) as enshrined in the ICESCR, but that it is certainly not an appropriate measure to protect the human rights of people living with a disability. This is an important message to member states who claim that they spend a lot of money for disabled persons and then submit reports which show that a large part of the budget is spent on impairment prevention policy.

However, as Tom Shakespeare has pointed out [52], not all impairment prevention policy is bad, and most disabled persons actually are in need of this kind of public health policy. In fact, the 2011 WHO World Report on Disability gives evidence that disabled persons experience poorer level of health due to a variety of factors, such as inaccessible health care services, risk of developing secondary conditions, higher risk of being exposed to violence, increased rates of health risk behavior ([90], pp. 57–60). This is also recognized in the CRPD in the context of the rights to health. There prevention is addressed not with relation to primary prevention but to secondary prevention programs to "prevent further disabilities including among children and older persons" ([1], art. 25 (b)). Article 25 CRPD is an example of framing the right of health of disabled persons in a human rights context. It demands equal access to general and specialized health care services for disabled persons. Services must be community based and sensitive to freedom rights and to the dignity of disabled persons. Discrimination through provision or denial of health care must be prohibited and prevented. As the WHO Report underlines:

Viewing disability as a human rights issue is not incompatible with prevention of health conditions as long as prevention respects the rights and dignity of people with disabilities, for example in the use of language and imagery...Preventing disability should be regarded as a multidimensional strategy that includes prevention of disabling barriers as well as prevention and treatment of underlying health conditions [90], p. 8.

4.2. Proposition 6: Poverty and Disability Are Interrelated but There Is a Roadmap for Change

As a sixth argument, I opine: Whereas the social model of disability can explain why 2/3 of the one billion disabled persons in this world live in relative poverty, the human rights model offers a roadmap for change.

---

[13] WPA para. 55 (emphasis added) [85].

From early on, social model proponents and critics acknowledged the close link between poverty and disability ([16], pp. 12–13). Indeed, the interrelatedness of poverty and disability was put forward as evidence that not only disability but also impairment is a social construct ([52], pp. 34–35). There is now abundance of evidence that impairment and poverty are mutually reinforcing ([90], pp. 10–11). Impairment may increase the risk of poverty and poverty may increase the risk of impairment. Lack of resources, lack of education, dearth of access to fundamental services are among the factors to be considered when trying to understand why 2/3 of the world population of disabled people live in the developing world. The social model has helped to understand that disability is a development issue. Social model advocates and disability studies researchers have had a significant impact on empowerment policies that address these issues ([86], pp. 206–59; [91], p. 15; [92–95]). The United Nations, the World Bank and other development agents have long acknowledged that disability is a development issue [96], however, disability was not mainstreamed in development policies. Thus, disability was initially not recognized as one of the issues in the Millennium Development Goals. Only after the adoption of the CRPD did this change dramatically, and disability became a central subject of international cooperation policy.

The CRPD is the first human rights treaty with a standalone provision on development. Article 32 CRPD on international cooperation was one of the major controversial provisions from the beginning to the end of the negotiations ([13], p. 132). Together with article 11 CRPD on situations of risk and humanitarian emergencies, it provides a solid roadmap for disability policy in international humanitarian und development cooperation. Article 32 CRPD demands that international cooperation is inclusive and accessible to disabled people; that disability is mainstreamed in all development programs; and that DPOs are involved in the monitoring of these activities. Article 11 CRPD demands that states take adequate actions to protect disabled persons in situation of natural disaster or humanitarian emergencies. This latter article was introduced after the Tsunami of 2004 in the Indian Ocean, which led to the death of several hundred thousand human beings, among them many disabled individuals who were excluded from rescue. By the end of the negotiations, the Lebanon war had started in July 2006, which increased the already politicized nature of the article. Under these circumstances, it was amazing to reach consensus on the text of these articles.[14] Both these articles bring at least three important aspects to the development and humanitarian policy: (1) a human rights based approach to development and humanitarian aid; (2) disability mainstreaming as a leitmotif of international cooperation; and (3) the importance of DPO involvement. These aspects are not new, they have been raised before but with the CRPD, they have become binding international law.

A human rights approach in development means that people living in poverty are not objects of welfare and charity but rights holders who have a say in the distribution of resources and needs assessment. Participation is a means, and a goal and strategies need to be empowering. Development projects need to target disadvantaged, marginalized and excluded groups. These are some of the principles that make up the UN common understanding of the human rights based approach to development cooperation which was adopted in 1997 [97]. While the new rights based approach in development is not without shortcomings [98], it is an important step into the direction of achieving social justice in times of globalization. Disability mainstreaming is an important strategy to overcome segregation structures implemented and maintained by traditional disability policies. Without active and equal participation of disabled people and their representative organizations, development strategies and programs will perpetuate and exacerbate discrimination against disabled persons. The impact of the CRPD in combating poverty can be seen in various development policies of State Parties, who have now incorporated disability inclusive development programs in their international cooperation policies. At the international level the impact can clearly be seen in the 2030 Agenda, which

---

[14] Actually, because there could not be reached consensus on a reference to foreign occupation in the treaty—initially in article 11, later in the preamble—this issue was the only part of the treaty which could not be approved by consensus. For details see ([13], p. 125).

was adopted on 25 September 2015 by the UN General Assembly and include the new Sustainable Development Goals (SDG) [99]. While disabled persons were not included in the predecessor, the Millennium Development Goals which were in force until 2015, the 2030 Agenda contains eleven references to persons with disabilities.[15] This gives hope that disabled persons will not be foreclosed from development initiatives and funding streams implementing the 2030 Agenda.

4.3. Developing the Social Model into a Human Rights Model of Disability

My intention is not to abandon the social model of disability, but to develop it further. The social model of disability was the most successful dictum during the negotiations of the CRPD. If there is one single phrase which summarizes the success story of the CRPD, it is that it manifests the paradigm shift from the medical to the social model of disability in international disability policy. Not everyone who used the term during the negotiation process was knowledgeable about disability studies. Indeed, I concur with Rosemary Kayess and Phillip French in their analysis that the enormous influence the social model had during the negotiations has come from a "populist conceptualization of the social model as a disability rights manifesto and its tendency towards a radical social constructionist view of disability, rather than from its contemporary expression as a critical theory of disability." ([12], p. 7). However, given that the drafting of international human rights norms is always a highly political undertaking, the reductionism in the use of the social model is comprehensible. The social model of disability had become the motto of the international disability movement and it served as a powerful tool to demand legal reform. My intention is not to denounce the social model but to carry it further. Like many other human rights projects, the CRPD once planted into this world through adoption by the General Assembly took a life of its own. The impact has been significant in many areas, such as human rights monitoring, international cooperation, accessibility and legal capacity discourse, or inclusive education to name but a few. In our background study, we found that while the disability rights movement had embraced the idea of human rights, many disability rights organizations had not become human rights organizations in terms of agents in the system, comparable to mainstream human rights organizations like Amnesty International or Human Rights Watch ([14], pp. 256–70). Today, DPOs have influential agents in the UN human rights system. Thus, it could be concluded that political activism has turned to human rights and the CRPD is a codification of the human rights model of disability. The Committee has embraced the term human rights model of disability in its concluding observations.[16]

5. CRPD as an Equality Treaty

The CRPD has been modeled on existing treaties, notably the International Covenant on Civil and Political Rights (ICCPR) [37], the International Covenant on Economic, Social and Cultural Rights (ICESCR) [34], the Convention on the Elimination of all Form of Racial Discrimination (CERD) ([102], p. 195), the Convention Against All Forms of Discrimination Against Women (CEDAW) [43], and the Convention on the Rights of the Child (CRC) ([103], p. 3). While first two treaties belong to what is called the International Bill of Human Rights[17] and comprise the globally recognized core catalogue of human rights, the latter are group focused and are of different legal character. CERD and CEDAW are known to be anti-discrimination instruments, CRC is recognized

---

[15] Three instances in the Declaration relating to human rights (para. 19), vulnerable groups (para. 23) and education (para. 25) and seven instances in the SDG: goal 4 (education), goal 8 (employment), goal 10 (reducing inequalities), goal 11 (inclusive cities) goal 17 (means of implementation and data) and one instance in follow up and review relating to data disaggregation (para. 74, (g)) [100].

[16] Concluding Observations on the initial report of Argentina as approved by the Committee at its eighth session (17–28 September 2012), CRPD/C/ARG/CO/1, 8 October 2012, para. 7–8; concluding Observations on the initial report of China, adopted by the Committee at its eighth session (17–28 September 2012), CRPD/C/CHN/CO/1, 15 October 2012, para. 9–10, 16, 54 [101].

[17] Together with the Universal Declaration of Human Rights of 1948 [33].

as a more holistic treaty, comprising more than pure anti-discrimination rights. When the CRPD was negotiated between 2002 and 2006, there was an early consensus, that the legal character shall be a hybrid of both models. Thus, the CRPD demands State Parties to take positive measures with respect to many areas of public and private live, such as infrastructure ([1], art. 9), international cooperation and emergencies ([1], art. 32 and 11), inclusive education and employment ([1], art. 24 and 27), living ([1], art. 19), mobility ([1], art. 20), and decision-making in daily life ([1], art. 12). However, there is no doubt that equality and anti-discrimination is at the heart of the Convention. Every single substantive article includes an equality or anti-discrimination reference, the most typical being "on an equal basis with others". In addition there are two articles specifically dealing with the right to equality and non-discrimination. ([1], art. 5 and 6). Furthermore, equality and discrimination appear in the preamble ([1], preamble, para. (a), (c), (e), (h) (f), (k), (p), (r) and (y)), in the general principles of the Convention ([1], art. 3(b), (e), and (g)) and in the definition article ([1], art. 2). There are at least two reasons for the strong emphasis of equality and non-discrimination in the Convention. There was consensus that the CRPD should not create new human rights or special rights for disabled persons and thus, the goal was to provide human rights for disabled persons on an equal basis with the general population in each member state. Secondly, the shift to non-discrimination and equality reflects the supersession of the medical model with the social model. Recognizing disability as a social construct turns the focus on the elements in our world, which contribute to the social construction of disability. Discrimination is certainly one of the main factors in this regard. However, the CRPD did not stop short at embracing the non-discrimination and equality principles and contextualizing them to disability. It went further, in that it introduced new equality and non-discrimination concepts into international human rights law and a new definition of discrimination.

6. Disability-Based Discrimination Transcending Concepts in International Law

Clauses of non-discrimination and recognition of the right to equality can be found in most of the core international human rights treaties.[18] The right to equality is considered one of the most fundamental human rights in public international law. The early human right treaties do not contain definitions of discrimination. ICPPR and ICESCR both prohibit discrimination and promote equality in several of their provisions ([34], art. 3, 7, 13; [37], art. 2(1), 3, 14, 23, 25, 26),[19] however, the definition of discrimination and equality was left for the treaty bodies to be elaborated in General Comments.[20] Only the more group focused treaties provided for a definition. According to CERD, racial discrimination is defined as "any distinction, exclusion, restriction or preference based on race, colour, descent, or national or ethnic origin which has the purpose or effect of nullifying or impairing the recognition, enjoyment or exercise, on an equal footing, of human rights and fundamental freedoms in the political, economic, social, cultural or any other field of public life." ([1], art. 1 (1)). Similarly, CEDAW defines discrimination against women as "any distinction, exclusion or restriction made on the basis of sex which has the effect or purpose of impairing or nullifying the recognition, enjoyment or exercise by women, irrespective of their marital status, on a basis of equality of men and women, of human rights and fundamental freedoms in the political, economic, social, cultural, civil or any other field." ([103], p. 3, art. 1). The CRPD adopts this definition but goes beyond. Disability-based discrimination is defined as "any distinction, exclusion or restriction on the basis of disability which has the purpose or effect of impairing or nullifying the recognition, enjoyment or exercise, on an equal basis with others, of all human rights and fundamental freedoms in the political, economic, social, cultural, civil or any other field. It includes all forms of discrimination, including denial of reasonable

---

18 For an overview see [104].
19 Art. 2 (1), Art. 3, Art. 14, Art. 23, Art. 25, Art. 26 ICCPR; Art. 2 (2), Art. 3, Art. 7, Art. 13 ICESCR.
20 The Human Rights Committee adopted General Comment No. 4 on equal rights between men and women in 1981 and replaced it with General Comment No. 28 in 2000. General Comment No. 18 on non-discrimination was adopted in 1989. The CESCR adopted GC No. 16 on equal rights of men and women in 2005 and GC No. 20 on non-discrimination in 2010.

accommodation." ([1], art. 2). The latter is defined as "necessary and appropriate modification and adjustments not imposing a disproportionate or undue burden, where needed in a particular case, to ensure to persons with disabilities the enjoyment or exercise on an equal basis with others of all human rights and fundamental freedoms." ([1], art. 2). Thus, the CRPD extends the officially recognized definition of discrimination by explicitly embracing all forms of discrimination and by adding state duties to provide for adjustments and modifications in order to eliminate barriers which prevent disabled persons from equal enjoyment of human rights. Such a duty acknowledges the fact that structural, environmental, communicative or other barriers exist in society which amount to discrimination against disabled persons. In order to combat discrimination it is not sufficient to refrain from "distinction, exclusion or restriction" some active measures need to be taken in order to make society accessible. Similarly article 9 CRPD on accessibility demands that positive measures are taken to eliminate barriers in the built environment, in information and communication and with regard to transportation. In its General Comment No 2 of 2014 on accessibility the CRPD Committee has distinguished the duty to provide reasonable accommodation from the duty to provide accessibility. While the measures for creating accessibility—e.g., building a ramp—might be the same, the personal scope is different. Accessibility duties target groups of disabled persons whereas reasonable accommodation is oriented towards the individual. The duty to provide accessibility is according to the General Comment No 2 "an *ex ante* duty. States parties therefore have the duty to provide accessibility before receiving an individual request to enter or use a place or service. States parties need to set accessibility standards, which must be adopted in consultation with builders and other relevant stakeholders. Accessibility standards must be broad and standardized [105]." In contrast, "[t]he duty to provide reasonable accommodation is an *ex nunc* duty, which organizations of persons with disabilities, and they need to be specified for service-providers, means that it is enforceable from the moment an individual with an impairment needs it in a given situation (workplace, school, etc.) in order to enjoy her or his rights on an equal basis in a particular context. Here, accessibility standards can be an indicator, but may not be taken as prescriptive. Reasonable accommodation can be used as a means of ensuring accessibility for an individual with a disability in a particular situation. Reasonable accommodation seeks to achieve individual justice in the sense that non-discrimination or equality is assured, taking the dignity, autonomy and choices of the individual into account." ([1], general comment No. 2 CRPD/C/GC, 22 May 2014 para. 26). The Committee has also interpreted accessibility as part of the equality principle in that "denial of access to the physical environment, transportation, including information and communication technologies, and facilities and services open to the public should be viewed in the context of discrimination" ([1], general comment No. 2 CRPD/C/GC, 22 May 2014 para. 23). Thus, the non-discrimination and equality concept enshrined in the CRPD has a group component extending the notion of non-discrimination as purely individual. While the right to non-discrimination as enshrined in art. 5 CRPD is designed as a traditional individual right, equality is also understood as a group principle, which needs interaction with representative organizations of persons with disabilities in order to be realized. This group component can be derived from General Comment 2 but also from the text of the Convention itself. More than other human rights treaties, the CRPD gives space to civil society as agents in human rights implementation. Article 4 (3) demands that State parties closely consult with disabled persons and their representative organisations. Similarly, article 33 (3) demands that civil society can fully participate in the national monitoring process. The strong recognition of representative organizations of disabled persons—usually called DPO (disabled persons' organizations)—as instrumental in implementing and monitoring the CRPD can be attributed to the process of negotiation of the treaty. It is well known, that civil society had a particularly high influence in the making of the convention [12,13,106]. Disabled persons were actors in all stake holder groups: Delegations of state parties, non-governmental organizations—most of them being DPOs—UN organizations and National Human Rights Institutions. The majority of disabled experts were representatives of DPOs. At the end of the negotiations, more than 400 NGOs had been accredited to the Ad Hoc Committee, the body in charge of the drafting of the treaty. The "new diplomacy" obtained through negotiations such as the CRPD treaty[21] gives voice to groups who have been invisible in international human rights law because of systemic wide spread discrimination. Giving voices to these groups in international human rights instruments also means to acknowledge that discrimination effects individuals as members of social groups and hence non-discrimination measures need to target individuals and groups. The duty to provide reasonable accommodation and the accessibility obligations as well as the participation provisions relating to DPOs reflects this dual approach to non-discrimination. Both, individuals who are at risk of discrimination as well as their collective voices need to be protected and empowered by non-discrimination measures. In addition, the CRPD is the first human rights treaty to explicitly acknowledge intersectional discrimination. Art. 6 CRPD speaks of multiple discrimination of disabled women and demands that State Party take appropriate measures against it. With relation to disabled women and girls multiple and intersectional discrimination is clearly recognized. Thus, it is acknowledged that individuals experience discrimination as members of a (or several) groups but these groups are not homogenous. All group members are individuals with multiple layers of identities, statuses and life circumstances. Thus, the CRPD provides for a new concept of equality which takes into account individual and structural as well as intersectional discrimination. This new equality concept falls within a modern equality concept that has been called transformative equality ([4], p. 36; [107], p. 56). According to Sandra Fredman transformative equality requires not only the removal of barriers to inclusion but also positive measures to initiate a real change that also addresses hierarchical power relations ([107], p. 115; [108]). Andrea Broderick describes the transformatory approach to equality as seeking to "address the socially constructed barriers, stereotypes, negative customs and practices which hinder the full enjoyment of rights by marginalized groups." ([4], p. 36). The transformative equality concept is distinguished from other concepts of equality, most notably the substantive and the formal equality concept. Formal equality seeks to combat direct discrimination by treating similarly situated persons similar and differently situated persons differently. The problem with the formal equality concept is that it only works when ignorance towards differences among human beings has equality effects. Typically it helps when it results in the eradication of harmful stereotyping. It fails, however, when differences—such as impairment—are taken as rational grounds for denial of rights. Furthermore, the formal equality concept does not recognize the "dilemma of difference" as explained by Martha Minow. According to her the "stigma of difference may be recreated both by ignoring and by focusing on it" ([109], p. 20). The substantive equality model in contrast seeks to address structural and indirect discrimination and takes into account power relations. Discrimination is seen less as an issue of differential treatment but as treatment in the context of domination and oppression. Substantive and transformative equality concepts have much in common, but as Andrea Broderick clarifies, the difference lies in the role for positive measures to change structures and systems ([4], pp. 146–47). While the substantive equality model seeks to combat discriminatory behavior, structures and systems, the transformative equality concept targets changing these structures and systems with a variety of positive measures.

The evolution of these equality concepts coincides with recognition of the social construction of identity markers. Once it was understood that discrimination operates as a process and within hierarchical structures rather than being triggered by immutable and natural personal traits, the shortcomings of the formal equality concept became obvious. Legal theory on discrimination and equality evolved over different eras. For the realm of international human rights law Oddny Mjöll Arnadottir has most convincingly introduced three eras of equality concepts in international human rights law and she describes the CRPD as a "legitimate child" of these developments ([110], p. 47). The first era, which spans from 1950s to the 1970s, she calls universal sameness ([110], p. 47). In this phase, the formal equality concept prevails in which equality rights are linked to sameness and

---

21   According to Sabatello, similar processes of civil society involvement took place in relation to the Rome Statute of the International Criminal Court and the Ottawa Mine Ban Treaty ([97], pp. 239–58).

symmetrical treatment approaches. The second phase runs from the 1970s to 1990s and is called specific difference and the focus is on specific discrimination grounds, which were seen as natural or immutable. During this phase, it is acknowledged that, as an exception to the rule of formal equality, some differences need to be accommodated. CERD and CEDAW are children of this era and Arnadottir names the equality model of this second era as substantive difference model ([110], p. 50). The third era is called multidimensional disadvantage era and is linked to contemporary equality law, which started in the 1990s. Concepts of multidimensional and structural disadvantage shape the thinking about discrimination in this era. The equality concept in this phase is the substantive disadvantage model. "It is a contextual approach that focuses on the asymmetrical structures of power, privilege and disadvantage that are at work in society. [...] This approach has been elaborated as a response to the weakness of the other approaches that frame questions of equality in terms of the comparative concepts of sameness and difference." ([110], p. 54). The school of thought which brought about this equality concept is framed as "social construction feminism." ([110], p. 54). In this era, the state has a more proactive role to bring about change in relation to eliminate discriminatory social and political structures. While Arnadottir uses different terminology, I think it is possible to associate these three eras with the concepts of formal, substantive and transformative equality.[22] These eras correlate to different models of disability. Most authors agree that the era of formal equality clearly correspond with the medical model of disability ([4], p. 33 with further references). Disability is seen as a personal characteristic which inhibits equality and thus disabled persons are kept outside the equality and discrimination debate. Various opinions seem to exist regarding the two other concepts of equality and their relation to different models of disability. Arnadottir clearly associates the social model of disability with the third era of equality law and hence with transformative equality or in her terms to substantive disadvantage ([110], p. 60). However, she does not reflect on any other model of disability despite medical and social model. For her the CRPD "is expressly based on the social model of disability." ([110], p. 59) Broderick in contrast sees the CRPD as endorsing several models of disability, among them "a holistic human-rights based model" of disability ([4], p. 149), the capability model as well as the universalist model of disability ([4], pp. 141–42). Both, the universalist model of disability as well as the human rights model of disability she associates with the third era of equality law, the transformative equality concept ([4], pp. 45, 146). On the basis of the three phase division regarding the evolution of equality law, I would associate the medical model of disability with the first era of formal equality, the social model of disability with the second era of substantive equality and the human rights model with transformative equality. The medical model of disability is associated with formal equality because impairment is regarded as a difference that either must to be ignored or which might legitimizes different, unfavorable treatment. The social model of disability can be linked to the substantive model of equality, since impairment is seen as a difference that needs to be accommodated in order to prevent the social construction of disability. The human rights model of disability can neatly be fitted with transformative equality in that it provides the roadmap for change. However, it would be a mistake to assume that formal or substantive equality are to be abolished. The CESCR has endorsed different concepts of equality and discrimination in its recent General Comment No. 20, among them formal and substantive equality. The General Comment emphasizes that discrimination of any kind must be eradicated, both formally and substantively ([111], para. 8). Likewise the CRPD demands that "all discrimination on the basis of disability" ([1], art. 5 (2)) is combated. Formal equality helps to target direct discrimination and it should be kept in mind that disabled persons are often at risk of direct discrimination. To refuse intellectually disabled persons entrance to a dance hall because other guests might feel uneasy, cannot be sanctioned with the duty to provide reasonable accommodation. Such discrimination must be tackled with a formal equality approach. Because discrimination is a

---

[22] I think I am here in line with Andrea Broderick who argues, "that substantive disadvantage equality also takes a step into the realm of transformative equality by seeking to target structural inequalities." See ([4], p. 45).

process and takes different forms, the CRPD endorses a wide concept of discrimination, and takes collective as well as individual aspects into account. The shift to the human rights model of disability and transformative equality does not replace older models of disability or equality. However it should prevent models from legitimizing the denial or restrictions of human rights.

7. Conclusions

The CRPD was initially drafted as a human rights convention that replaces the medical model of disability with the social model of disability. However, the drafters went beyond the social model of disability and codified a treaty that is based on the human rights model of disability. While the medical model of disability reduces the disabled individual to her impairment, the social model dissects disability as a social construct and debunks exclusion and denial of rights on the basis of impairment as ideological constructions of disability. The human rights model builds on the social model in that it is built on the premise that disability is a social construct but it develops it further. There are six propositions for this assertion. First, the human rights model can vindicate that human rights do not require a certain health or body status, whereas the social model can merely explain that disability is a social construct. Secondly, the human rights model encompasses both sets of human rights, civil and political as well as economic, social and cultural rights and thus not only demands anti-discrimination rights for disabled persons. Thirdly, the human rights model embraces impairment as a condition which might reduce the quality of life but which belongs to humanity and thus must be valued as part of human variation. Fourthly, the human rights model values different layers of identity and acknowledges intersectional discrimination. The fifth proposition is that unlike the social model, the human rights model clarifies that impairment prevention policy can be human rights sensitive. Lastly, it is opined that the human rights model not only explains why 2/3 of the world's disabled population live in developing countries, but that it also contains a roadmap for change.

The CRPD additionally develops international equality law further. It introduces a new definition of discrimination by amending "denial of reasonable accommodation" as a form of discrimination. It further introduces a concept of discrimination that is both group and individual oriented. The duty to provide accessibility and the duty to involve representative organizations of disabled people are both group oriented obligations. They are supposed to overcome (past) barriers and discrimination and bring the voices of disabled persons to the mainstream of society and help to transform it to become more inclusive. The duty to combat discrimination, including the duty to provide reasonable accommodation, is oriented towards the individual. Accessibility standards at times might be inappropriate to meet the needs of an individual with rare impairments or a person who chooses to do things differently.

The CRPD is based on a modern equality concept which has evolved over different phases of equality law with different notions of equality. The first, formal equality seeks to combat direct discrimination but fails to take account of the "dilemma of differences." The second, substantive equality seeks to address differences among individuals and power relations among them. The third is coined transformative equality and thrives to overcome structural, institutional, as well as direct and indirect discrimination by introducing positive duties to transform society. The human rights model is based on this latter concept of transformative equality, while the medical model of disability correlates to formal equality and the social model of disability corresponds to the substantive equality concept.

While formal and substantive equality theories have their shortcomings it would be premature to drop them from anti-discrimination law and policy. The CRPD encompasses all concepts of equality and, thus implicates formal, substantive and transformative equality duties for State parties. State parties have to prohibit direct and indirect discrimination against disabled persons and they have to provide accessibility and reasonable accommodation. They also have to enable meaningful participation for organizations of disabled persons in the implementation and monitoring of the Convention. Most State Parties have not yet comprehended the scope of these obligations. After all, the CRPD was not intended to create "new rights", why then should it lead to new human rights obligations? However, this is exactly what the CRPD is about.

Conflicts of Interest: The author declares no conflict of interest.

References

1. United Nations. "Convention on the Rights of Persons with Disabilities." *United Nations Treaties Series*, 2008, vol. 2515, p. 3. Available online: https://treaties.un.org/doc/publication/unts/volume%202515/v2515.pdf (accessed on 19 August 2016).
2. Alison Kafer. *Feminist, Queer, Crip*. Bloomington and Indianapolis: Indiana University Press, 2013.
3. United Nations General Assembly. "Promotion and protection of human rights: Human rights questions, including alternative approaches for improving the effective enjoyment of human rights and fundamental freedoms. A/C.3/70/L.56." 2 November 2015. Available online: http://www.un.org/disabilities/documents/gadocs/a_c.3_70_l.56.pdf (accessed on 19 August 2016).
4. Andrea Broderick. "The Long and Winding Road to Equality and Inclusion for Persons with Disabilities." Ph.D. Dissertation, Maastricht University, Maastricht, The Netherlands, 20 November 2015.
5. Theresia Degener. "A human rights model of disability." In *Routledge Handbook of Disability Law and Human Rights*. Edited by Blanck Peter and Flynn Eilionoir. London and New York: Routledge, 2017, pp. 31–50.
6. Jerome Bickenbach. *Physical Disability and Social Policy*. Toronto, Buffalo and London: University of Toronto Press, 1992.
7. Barbara Altmann. "Disability Definitions, Models, Classification Schemes, and Application." In *Handbook of Disability Studies*. Thousand Oaks: Sage Publication, 2001, pp. 97–122.
8. Tom Shakespeare. *Disability Rights and Wrongs*. New York: Routledge, 2006.
9. Michael Oliver. *The Politics of Disablement*. New York: St. Martin's Press, 1990.
10. Amita Dhanda. "Legal capacity in the disability rights convention." *Syracuse Journal of International Law and Commerce* 34 (2007): 429–62.
11. Eilionoir Flynn, and Anna Arstein-Kerslake. "Legislating Personhood: Realising the Right to Support in Exercising Legal Capacity." *International Journal of Law in Context* 10 (2014): 81–104. [CrossRef]
12. Rosemary Kayess, and Philipp French. "Out of Darkness into Light?" *Human Rights Law Review* 1 (2008): 1–34. [CrossRef]
13. Stefan Trömel. "A Personal Perspective on the Drafting History of the United Nations Convention on the Rights of Persons with Disabilities." In *European Yearbook of Disability Law*. Edited by Gerard Quinn and Lisa Waddington. Antwerpen: Intesentia, 2009, pp. 115–38.
14. Gerard Quinn, and Theresia Degener. *Human Rights and Disability*. New York and Geneva: United Nations, 2002, p. 14.
15. Rannveig Traustadottir. "Disability Studies, the Social Model and Legal Developments." In *The UN Convention on the Rights of Persons with Disabilities*. Edited by Oddný Mjöll Arnadóttir and Gerard Quinn. Leiden: Martinus Njhoff, 2009, pp. 3–16.
16. Michael Oliver. *Understanding Disability*. New York: St. Martin's Press, 1996.
17. Lisa Waddington. *From Rome to Nice in a Wheelchair*. Groningen: European Law Publisher, 2006.
18. Theresia Degener, and Gerard Quinn. "A Survey of International, Comparative and Regional Disability Law Reform." In *Disability Rights Law and Policy*. Edited by Mary Lou Breslin and Silvia Yee. New York: Transnational, 2002, pp. 3–128.
19. Anna Lawson. *Disability and Equality Law in Britain: The Role of Reasonable Adjustment*. Oxford: Hart, 2008.
20. Anna Lawson, and Caroline Gooding. *Disability Rights in Europe. From Theory to Practice*. Oxford: Hart, 2005.
21. Vic Finkelstein. "The 'Social Model of Disability' and the Disability movement." 2007. Available online: http://www.leeds.ac.uk/disability-studies/archiveuk/finkelstein/The%20Social%20Model%20of%20Disability%20and%20the%20Disability%20Movement.pdf (accessed on 23 May 2016).
22. Mark Priestley. "We're all Europeans now! The social model of disability and European social policy." In *The Social Model of Disability*. Edited by Colin Barnes and Geoff Mercer. Leeds: Disability Press, 2005.
23. Caroline Gooding. *Disabling Laws, Enabling Acts*. London: Pluto Press, 1994, pp. 10–13.
24. Colin Barnes. *Disabled People in Britain and Discrimination*. London: Hurst, 1991.

25. European Union. "European Disability Strategy 2010–2020." Available online: http://eur-lex.europa.eu/LexUriServ/LexUriServ.do?uri=CELEX:52010DC0636:en:NOT (accessed on 14 March 2013).
26. Lennard Davis. *The Disability Studies Reader*. New York: Routledge, 1997.
27. Lisa Vanhala. *Making Rights a Reality?* Cambridge: Cambridge University Press, 2011.
28. Björn Hvinden. "Redistributive and Regulatory Disability Provision: Incompatibility or Synergy?" In *European Yearbook of Disability Law*. Edited by Gerard Quinn and Lisa Waddington. Antwerp: Intersentia, 2009, pp. 5–28.
29. Theresia Degener. "Personal assistance services and laws: A commentary." Paper presented at International Symposium on Personal Assistance Models, World Institute on Disability and Rehabilitation International, Oakland, CA, USA, 1991.
30. Andrew Power, Janet Lord, and Allison DeFranco. *Active Citizenship and Disability*. New York: Cambridge University Press, 2013.
31. Ruth Townsley. "The Implementation of Policies Supporting Independent Living for Disabled People in Europe: Synthesis Report." Centre for Disability Studies, University of Leeds, Leeds, UK. 2010.
32. Roger Normand, and Sarah Zaidi. *Human Rights at the UN*. Bloomington: Indiana University Press, 2008.
33. United Nations. "Universal Declaration of Human Rights." Available online: http://www.un.org/en/universal-declaration-human-rights/index.html (accessed on 31 July 2016).
34. United Nations. "International Covenant on Social, Economic and Cultural Rights." *United Nations Treaties Series*, 1966, vol. 993, p. 3. Available online: http://www.refworld.org/docid/3ae6b36c0.html (accessed on 19 August 2016).
35. Ivan Simonovic. "Deposit of the 10th instrument of ratification of the OP-IESR New York." 5 February 2013. Available online: www2.ohchr.org/english/bodies/cescr/index.htm (accessed on 4 March 2013).
36. United Nations General Assembly. "Vienna Declaration and Programme of Action. A/CONF.157/23." 12 July 1993. Available online: http://www.unhcr.org/refworld/docid/3ae6b39ec.html (accessed on 14 March 2013).
37. United Nations. "International Covenant on Civil and Political Rights." *United Nations Treaties Series*, 1976, vol. 999, p. 171. Available online: https://treaties.un.org/doc/Publication/UNTS/Volume%20999/volume-999-I-14668-English.pdf (accessed on 19 August 2016).
38. Theresia Degener, and Yolan Koster-Dreese. *Human Rights and Disabled Persons: Essays and Relevant Human Rights Instruments*. Dordrecht: Martinus Nijhoff, 1995.
39. Camilla Parker. *A Community for All: Implementing Article 19*. New York: Open Society Foundation, 2011.
40. Gerard Quinn, and Susan Doyle. "Getting a Life. Living Independently and Being Included in the Community. A Legal Study to the Current Use and Future Potential of the EU Structural Funds to Contribute to the Achievement of Article 19 of the United Nations Convention on the Rights of Persons with Disabilities." 2012. Available online: http://www.europe.ohchr.org/documents/Publications/getting_a_life.pdf (accessed on 19 August 2016).
41. United Nations General Assembly. "Universal Declaration of Human Rights. 217 A (III)." 10 December 1948. Available online: http://www.refworld.org/docid/3ae6b3712c.html (accessed on 18 August 2016).
42. United Nations General Assembly. "Convention on the Elimination of All Forms of Racial Discrimination." *United Nations Treaties Series*, 1965, vol. 660, p. 165. Available online: http://www.refworld.org/docid/3ae6b3940.html (accessed on 19 August 2016).
43. United Nations General Assembly. "Convention on the Elimination of All Forms Elimination of Discrimination against Women." *United Nations Treaties Series*, 1979, vol. 1249, p. 13. Available online: http://www.refworld.org/docid/3ae6b3970.html (accessed on 19 August 2016).
44. Committee on Economic, Social and Cultural Rights. "International Covenant on Economic, Social and Cultural Rights, General Comment No. 5." 1995. Available online: http://tbinternet.ohchr.org/_layouts/treatybodyexternal/TBSearch.aspx?Lang=en&TreatyID=9&DocTypeID=11 (accessed on 31 July 2016).
45. Jim Mansell, Martin Knapp, Julie Beadle-Brown, and Jeni Beecham. *Deinstitutionalization and Community Living—Outcomes and Costs*. Canterbury: Tizard Centre of University of Kent, 2007.
46. European Union Agency for Fundamental Rights (FRA). "Choice and Control: The Right to Independent Living." 2012. Available online: http://fra.europa.eu/sites/default/files/fra_uploads/2129-FRA-2012-choice-and-control_EN.pdf (accessed on 19 August 2016).

47. Thomas Hammerberg. "Commissioner for Human Rights: The Right of People with Disabilities to Live Independently and Be Included in the Community." 2012. Available online: https://wcd.coe.int/ViewDoc.jsp?p=&id=1917847&direct=true (accessed on 19 August 2016).
48. Jenny Morris. *Pride against Prejudice*. Philadelphia: New Society Publishers, 1991.
49. Jenny Morris. "Impairment and disability: constructing an ethics of care which promotes human rights." *Hypatia* 16 (2001): 1–16. [CrossRef]
50. Mairian Corker, and Sally French. *Disability Discourse*. Buckingham and Philadadelphia: Open University Press, 1999.
51. Bill Hughes, and Kevin Paterson. "The Social Model of Disability and the Disappearing Body: Towards a sociology of impairment." *Disability & Society* 12 (1997): 325–40. [CrossRef]
52. Tom Shakespeare. *Disability Rights and Wrongs Revisited*. New York: Routledge, 2014.
53. Niels Petersen. "Human Dignity, International Protection." In *The Max Planck Encyclopaedia of Public International Law*. Edited by Rüdiger Wolfrum. Oxford: Oxford University Press, 2012.
54. Ronald Dworkin. *Taking Rights Seriously*. Cambridge: Harvard University Press, 1978.
55. Lee Ann Basser. "Human Dignity." In *Critical Perspectives on Human Rights and Disability Law*. Edited by Marcia H. Rioux, Lee Ann Basser and Melinda Jones. Leiden: Martinus Nijhoff Publishers, 2011, pp. 17–36.
56. Axel Honneth. *The Struggle for Recognition*. Cambridge: MIT Press, 1996.
57. Nick Watson. "The Dialectics of Disability: A social model for the 21st century?" In *Implementing the Social Model of Disability*. Edited by Colin Barnes and Geof Mercer. Leeds: Disability Press, 2004, pp. 101–17.
58. Berth Danermark, and Conniavitis L. Gellerstedt. "Social justice: Redistribution and recognition—A non-reductionist perspective on disability." *Disability & Society* 19 (2004): 339–53. [CrossRef]
59. Ashley M. Stein. "Disability Human Rights." *California Law Review* 95 (2007): 75–122.
60. Paddy Ladd. *Understanding Deaf Culture*. Clevedon, England and Buffalo: Multilingual Matters, 2003.
61. Mairian Corker. *Deaf Transitions*. London, Bristol and Philadelphia: J. Kingsley Publishers, 1996.
62. "World Blind Union." Available online: http://www.worldblindunion.org/English/Pages/default.aspx (accessed on 1 August 2016).
63. "World Federation of the Deaf." Available online: http://wfdeaf.org/ (accessed on 1 August 2016).
64. Peter Beresford. "Madness, Distress, Research and a Social Model." In *Implementing the Social Model of Disability*. Edited by Collin Barnes and Geof Mercer. Leeds: Disability Press, 2004, pp. 208–22.
65. Adrianne Asch, and Michelle Fine. "Nurturance, Sexuality, and Women with Disabilities." In *The Disability Studies Reader*. Edited by Lennard J. Davis. New York: Routledge, 1997, pp. 241–59.
66. Susan Wendell. "Toward a Feminist Theory of Disability." In *The Disability Studies Reader*. Edited by Lennard J. Davis. New York: Routledge, 1997, pp. 260–78.
67. Rosemarie Garland Thompson. "Feminist Theory, the Body, and the Disabled Figure." In *The Disability Studies Reader*. Edited by Lennard J. Davis. New York: Routledge, 1997, pp. 279–94.
68. Christopher M. Bell. *Blackness and Disability*. Münster: Lit Verlag, 2011.
69. Ayesha Vernon. "Multiple Oppression and The Disabled People's Movement." In *The Disability Reader*. Edited by Tom Shakespeare. London and New York: Cassell, 1998, pp. 201–10.
70. Anita Silvers. "Triple Difference: Disability, Race, Gender and the Politics of Recognition." In *Disability, Divers-ability and Legal Change*. Edited by Lee Ann B. Marks and Melinda Jones. The Hague, Bosten and London: Martinus Nijhoff, 1999, pp. 75–100.
71. Roland Burke. *Decolonization and the Evolution of International Human Rights*. Philadelphia: University of Pennsylvania Press, 2010.
72. Clifford Bob. *The International Struggle for New Human Rights*. Phildelphia: University of Pennsylvania Press, 2009.
73. Frederic Mégret. "The Disabilities Convention." *Human Rights Quarterly: A Comparative and International Journal of the Social Sciences, Humanities, and Law* 30 (2008): 494–516. [CrossRef]
74. Carol C. Gould. *Globalizing Democracy and Human Rights*. Cambridge and New York: Cambridge University Press, 2004.
75. Christine Chinkin, and Hilary Charlesworth. *The Boundaries of International Law: A Feminist Analysis*. Manchester: Manchester University Press, 2000.
76. Catharine A. MacKinnon. *Toward a Feminist Theory of the State*. Cambridge: Harvard University Press, 1989.
77. Mari J. Matsuda. *Where Is Your Body?* Boston: Beacon Press, 1996.

78. Angela P. Harris. "Race and Essentialism in Feminist Legal Theory." *Stanford Law Review* 3 (1990): 581–616. [CrossRef]
79. Theresia Degener. "Intersections between disability, race and gender in discrimination law." In *European Union Non-Discrimination Law and Intersectionality*. Edited by Dagmar Schiek and Anna Lawson. Burlington: Ashgate Publisher, 2011, pp. 29–46.
80. Johanna E. Bond. "International intersectionality: A theoretical and pragmatic exploration of women's international human rights violations." *Emory Law Journal* 52 (2003): 71–186.
81. Theresia Degener, and Swantje Köbsell. *Hauptsache es ist gesund?* Hamburg: Konkret Literatur, 1992.
82. Eric Parens, and Adrienne Asch. *Prenatal Testing and Disability Rights*. Washington: Georgetown University Press, 2000.
83. Anita Silvers, David Wasserman, and Mary Mahowald. *Disability, Difference, Discrimination*. Lanham: Rowman & Littlefield, 1998.
84. Marsha Saxton. "Why members of the disability community oppose prenatal diagnosis and selective abortion." In *Prenatal Testing and Disability Rights*. Edited by Eric Parens and Adrienne Asch. Washington: Georgetown University Press, 2000.
85. United Nations General Assembly. "World Programme of Action Concerning Disabled Persons. WPA A/37/351/Add.1 and Add.1/Corr.1, annex." Available online: https://www.un.org/development/desa/disabilities/resources/world-programme-of-action-concerning-disabled-persons.html (accessed on 5 March 2016).
86. United Nations General Assembly. "Standard Rules on the Equalization of Opportunities for Persons with Disabilities." Available online: http://www.un.org/esa/socdev/enable/dissre00.htm (accessed on 3 March 2016).
87. Diane Driedger. *The Last Civil Rights Movement*. New York: St. Martin's Press, 1989.
88. Theresia Degener. "Disabled Women and International Human Rights." In *Women and International Human Rights Law*. Edited by Kelly D. Askin and Dorean M. Koenig. Ardsley and New York: Transnational, 2001, vol. 3, pp. 267–82.
89. Osamu Nagase. "Difference, Equality and Disabled People." Master's Thesis, Institute of Social Studies, The Hague, The Netherlands, December 1995.
90. World Health Organisation, and World Bank. *World Report on Disability*. Geneva: WHO-Verlag, 2011.
91. Colin Barnes, and Geof Mercer. *The Social Model of Disability*. Leeds: Disability Press, 2005.
92. Brian Watermeyer. *Disability and Social Change*. Cape Town: HSRC Press, 2006.
93. Mark Priestley. *Disability and the Life Course*. Cambridge and New York: Cambridge University Press, 2001.
94. Emma Stone. *Disability and Development*. Leeds: Disability Press, 1999.
95. Bill Albert. *In or out of the Mainstream? Lessons from Research on Disability and Development Cooperation*. Leeds: The Disability Press, 2006.
96. Jeanine Braithwaite, and Daniel Mont. *Disability and Poverty: A Survey of World Bank Poverty Assessments and Implications*. Washington: World Bank, 2008.
97. United Nations. "The Human Rights Based Approach to Development Cooperation: Towards a Common Understanding among UN Agencies." Available online: http://hrbaportal.org/the-human-rights-based-approach-to-development-cooperation-towards-a-common-understanding-among-un-agencies (accessed on 3 August 2016).
98. Andrea Cornwall, and Celestine Nyamy-Musembi. "Putting the 'rights-based' approach to development into perspective." *Third World Quarterly* 8 (2004): 1415–37. [CrossRef]
99. United Nations. "UN Doc. A/RES/70/I 21 October 2015. Transforming our world: The 2030 Agenda for Sustainable Development." Available online: https://sustainabledevelopment.un.org/post2015/transformingourworld (accessed on 3 August 2016).
100. United Nations. "International Convention on the Protection of the Rights of All Migrant Workers and Members of Their Families." *United Nations Treaties Series*, 2004, vol. 2220, p. 3. Available online: https://treaties.un.org/doc/publication/unts/volume%202220/v2220.pdf (accessed on 19 August 2016).
101. United Nations Committee on the Rights of Persons with Disabilities. "Concluding Observations." Available online: http://tbinternet.ohchr.org/_layouts/treatybodyexternal/TBSearch.aspx?Lang=en&TreatyID=4&DocTypeID=5 (accessed on 3 August 2016).

102. United Nations. "Convention on the Elimination of all Form of Racial Discrimination." *United Nations Treaties Series*, 1965, vol. 160, p. 195. Available online: http://www.un-documents.net/icerd.htm (accessed on 19 August 2016).
103. United Nations. "Convention on the Rights of the Child." *United Nations Treaties Series*, 1999, vol. 1577, p. 3. Available online: https://treaties.un.org/doc/Publication/UNTS/Volume%201577/v1577.pdf (accessed on 19 August 2016).
104. Wouter Vandenhole. *Non-Discrimination and Equality in the View of the UN Human Rights Treaty Bodies.* Antwerp and Oxford: Intersentia, 2005.
105. Committee on the Rights of Persons with Disabilities. "CRPD General Comment No 2 CRPD/C/GC, 22 May 2014, para. 25." Available online: http://www.ohchr.org/EN/HRBodies/CRPD/Pages/GC.aspx (accessed on 3 August 2016).
106. Maya Sabatello. "The New Diplomacy." In *Human Rights and Disability Advocacy.* Edited by Maya Sabatello and Marianne Schulze. Philadelphia: University of Philadelphia Press, 2013.
107. Sandra Fredman. "Beyond the Dichotomy of Formal and Substantive Equality: Towards a New Definition of Equal Rights." In *Temporary Special Measures: Accellerating De Facto Equality of Women under Article 4 (1) UN Convention on the Elemination of All Forms of Discrimination Against Women.* Edited by Ineke Boerefijn, Fons Coomans, Jenny Goldschmidt, Rikki Holtmaat and Ria Wolleswinkel. Antwerp: Intersentia, 2003.
108. Sandra Fredman. *Human Rights Transformed. Positive Rights and Positive Duties.* Oxford: Oxford University Press, 2008.
109. Martha Minow. *Making All the Diffference*, 2nd ed. Ithaca and London: Cornell University Press, 1991.
110. Oddný M. Arnardottir. "A Future of Multimimensional Disadvantage Equality?" In *The UN Convention on the Rights of Persons with Disabilities.* Edited by Oddný M. Arnardottir and Gerard Quinn. Leiden and Boston: Martinus Nijhoff, 2009.
111. Committee on Economic, Social and Cultural Rights. "General Comment No 20 UN Doc. E/C.12/GC/20, 2 July 2009, para. 8." Available online: http://tbinternet.ohchr.org/_layouts/treatybodyexternal/TBSearch.aspx?Lang=en&TreatyID=9&DocTypeID=11 (accessed on 3 August 2016).

![laws logo] *laws*

MDPI

Article

Harmonisation and Cross-Fertilisation of Socio-Economic Rights in the Human Rights Treaty Bodies: Disability and the Reasonableness Review Case Study

Andrea Broderick

Department of International and European Law, Maastricht University, Maastricht 6211, The Netherlands; andrea.broderick@maastrichtuniversity.nl; Tel.: +353-861-016-706

Academic Editor: Frank Pasquale
Received: 19 May 2016; Accepted: 14 September 2016; Published: 25 September 2016

Abstract: In light of the recent adoption of the Optional Protocol to the International Covenant on Economic, Social and Cultural Rights (OP-ICESCR) and the Optional Protocol to the Convention on the Rights of Persons with Disabilities (OP-CRPD), there is a necessity for harmonisation among the treaty bodies, particularly in the area of socio-economic rights. The equality norm in the CRPD, including the duty to reasonably accommodate, is an important facilitator of socio-economic rights. This article sets forth the opportunities for cross-fertilisation of socio-economic rights, and disability rights in particular, at the level of international human rights law and beyond, as well as the potential that exists for social change at the domestic level. The CRPD Committee and the United Nations Committee on Economic, Social and Cultural Rights (UNCESCR) will undertake the task of assessing measures adopted by States related to alleged violations under the optional protocols and will determine compliance with treaty obligations under the State reporting procedure. In that regard, a framework of "reasonableness review" is proposed, which could provide the opportunity to merge individual rights' violations with broader issues of socio-economic inequalities and could also lead to coherent implementation of the normative content of socio-economic rights at the domestic level.

Keywords: disability; equality; reasonable accommodation; progressive realisation; socio-economic rights; reasonableness review

1. Introduction

There has been a marked shift towards harmonised and integrated human rights treaty body working methods at the international level. The treaty body reform and strengthening process has been ongoing for some time now, with arguably limited success. In light of the established, and expanding, system of individual communications under the core international human rights treaties, the "necessity of harmonization, consistency and coherence of jurisprudence" is deemed to be of "paramount importance" [1]. Nowhere does this statement ring truer than in the realm of disability rights. Rowena Daw notes that "disability was, until very recently, the forgotten dimension of human rights and went unacknowledged as a subject for a right to equality" ([2], p. 8). This situation has changed substantially with the entry into force of the United Nations Convention on the Rights of Persons with Disabilities (CRPD) and the establishment of the right to adjudication and remedy for claims under the Optional Protocol to the CRPD (OP-CRPD).

The CRPD is a progressive human rights treaty, which endorses a substantive and transformative model of equality. Substantive equality is concerned "with the effects of laws, policies and practices and with ensuring that they do not maintain, but rather alleviate, the inherent disadvantage that particular groups experience" ([3], para. 7). Transformative equality seeks to target the underlying structural inequalities that hinder the full enjoyment of rights by disadvantaged groups. Within the realm of its substantive equality norm, the CRPD includes the duty to reasonably accommodate persons with disabilities [4]. Reasonable accommodation entails positive measures—adaptations and modifications to the environment and to established practices—to address the unique needs of persons with disabilities in order to ensure the equal right to education and health, among others. The duty to reasonably accommodate persons with disabilities spans all human rights in the CRPD, both civil and political, as well as economic, social and cultural rights.

The equality norm is an important facilitator of socio-economic rights in the context of marginalised groups. Furthermore, socio-economic rights are "an integral means by which systemic disadvantage and inequalities are addressed" ([5] p. 220). Bruce Porter argues that "substantive equality requires a recognition that to realise an equal right to effective remedies for all, [economic, social and cultural rights] adjudication may have to meet different needs and develop new approaches" ([6], p. 41). This article contends that "reasonableness review" is one such approach, which could help to advance the realisation of socio-economic rights for disabled persons. Reasonableness review has evolved at both the national and the international level, with a view to providing a mechanism for adjudicating on the appropriateness of State action or inaction in realising progressively socio-economic rights. It seeks to ensure that the content of socio-economic norms is adjudicated upon in relation to the marginalised group in question, rather than basing an analysis on technical or abstract indicators and benchmarks.

This article sets forth the inter-connectedness of treaty body adjudication and the opportunities for harmonisation and cross-fertilisation of disability rights, and socio-economic rights more generally, at the level of international human rights law (and beyond, at the regional level). This article also addresses the potential that exists for a transformative human rights framework and for social change at the domestic level if the human rights treaty bodies work together towards the realisation of socio-economic rights, particularly in the context of persons with disabilities. The focus of this paper is on the CRPD and the International Covenant on Economic, Social and Cultural Rights (ICESCR), as well as the procedural mechanisms established under the two new optional protocols to those treaties. Those procedural mechanisms harbour the potential to advance disability discrimination and reasonable accommodation claims, provided that such claims are dealt with coherently by the respective treaty bodies. The CRPD Committee and the United Nations Committee on Economic, Social and Cultural Rights (UNCESCR) will both undertake the important task of assessing the measures taken by States related to alleged violations under the optional protocols and will determine compliance with treaty obligations under the State reporting procedure.

The core concern of this paper is to set forth the various criteria inherent in the duty to provide reasonable accommodation, contained in articles 2 and 5(3) of the CRPD, and to apply those criteria more generally to a framework of reasonableness review of socio-economic rights. The duty to accommodate, and the obligation to realise progressively socio-economic rights to the maximum of available resources, pursue different objectives—the reasonableness standard concerns the implementation of economic, social and cultural rights in general and the duty to provide reasonable accommodation relates to the prohibition of discrimination against disabled people. Notwithstanding this, both obligations reflect, on the one hand, the needs and interests of persons with disabilities and, on the other hand, the needs and interests of duty-bearers, including resource limitations and other non-financial considerations. It is envisaged that the criteria forming part of the reasonable accommodation norm may provide some degree of insight into the balancing of interests that is implicit in the implementation of other rights and obligations in the disability sphere that are subject to progressive realisation. These criteria will be drawn on throughout this article to shape a framework of reasonableness review, which could provide the relevant committees with the opportunity "to merge considerations of individual rights' violations with broader issues of socio-economic inequalities" ([5], p. 233) and could also lead to coherent implementation of the normative content of socio-economic rights at the domestic level. The primary example used throughout the paper to illustrate this framework of reasonableness review is the right to education.

In order to address the foregoing issues, this article is divided into six sections. The second section of this paper provides a brief overview of the treaty body reform and strengthening process. The third section outlines the relevance of the ICESCR and the CRPD, as well as the Optional Protocol to the ICESCR (OP-ICESCR) and the OP-CRPD to advancing the realisation of socio-economic rights in the context of disability. Section 4 details the constituent elements of the reasonable accommodation norm in the CRPD. Those elements can potentially aid in the construction of a harmonised standard of reasonableness review of measures taken to implement socio-economic rights (particularly in the disability context, but also more generally). Section 4 of this article also contains a brief overview of progressive realisation of disability rights via the proposed framework of reasonableness review. Section 5 of this article elaborates on the potential for social change that exists in the disability context, and on a wider scale, through harmonisation and cross-fertilisation of treaty body standards by means of a framework of reasonableness review. Finally, Section 6 contains concluding remarks.

2. Treaty Body Reform and Strengthening

It has been acknowledged for some time now that the UN human rights treaty body system "would benefit from institutional and other forms of strengthening in order to render it more efficient and effective" [7]. Treaty body reform has also been the subject of much academic commentary [8]. One of the most pressing challenges for the human rights committees is to ensure coordination of their activities with other treaty bodies and with other mechanisms within the UN seeking to ensure protection and promotion of human rights. Harmonisation of the current *modus operandi* has been high on the agenda of the treaty bodies since the reform and strengthening process began. However, success has been limited. It is not just the treaty body working methods that need to be improved. Most importantly of all, any reform and strengthening process must result in enhanced protection of human rights on the ground.

The state reporting procedure is a central feature of the human rights treaty body system. It offers an opportunity for each State Party to: Review the types of measures it has taken to "harmonize national law and policy with the provisions of the relevant international human rights treaties to which it is a party"; monitor progress in human rights implementation; assess future needs and goals for more effective implementation of the treaties; and "plan and develop appropriate policies to achieve these goals" [9]. The individual communications system, on the other hand, should provide a mechanism by which to ensure that human rights are given concrete meaning in the context of the lived experiences of disabled claimants.

The extent to which the jurisprudence and recommendations of the international human rights treaty bodies are taken into account at the national, and indeed at the regional level, has long been the subject of debate. Domestic courts and regional adjudicatory mechanisms, such as the European Court of Human Rights, refer intermittently to the views of the treaty bodies. National courts have described the general comments of the UNCESCR as "of importance for the interpretation and jurisprudential development [of the Covenant] though they are not directly binding" [10]. However, not all domestic courts have enthusiastically endorsed this source of international human rights law [11]. Perhaps this is, in part, due to the vagueness of the normative standards emerging from the treaty bodies and their lack of harmonisation *inter se*.

In the disability context, it is imperative that the treaty bodies develop coherent jurisprudence and guidance for States Parties in the assessment of State action in order to ensure a more effective realisation of the object and purpose of the relevant treaties at the national level. This paper seeks to address that issue by setting out defined criteria, drawn from a reasonableness review framework, to be considered by the human rights committees in their deliberations on disability rights, and socio-economic rights generally. Before setting out in section five of this paper the criteria deemed essential for consideration by the treaty bodies, section three of this paper demonstrates the links between the ICESCR, the CRPD and the advancement of socio-economic rights in the disability context by means of a framework of reasonableness review and section four sets out defined criteria stemming from the reasonable accommodation norm, to be applied and elaborated on in Section 5.

3. The ICESCR, the CRPD and their Optional Protocols: Advancing the Realisation of Socio-Economic Rights in the Context of Disability

There are clear overlaps between standards in different human rights treaties and, as a result, harmonisation and cross-fertilisation of the views of the human rights treaty bodies is not only desirable, but essential, in order to ensure coherence of international and regional human rights standards and effective implementation at the domestic level. This section of the paper provides an overview of the relevance of the ICESCR and the CRPD, as well as their individual communications mechanisms, to advancing socio-economic rights realisation in the disability context.

3.1. The ICESCR and Its Optional Protocol

The rights contained in the ICESCR are of great relevance to all marginalised groups, not least persons with disabilities. The prohibited grounds of discrimination [12] listed in Article 2(2) of the ICESCR do not include disability expressly. However, the inclusion of "other status" in Article 2(2) emphasises the fact that the list is not exhaustive. General Comment 5 (1994) of the UNCESCR confirms that disability-based discrimination falls under the label of "other status" in the ICESCR ([13], para. 5). It details the manner in which the treaty should be interpreted in order to ensure the equal enjoyment of the rights specified therein by persons with disabilities. Akin to the CRPD, General Comment 5 endorses the social constructionist approach to disability, by acknowledging the fact that the rights of disabled people are hindered in circumstances where discriminatory societal barriers exist ([13], para. 22). It also acknowledges explicitly the link between equality norms on the one hand, and participation and inclusion in society for persons with disabilities, on the other hand ([13], para. 15). Significantly, it includes within the definition of disability-based discrimination a denial of reasonable accommodation ([13], para. 15).

The UNCESCR has explained the reason for the absence of an explicit disability-related provision in the ICESCR, attributing this "to the lack of awareness of the importance of addressing this issue explicitly, rather than only by implication, at the time of the drafting of the Covenant over a quarter of a century ago" ([13], para. 6). The mere fact that the ICESCR was drafted without explicit mention of the rights of persons with disabilities demonstrates the necessity for cross-fertilisation and harmonisation among the treaty bodies in the review of State progress on the implementation and realisation of socio-economic rights.

The travaux préparatoires of the OP-ICESCR demonstrate the fact that there was controversy amongst the participating States on the issue of "justiciability" [14]. In spite of this controversy, consensus was reached among delegates at the negotiation sessions regarding the insertion of a standard of review of steps to be adopted under the ICESCR in accordance with Article 2(1) of the treaty (pertaining to progressive realisation of rights to the maximum of available resources). Article 8(4) OP-ICESCR provides as follows:

> When examining communications under the present Protocol, the Committee shall consider the reasonableness of the steps taken by the State Party in accordance with part II of the Covenant [...].

The UNCESCR has acknowledged the fact that measures taken by States to fulfil socio-economic rights must be "adequate" or "reasonable" [15] and has outlined certain factors as being pertinent considerations in assessing whether steps adopted by States are reasonable. [1] Those factors have been

---

[1]   The factors listed by the UNCESCR as being relevant to a consideration of measures adopted by States are as follows: (a) the extent to which the measures taken were deliberate, concrete and targeted towards the fulfilment of economic,

deemed to demonstrate "a strong commitment to the principle of effective remedies" ([6], p. 46). As Lillian Chenwei rightly points out, "the reasonableness standard in the Optional Protocol acknowledges the institutional roles and limitations in giving effect to the right to effective remedies for socio-economic rights violations" ([16], p. 756).

Since many ICESCR rights are relevant to persons with disabilities ([17], p. 80), the standard of reasonableness to be developed by the UNCESCR must be harmonised with the standard of reasonableness to be developed by the CRPD Committee, through its jurisprudence under the individual communication procedure and in its general comments related to the assessment of positive equality claims and socio-economic claims via the reasonable accommodation obligation. Bruce Porter notes that the standard of review to be developed by the UNCESCR under Article 8(4) OP-ICESCR will "inform and be informed by the way in which the principle of reasonableness review of substantive social rights claims evolves at other treaty monitoring bodies, in regional systems and in domestic law" ([6], p. 42).

3.2. The CRPD and Its Optional Protocol

The CRPD has the potential to be a truly transformative human rights treaty, if its provisions are coherently interpreted and applied. The OP-CRPD allows for individual complaints to be submitted to the CRPD Committee by individuals and groups of individuals, or by a third party on behalf of individuals and groups of individuals, alleging that their rights have been violated under the Convention. In order to ensure that the transformative potential of the CRPD is capitalised upon, it is vital to place a framework around the progressive implementation of CRPD norms, both in terms of resource allocation and programmatic design of socio-economic rights. This would serve to ensure an appropriate balancing of the needs of disabled persons and the tasks of duty-bearers.

As *lex specialis*, the CRPD can be used to contribute to a better understanding of the normative content of socio-economic rights in the context of disabled persons. For instance, Article 24 of the CRPD contains a detailed elaboration on the right of persons with disabilities to inclusive education, whilst the ICESCR articulates the vague right of everyone to the enjoyment of accessible education at all levels in Article 13 thereof. The CRPD can be used as a tool to compel States to include in their reports to the UNCESCR the specific implementation measures adopted by States with respect to ensuring the accessibility, and full enjoyment, of education for persons with disabilities. Moreover, the CRPD Committee can use the Convention to offer guidance to other human rights treaty bodies (both international and regional) in their work in the field of disability.

Of course, it is not only ICESCR rights that should be cross-referenced with the CRPD, nor is it merely in the realm of socio-economic rights that cross-referencing and harmonisation of disability rights should occur. The interpretation of the rights of children with disabilities should also be harmonised under the Convention on the Rights of the Child (CRC) and the CRPD. Moreover, the Human Rights Committee should keep a keen eye on pronouncements made by the CRPD Committee regarding the inter-dependency of civil and political rights and socio-economic rights. Many of the substantive articles in the CRPD can be termed "hybrid" rights on account of the fact that they fuse elements of immediately realisable civil and political rights, as well as progressively realisable socio-economic rights.

The CRPD Committee can potentially advance the actualisation of disability rights by means of a coherent elaboration on the standard of reasonableness to be applied across the substantive rights in the

---

social and cultural rights; (b) whether the State party exercised its discretion in a non-discriminatory and non-arbitrary manner; (c) whether the State party's decision (not) to allocate available resources is in accordance with international human rights standards; (d) where several policy options are available, whether the State party adopts the option that least restricts Covenant rights; (e) the time frame in which the steps were taken; (f) whether the steps had taken into account the precarious situation of disadvantaged and marginalized individuals or groups and, whether they were non-discriminatory, and whether they prioritized grave situations or situations of risk.

CRPD. By integration of the equality norm (via the reasonable accommodation duty) in its assessment of measures adopted by States to realise socio-economic rights progressively, the Committee can also put forth a good example, which can serve to enhance the realisation of socio-economic rights more generally. Bruce Porter notes that the CRPD offers an exceptional model of "convergent paradigms of rights and remedies" on account of the "convergence of the right to equality and non-discrimination and the economic, social and cultural rights" ([6], p. 42) of persons with disabilities in the Convention. Furthermore, he draws attention to the fact that the standard adopted by the CRPD Committee will be hugely important "in reviewing the right to positive measures in light of available resources in the context of both equality rights and [economic, social and cultural] rights" ([6], p. 42). In light of the foregoing, the next section of this paper outlines the constituent elements of the standard of review to be adopted under the CRPD, before an elaboration in Section 5 on those various elements.

4. The Duty to Reasonably Accommodate: Its Constituent Elements and the Link to Progressive Realisation of Disability Rights

In light of the importance of the reasonable accommodation duty to the implementation of the equality norm and, in turn, the importance of the equality norm to the eradication of socio-economic disadvantage, this section provides an overview of the constituent elements of the reasonable accommodation duty ([18], pp. 151–76). These elements could potentially aid the CRPD Committee in outlining its standard of reasonableness review and could serve as a helpful standard of review for the UNCESCR in its assessment of disability-related measures adopted by States Parties to the Covenant. The types of criteria applied to disability rights could also potentially aid the other treaty bodies in their assessment of equality and socio-economic claims by marginalised groups generally.

4.1. The Constituent Elements of the Reasonable Accommodation Duty

In a similar vein to progressive realisation of disability rights, the reasonable accommodation duty entails "a balancing of needs and interests" ([5], p. 151) between the disabled person and the duty-bearer. It therefore represents a microcosm of the overall measures to be adopted by States Parties to the Convention. The interests of disabled people and duty-bearers are captured by the requirement that all accommodation measures must be "necessary and appropriate" in order "to ensure to persons with disabilities the enjoyment or exercise on an equal basis with others of all human rights and fundamental freedoms" [4]. The interests of duty bearers (States and entities), on the other hand, are spelt out in the requirement that accommodation measures must not impose a "disproportionate or undue burden" [4] on the duty-bearer. The necessity criterion signifies the duty to take all essential measures to ensure access to, and enjoyment of, CRPD rights for persons with disabilities ([5], p. 160). The use of the word "appropriate" in the definition of reasonable accommodation implies that accommodations must be effective in ensuring realisation of the rights of disabled persons, including socio-economic rights ([5], p. 160). The criterion of effectiveness is confirmed by a contextual reading of the Convention. This is borne out by General Obligation 4(1), which links the word "appropriate" with the full realisation of rights [19].

In order to determine the effectiveness of measures adopted under the duty to accommodate, one must also consider the object and purpose of the duty itself. The specific objective of the duty to accommodate is to promote equality and to eliminate discrimination. Equality considerations will therefore be paramount in determining the effectiveness of measures adopted with a view to reasonably accommodating disabled persons. Linked to the criterion of effectiveness and the equality norm is the core notion of the inherent dignity of persons with disabilities. The duty to accommodate is "based on the values underlying the Convention as a whole—human dignity and respect for difference" ([5], p. 175). Where States or entities fail to accommodate a person with a disability, or where they provide an ineffective accommodation, this will inevitably result in marginalisation and exclusion of the disabled person from the enjoyment of rights and will, therefore, harm the inherent dignity of persons with disabilities.

The duty to reasonably accommodate "seeks to balance the rights of, and burdens and benefits to, all persons affected by the proposed accommodation" ([5], p. 176). The primary consideration under the CRPD will be "a detailed balancing of the costs and benefits of the proposed measure to the entity providing it" ([5], p. 176). In addition, third-party benefits should be factored in as a "tangential consideration" ([5], p. 176) in the assessment of the reasonableness of measures adopted under the CRPD. In other words, where granting an accommodation to a particular individual results in benefits to others, this can potentially be used to offset cost arguments advanced by States or entities.

4.2. Progressive Realisation and Reasonableness Review of Socio-Economic Rights in the Disability Context

The concept of progressive realisation has been described by the Office of the High Commissioner for Human Rights (OHCHR) as "a practical device that acknowledge(s) the real world challenges" and "helps to avoid overburdening [S]tates, employers and other duty-bearers" ([20], p. 5). Much like the (individualised) balancing of burdens and interests inherent in the reasonable accommodation norm, the progressive realisation norm entails a similar balancing act on a larger scale.

The reasonableness review model first evolved in South African jurisprudence as a means by which to evaluate the right to positive measures under the South African Constitution and the actions taken by States thereunder to realise socio-economic rights. There are some criticisms of reasonableness review, particularly related to the fact that it is not an appropriate standard by which to develop the substantive content of socio-economic rights. Fons Coomans, for instance, notes that reasonableness is an "inherently vague" and "elastic" ([21], p. 187) notion. Any use of a reasonableness review standard by the human rights treaty bodies must, therefore, be carefully balanced with the minimum core content of human rights.

Reasonableness review came to the fore at the international level when the UNCESCR created a 'reasonableness standard' under Article 8(4) OP-ICESCR. That standard essentially mandates that States use limited resources in a reasonable, non-arbitrary, non-discriminatory manner and, furthermore, that States should be held accountable for the manner in which they use their resources in the implementation of socio-economic rights [22].

Invoking reasonableness review to assess alleged violations of disability rights compels an assessment that is tailored to the specific national context at issue and the socio-economic disadvantage faced by persons with disabilities in that context ([5], p. 210). Under the OP-CRPD and the OP-ICESCR, the respective committees will have to ensure that rights are being realised effectively in the circumstances of the individual's lived experience, relative to the particular disadvantage experienced by the petitioner. As Bruce Porter and Sandra Liebenberg observe, reasonableness review in the context of the OP-ICESCR provides "for a dialectic between an individual rights claim and the consideration of other needs and interests, to ensure consistency with broader values and purposes of the Covenant in the context of limited resources" ([23], pp. 6–7).

In the next section of this paper, the various components of the proposed reasonableness review framework for disability rights will be elaborated upon, taking (at various junctures) the right to education as an example. It is hoped that this could provide the basis for a transformative human rights framework, provided that the treaty bodies work together towards harmonisation and cross-fertilisation of socio-economic rights in the context of disability. Such a transformative framework could also have a wider impact on the interpretation and implementation of socio-economic rights for other marginalised groups.

5. The Potential for Social Change: Harmonisation and Cross-Fertilisation of Disability Rights at the International Level and Beyond

Reform of the treaty body system should not just result in enhanced efficiency at the international level but should also "strengthen the capacity of rights-holders to enjoy their human rights and support States to carry out their obligations to implement fully these rights" ([7], para. 7). Any standard of review adopted by the treaty bodies should serve to ensure that failures by States to meet their obligations, for instance, under Article 2(1) of the ICESCR and under Article 4(2) CRPD, result in effective remedies for individual victims of violations.

Since the human rights treaty bodies only began to harmonise the procedural aspects of their working methods in recent times, some authors claim that "widespread formal efforts at substantive coherence are likely far off but not unfathomable" ([24], p. 158). There is already some evidence of harmoinsation of standards across the board. For example, General Comment 5 of the UNCESCR was drawn on by many national representatives at the CRPD negotiation sessions in order to forge a link in the CRPD between the duty to reasonably accommodate and the equality and non-discrimination norms [25].

Back in 2002, Gerard Quinn and Theresia Degener conducted several case studies on the use of the ICESCR in the context of disability, specifically analysing State Party reports in that regard. Those case studies revealed that the two key messages of General Comment 5 (equality and participation/inclusion of persons with disabilities in society) had "not percolated through to the point where they influence all (or even most) policies and measures relating to disability in the areas covered by the ICESCR" ([26], p. 112). To date, the overall implementation regime of international human rights law is greatly lacking ([27], p. 358). Invoking a reasonableness standard of review across the core human rights treaty bodies could provide a means by which to harmonise socio-economic rights claims and equality claims, particularly in the context of disability, and this could trickle down to the national level. The core treaty bodies might look to the CRPD Committee's elaboration of its standard of review via the reasonable accommodation obligation. In turn, the CRPD Committee might draw some guidance from the manner in which interpretation of Article 8 OP-ICESCR unfolds, through statements of the UNCESCR on what constitute "reasonable" measures, as well as decisions of the Committee in which it deals with socio-economic rights claims.

In the following sub-sections of this paper, a framework of reasonableness review will be proposed, taking into account the various criteria highlighted above as being primary objectives of any measures taken to reasonably accommodate persons with disabilities.[2]

5.1. The Effectiveness of Measures Adopted by States

As highlighted above, the criterion of effectiveness is one of the constituent elements of a standard of review based upon the reasonable accommodation duty in the CRPD. If we take the right to education in both the CRPD and the ICESCR as an example, we can observe that both provisions refer to the criterion of effectiveness. Article 24 of the CRPD provides that States Parties should ensure that "persons with disabilities receive the support required, within the general education system, to facilitate their *effective* education". Similarly, Article 13(1) of the ICESCR provides that States Parties to the Covenant agree that "education shall enable all persons to participate *effectively* in a free society". In its concluding observations on States Parties' reports, the CRPD Committee has already recommended that the Australian authorities should conduct research into the effectiveness of current inclusive education policies, including the extent to which the relevant disability standards in education are being implemented in each State and territory ([28], para. 46b). The Committee has also urged States to "set targets to increase participation and completion rates by students with disabilities in all levels of education and training" ([28], para. 46c). However, the Committee has not commented further on the criterion of effectiveness in the context of education.

In its non-binding (but authoritative) statement outlining criteria pertinent to whether measures taken by States to fulfil socio-economic rights are "adequate" or "reasonable," the UNCESCR asserts that a relevant consideration is whether the State adopts the option that least restricts Covenant rights, in circumstances where several options are available ([15], para. 8d). However, the UNCESCR has

---

[2] Sections 5.1–5.5 of this article draw on, and elaborate on considerably, where relevant to this article, the ideas and the categorisations contained in ([5], pp. 213–31).

not commented to any great extent on this criterion of effectiveness and therefore States are lacking guidance on this vital aspect of fulfilment across each of the substantive socio-economic rights in both the CRPD and the ICESCR.

In order to buttress the substantive and transformative framework of equality in the Convention, and in order to go beyond merely normative discussions, it would be most helpful if the CRPD Committee would elaborate further on the types of positive measures that might be effective in ensuring fulfilment of the socio-economic rights contained in the Convention. The UNCESCR, and the other treaty bodies, should keep a keen eye on the CRPD Committee's standard of review in that regard. There are many tools that can be used by the human rights treaty bodies to monitor the progressive realisation of socio-economic rights [29]. The committees might bear in mind quantitative tools, such as specific indicators, related to each of the substantive rights in the respective treaties and tailor their assessments of measures taken by States to meet those indicators to the domestic context at issue. With regard to the right to education, specific structural, process and outcome indicators, such as those elaborated upon by Inclusion International [30] or by the Right to Education project [31], could be drawn on as a tool to help States measure their progress in realising the right to education. States themselves could tailor the indicators to their national context and collect data for application of the indicators [32]. Such tools could also be used as a basis for the committees to reflect more deeply on the types of measures that might be effective in realising the normative content of inclusive education under Article 24 of the CRPD.

5.2. Equality Considerations

The adoption of the CRPD was deemed necessary in order to ensure that *de facto* equality is attained—in other words, that the systemic inequalities and substantive disadvantage experienced by persons with disabilities is remedied. The equality norm runs like a "red thread" through the substantive provisions of the CRPD, and the reasonable accommodation duty breathes new life into the practical application of both civil and political and socio-economic rights for persons with disabilities.

Sandra Liebenberg and Beth Goldblatt contend that "the most severe forms of disadvantage are usually experienced as a result of an intersection between group-based forms of discrimination and socio-economic marginalisation" ([33], p. 339). There are many recognised benefits to including equality as a relevant criterion in the assessment of measures taken by States in the context of realising socio-economic rights generally, and disability rights more specifically ([33], pp. 351–52). If the equality norm were to feature prominently in socio-economic rights adjudication, and also in the consideration of measures adopted by States under the reporting system, States "would be required to provide heightened justifications for any alleged rights' violations" ([5], p. 223). This is particularly so "in circumstances where denying access to the right(s) in question would cause further entrenchment of inequalities or marginalisation for persons with disabilities" ([5], p. 223). Integration of an equality perspective would also serve to ensure a deeper understanding of the "multi-dimensional disadvantage" experienced by disabled persons in the enjoyment and exercise of socio-economic rights ([5], p. 223).

The link between the actualisation of socio-economic rights and the principles of non-discrimination and equality has been remarked upon by the UNCESCR in its general comments [34]. Furthermore, in its 2007 statement outlining the guiding criteria for interpreting the reasonableness standard incorporated in Article 8(4) OP-ICESCR, the Committee asserts that exercise by a State of discretion in a non-discriminatory and non-arbitrary manner ([15], para. 8) will be relevant in any consideration of whether States fulfil the "reasonableness" criterion under Article 8(4) OP-ICESCR.

Lack of access to education, culminating in unequal opportunities, has been recognised as a "dominant problem in the disability field" [35] for both children and adults with disabilities. The CRPD Committee has emphasised the fact that States Parties to the Convention must intensify their efforts to ensure that disabled children can benefit to the same extent as non-disabled children from any system of compulsory education established by domestic authorities ([36], para. 38). The Committee should now begin to adjudge any violations of the right to education (and indeed, all other socio-economic rights) with regard to the "position of the claimant group in society, the nature of the resource or service claimed and the impact of the denial of access to the service or resource in question on the claimant group" ([37], pp. 89–90) as mandated by frameworks of reasonableness review. In circumstances where the denial of the right results in entrenched inequalities, as is the case with denial of the right to inclusive education, the committees must apply a heightened standard of review. Among other things, the treaty bodies should enquire whether, in their enjoyment of the right to education, disabled people have been granted equality before and under the law, equal benefit and equal protection of the law. The treaty bodies will also have to enquire into the affirmative action measures adopted by States to guarantee equal access for persons with disabilities to inclusive education. In circumstances where the UNCESCR is adjudicating complaints of discrimination in relation to access to education, it should take into account the specific approach developed by the CRPD Committee with regard to reasonable accommodation.

In light of the overlapping issues that arise in the context of the work of the UNCESCR, on the one hand, and the CRPD Committee, on the other hand, it is essential that the emerging standards of equality, as elaborated upon by the CRPD Committee, should be factored into any consideration by the UNCESCR of the standard of reasonableness it applies to disability rights. More generally, the elaboration by the CRPD Committee of a substantive and transformative framework of equality (through its jurisprudence and general comments) can potentially guide the other human rights treaty bodies in adjudication related to the socio-economic rights of all marginalised groups. At the level of international and regional human rights law, the understanding of the equality norm has evolved greatly in recent times, from embodying the formal model of equality to endorsing a more substantive, and even transformative, conception of equality ([38], pp. 47–64). Thus, there is scope for the treaty bodies to learn lessons from the values underlying the CRPD and the CRPD Committee's approach to interpretation of the equality norm contained in the Convention.

5.3. Dignity Considerations

In any consideration of the core principle of equality, one must factor into account the inherent dignity of disabled individuals as a pertinent concern. The Preamble of the CPRD recognises that "discrimination against any person on the basis of disability is a violation of the inherent dignity and worth of the human person" [39]. The object and purpose of the CRPD includes the promotion of respect for the inherent dignity of disabled persons. Dignity also features as a central concern in General Principle 3(d), which mandates "respect for difference and acceptance of persons with disabilities as part of human diversity and humanity" [40]. The CRPD aims at overturning the stereotyped image of persons with disabilities as lacking capabilities and aims to develop such capabilities and human potential through the provision, by States and public and private entities, of sufficient resources and other forms of assistance. The reasonable accommodation duty, which spans the socio-economic provisions of the CRPD, is also based on the core norm of human dignity.

At the international level, dignity issues can be brought to life by claimants from marginalised groups, including disabled claimants, under the individual communication mechanism. Dignity considerations must therefore be central to any assessment of reasonableness by the respective human rights committees in their adjudication and pronouncements on socio-economic rights. The UNCESCR has already acknowledged, in its General Comment 5, that all services for persons with disabilities "should be provided in such a way that the persons concerned are able to maintain full respect for their rights and dignity" ([13], para. 34). However, the notion of "dignity" remains a vague normative concept and some guidance is required at the level of the treaty bodies in order to harmonise this fundamental principle for disabled persons (and, by extension, other marginalised groups) in the application of socio-economic rights ([41], p. 20).

In spite of the many criticisms of its use as a normative standard for human rights protection ([42], p. 5), it has been argued elsewhere ([5], pp. 224–28) that there are two strands to the concept of human dignity in human rights law generally, and, particularly, dignity as a guiding normative value under the CRPD. The first strand of human dignity reflects the urgency of needs of marginalised groups and requires that priority consideration be given to those needs by States. This interpretation is mirrored in the various pronouncements of the UNCESCR, among others, related to the necessity to cater for the needs of those in most dire circumstances ([15], para. 4). The second strand of human dignity at the international level correlates with the equality norm and requires consideration of the equal worth of all human beings. States must ensure to implement the rights of persons with disabilities in a manner which respects the differential characteristics and ensures that disabled persons are not forced to endure degrading circumstances in the exercise of their human rights.

Take, for instance, the right to education in both the CRPD and the ICESCR. Article 24 of the CRPD provides that States Parties shall ensure an inclusive education system at all levels and life-long learning directed to "the full development of human potential and sense of dignity [...] and the strengthening of respect for [...] human diversity" [43]. In a similar vein, Article 13(1) of the ICESCR provides that "education shall be directed to the full development of the human personality and the sense of its dignity, and shall strengthen the respect for human rights and fundamental freedoms" [44]. Without further guidance at the level of the treaty bodies, it is difficult to expand on the notion of human dignity in the context of individual rights.

The CRPD is based upon a human rights-based and capabilities-based approach [45] to disability, which recognises the dignity and worth of each individual ([46], p. 775) and, therefore, the CRPD Committee should always take human dignity into account when determining the reasonableness of measures adopted by States. The CRPD does not provide any guidance as to priority setting - in other words, which measures should be taken when a given State cannot ensure all capabilities immediately in the same timeframe. However, as Caroline Harnacke rightly points out, "the focus of justice is not on the question of what resources the State has to spend on every person but on the question of what outcome is attained" ([46], p. 777).

The domestic case law of the Canadian Supreme Court expands on the notion of human dignity in the context of persons with disabilities. In *Law v Canada (Minister of Employment and Immigration)*, the Court observes that "human dignity is harmed by unfair treatment premised upon personal traits or circumstances which do not relate to individual needs, capacities, or merits" and, furthermore, that "it is enhanced by laws which are sensitive to the needs, capacities, and merits of different individuals, taking into account the context underlying their differences" [47]. In connection with the right to inclusive education, the treaty bodies should maintain a focus on the effects of laws and policies on the needs and capabilities of disabled people. Charles Ngwena claims that the "repeated emphasis in the CRPD, including in Article 24, on the State's duty to accommodate human diversity by, *inter alia*, providing individualised support, is the Convention's greatest transformative modality" ([48], p. 478). He asserts that by placing responsibility on society, rather than on disabled learners and their carers (in terms of the economic cost of accommodation measures), Article 24 seeks to "repair, more holistically, the historical marginalisation and exclusion of disabled learners from not just the education system, but also other socio-economic systems that have been constructed on the assumption of able-bodiedness" ([48], p. 478). He further asserts that "under the CRPD, human dignity cannot depend on functional capacities. Achieving, as a prerequisite, a certain prescribed baseline of functional capacity cannot be what entitles a disabled person to have an equal claim on resources, but the fact of being human" ([48], pp. 478–79). The CRPD Committee should endeavour to frame its own capabilities-based approach and, by that token, evaluate the various measures adopted by States under the right to inclusive education in order to ensure that Article 24 of the Convention is coherently implemented.

In its draft General Comment 9, the CRPD Committee referred to the inherent dignity of persons with disabilities as "a crucial element to be considered, including in the context of reasonable accommodation" ([49], para. 24). In the provision of reasonable accommodations and in the overall enjoyment of the right to education, full account must be taken of the physical and psychological integrity and empowerment, as well as the equal self-worth of disabled people. Persons with disabilities should not be expected to exercise the right to inclusive education in conditions which are degrading or humiliating.

Interestingly, the concept of dignity has been linked by the CRPD Committee to the notion of costs. When elaborating on measures to be adopted to guarantee the general accessibility of the environment, the Committee stated that "in adapting existing buildings, reasonableness of costs must be balanced against respect for the inherent dignity of persons with disabilities" ([49], para. 24). However, the Committee did not go on to refer to dignity in such terms in the final version of General Comment 9. The CRPD Committee should take the opportunity to expand on this normative value relative to the rights contained in the Convention in order to ensure coherence in their application. This could serve to aid the other treaty bodies in the application of the concept of "human dignity" in relation to socio-economic rights realisation.

5.4. Participatory Processes/Accountability

In the application of Article 8(4) OP-ICESCR, and in any analysis by the CRPD Committee of the reasonableness of measures adopted by States under the State reporting procedure and the individual communications mechanism, the fundamental notion of participatory processes should be factored into account. General Obligation 4(3) of the CRPD recognises the pivotal importance of participation of persons with disabilities and their representative organisations in every aspect of implementation of the Convention. In order to achieve full and effective participation in society, the UNCESCR has noted that "the specific measures necessary to realise the rights of persons with disabilities must be developed in cooperation with representatives of persons with disabilities" ([13], para. 14). Furthermore, the UNCESCR has asserted that the reporting process should also "encourage and facilitate, at the national level, popular participation, public scrutiny of government policies and constructive engagement with civil society [...]" ([9], para. 10).

Bruce Porter contends that in order to realise socio-economic rights more effectively, the UNCESCR "may have to create procedures that are new to treaty bodies, in order, for example, to hear the evidence of rights claimants, access independent experts, or hear from NGO interveners" ([6], p. 53). Porter and Sandra Liebenberg contend that the OP-ICESCR "provides a new opportunity for claimants to assist the Committee in elaborating on the content of rights, properly informed by the voice and understanding of those affected." The onus would then shift "to the respondent to explain the basis for its policies or decisions" ([23], p. 7). In the context of the CRPD, non-State actors play an important role, in particular in the implementation of the individualised reasonable accommodation duty. On account of this, it will be vitally important that the respective treaty bodies develop new processes to ensure that adequate weight is given to the voice of disabled applicants and their representative organisations, as well as to non-State actors (who often have a great impact on ensuring respect for human rights) [50], in the application of human rights norms in particular national contexts and in the implementation of appropriate remedies. In arguing for aligned models of interaction between treaty bodies, national human rights institutions and civil society, Suzanne Egan notes that "there is much room to harmonise [the treaty body] working practices so as to create a less confusing landscape for these key contributors to the process" ([51], p. 228).

A consultative process of exchange of views between all stakeholders would make it easier for the treaty bodies to determine whether steps taken by States are reasonable in conception and implementation and, moreover, whether they are in compliance with the obligations contained in the respective human rights treaties. Involving persons with disabilities in socio-economic rights realisation, through, for example, drafting human rights action plans, results in increased potential for actual needs to be met and also serves to ensure that remedies are moulded to address the particular needs and contextual background against which claims have been advanced. In the context of the right to education, such plans can serve to ensure that barriers to inclusive education are eradicated and that goals towards achievement of fully inclusive systems are met, taking into account the recommendations of the human rights treaty bodies. However, these plans must not merely be a token gesture on the part of States and must be followed through on.

In addition, outcome accountability is essential. The focus of Article 24 of the CRPD is on both equality of opportunities and outcomes. In order to ensure that these objectives are being met, accountability provisions must be enacted in national laws and policies to enhance the effectiveness of services for pupils with special educational needs, as well as to enhance the outcomes for all learners. Outcomes for students with special educational needs must be consistently monitored in order to ensure that learners with disabilities are making progress commensurate with their ability and that State resources are being used to optimal effect. With regard to implementation and monitoring tools, Gauthier de Beco points to the fact that the CRPD Committee could also "encourage international collaboration to provide an overall review of relevant experiences to date and to undertake an examination of the way in which these experiences could help to improve such tools within their particular context" ([52], pp. 58–59). Disabled people should naturally be involved in all of these processes. In order to measure progress towards the full realisation of the right to inclusive education for disabled people, de Beco maintains that "when national human rights action plans and human rights indicators are available, the Committee could request [State Parties] to provide information on them and evaluate the [State Party's] capacity to implement Article 24 of the CRPD" ([52], pp. 58–59). The Committee could then "indicate to [State Parties] which targets [within their national human rights plans] need to be achieved by the national human rights action plans and evaluated by the human rights indicators for the next reporting cycle" ([53], p. 276).

5.5. Disproportionate Burden and Third-Party Benefits

The notion of disproportionate burden contained in the reasonable accommodation norm requires an individualised balancing act between the needs and interests of disabled persons, on the one hand, and duty-bearers, on the other hand. A balancing of needs and interests also takes place in the context of the obligation to realise disability rights progressively to the maximum of available resources, albeit on a different scale. There is little research available on the latter obligation and this has inevitably hindered the realisation and enforcement of rights at the national level. As de Beco points out, the progressive realisation of socio-economic rights remains problematic on account of both timing and prioritisation issues, in particular which criteria will be applied "in determining whether a State's priorities are acceptable" or the "best option" in the context of the maximum of available resources ([53], p. 276).

Without principled guidelines in human rights implementation, Jos Philips maintains that "priority setting risks becoming an ad-hoc exercise, which may harm the cause of disabled persons as well as the cause of human rights" ([54], pp. 150–51). While budget analysis is a "powerful tool for understanding government's priorities" ([55], p. 36), many questions remain unanswered with regard to "how effectively or efficiently the money is being spent, or whether the resources allocated are reaching their intended purpose" ([55], p. 36). Concerning the duty to use the maximum of available resources, Sandra Fredman has stated that three elements of government appropriations are capable of concrete assessment, namely (a) the sufficiency of government spending/investment; (b) the equity of expenditure patterns; and (c) the efficiency of expenditure ([56], p. 82). The human rights treaty bodies can look to these various aspects of resource allocation by States Parties to the Convention in determining the reasonableness of State action. The committees must look to the resource prioritisation and resource optimisation efforts of States and should pay close attention to arguments brought forward by non-governmental organisations, in particular, regarding State capacity and failure to meet benchmarks set for the full realisation of disability rights. National authorities should develop performance-based budgets, which seek to allocate resources for the achievement of certain objectives and, thereby, allow assessment of the cost-effectiveness of measures taken relative to achieving the desired result for all those in need.

In addition to consideration of the financial and other costs imposed by particular measures on States or private entities, another potentially relevant consideration is the issue of the benefits of the requested measures accruing to persons other than the disabled individual in question. In the wider context of progressive realisation, the treaty bodies might consider whether measures adopted for the benefit of one particular target group could result in benefits to a wider cohort of individuals and this may be a factor mitigating against cost arguments advanced by States. Christopher Brown notes that courts (and, by extension, the treaty bodies) could "correct the asymmetric treatment of costs by recognizing the existence of positive externalities of accommodation and taking these into account when evaluating whether a proposed accommodation is reasonable" ([57], p. 329). In that regard, Brown elaborates on the positive externalities inherent to third-party benefit analysis of reasonable accommodations on three levels in the context of employment, namely benefits to all disabled employees, benefits to the firm itself and the net social benefits model ([57], p. 329). A similar analysis could apply in the context of the progressive realisation of inclusive education. It has been argued elsewhere ([5], p. 231) that "ensuring accessibility of the educational curriculum arguably benefits other students in terms of learning outcomes (both disabled students and non-disabled students)" ([5], p. 231). Therefore, "measures taken to ensure accessibility of the curriculum could contribute to the implementation of the right to education for all" ([5], p. 231). In addition, ensuring that disabled people receive an appropriate education, and can therefore transition to full employment, has clear net social and economic benefits [58].

While each treaty body will be directly concerned with the rights of those bringing the particular claim at issue, the treaty bodies may factor into account the issue of third-party benefits in the overall consideration of whether a measure constitutes a disproportionate burden for a State or entity. This may prove to be another area in which the human rights treaty bodies can learn from each other in order to harmonise implementation of socio-economic rights and to ensure a more effective implementation at the domestic level.

6. Conclusions

This article has demonstrated the necessity for cross-fertilisation and harmonisation of socio-economic rights in the context of the international human rights treaty bodies and beyond. A particular focus was maintained on cross-fertilisation of disability rights under the CRPD and the ICESCR. It was argued throughout this article that the intersection of equality and socio-economic rights in the CRPD may provide a key to unlocking the structural inequalities which disabled people, and by extension other marginalised groups, have encountered for too long now. In turn, this has the potential to result in a transformative application of socio-economic rights at the international, national and regional levels.

As Janet Lord and Rebecca Brown point out, the OP-CRPD taken in conjunction with the OP-ICESCR "provide new entry points for claimants with disabilities and their representative organizations with the opportunity to enrich human rights advocacy through the application of reasonable accommodation across all spheres of life" ([59], p. 273). The interpretation of the CRPD by the CRPD Committee can inform socio-economic rights interpretation by all of the treaty bodies. Furthermore, the CRPD Committee might learn from the UNCESCR in its elaboration of the standard of reasonableness to be applied under the OP-ICESCR. This has the potential to advance socio-economic claims, and to harmonise disability rights (and indeed the rights of other marginalised groups), at the level of the human rights treaty bodies.

Bruce Porter argues that "the guiding principle of reasonableness review should be the right to adjudication and effective remedies" for socio-economic rights claimants, with "a particular focus on the claims advanced by marginalised and disadvantaged groups" [60]. The CRPD, as a transformative human rights treaty, taken together with the OP-CRPD and the OP-ICESCR, holds great potential for social change in the realm of socio-economic rights. The CRPD Committee and the UNCESCR, in particular, should set out coherent criteria based, *inter alia*, on the types of criteria outlined in this article and should tailor them to diverse national contexts. It should, furthermore, require from each State an account of how these criteria are being applied and implemented at the domestic level relative to socio-economic rights. This would allow the CRPD Committee to judge the diverging priority choices of States according to their overall reasonableness. Then, and only then, can persons with disabilities (and other marginalised groups) begin to enjoy their human rights on an equal basis with others.

Conflicts of Interest: The author declares no conflict of interest.

Abbreviations

The following abbreviations are used in this manuscript:

CRC	Convention on the Rights of the Child
CRPD	Convention on the Rights of Persons with Disabilities
ICESCR	International Covenant on Economic Social and Cultural Rights
OHCHR	Office of the High Commissioner on Human Rights
OP-CRPD	Optional Protocol to the Convention on the Rights of Persons with Disabilities
OP-ICESCR	Optional Protocol to the International Covenant on Economic Social and Cultural Rights
UNCESCR	United Nations Committee on Economic, Social and Cultural Rights

References and Notes

1. Ibrahim Salama. "Opening Address by Mr. Ibrahim Salama, Director, Human Rights Treaties Division, to the Committee on Enforced Disappearances, 5th session." November 2014. Available online: http://www.ohchr.org/en/NewsEvents/Pages/DisplayNews.aspx?NewsID=14048&LangID=E (accessed on 12 July 2016).
2. Rowena Daw. *The Impact of the Human Rights Act on Disabled People.* London: Disability Rights Commission, 2000.
3. UNCESCR, General Comment 16 (2005) on the equal right of men and women to the enjoyment of all economic, social and cultural rights (Article 3 of the ICESCR), adopted at the thirty-fourth session of the Committee, Geneva, 25 April-13 May 2005, UN Doc. E/C.12/2005/4.
4. See Article 2 and Article 5(3) of the CRPD.
5. Andrea Broderick. *The Long and Winding Road to Equality and Inclusion for Persons with Disabilities: The United Nations Convention on the Rights of Persons with Disabilities.* Antwerp: Intersentia, 2015.
6. Bruce Porter. "The Reasonableness of Article 8(4)—Adjudicating Claims from the Margins." *Nordisk Tidsskrift for Menneskerettigheter* 27 (2009): 39–53.
7. OHCHR. "The Dublin Statement on the Process of Strengthening of the United Nations Human Rights Treaty Body System, para. 4." Available online: http://www2.ohchr.org/english/bodies/HRTD/docs/DublinStatement.pdf (accessed on 18 July 2016).
8. See for instance, Michael O'Flaherty, and Claire O'Brien. "Reform of UN Human Rights Treaty Monitoring Bodies: A Critique of the Concept Paper on the High Commissioner's Proposal for a Unified Standing Treaty Body." *Human Rights Law Review* 7 (2007): 141–72.
9. Office of the High Commissioner for Human Rights. "Guidelines on an expanded core document and treaty-specific targeted reports and harmonized guidelines on reporting under the international human rights treaties, HRI/MC/2004/3, Annex, para. 9 (drawing on UNCESCR, General Comment No 1)." Available online: http://tbinternet.ohchr.org/_layouts/treatybodyexternal/Download.aspx?symbolno=HRI%2FMC%2F2004%2F3&Lang=en (accessed on 12 July 2016).
10. *A and B v Regierungsrat des Kantons Zürich*, Judgment of 22 September 2000, para. 2(g), Swiss Federal Supreme Court (Bundesgerichtf).
11. See, for instance, the Judgment of 15 October 1999, Osaka High Court, 1718 HANREI JIHO 30 (stating that "[general] comments of the Human Rights Committee do not legally bind the interpretation of the ICCPR and the ICESCR by Japanese courts").
12. The prohibited grounds of discrimination in Article 2(2) ICESCR are: "race, colour, sex, language, religion, political or other opinion, national or social origin, property, birth or other status."
13. See UNCESCR, General Comment 5 on Persons with Disabilities, adopted on 09/12/94 at the Eleventh Session of the Committee, U.N. Doc E/1995/22.

14. Commission on Human Rights. "Report of the Open-Ended Working Group to Consider Options Regarding Elaboration of an Optional Protocol to the ICESCR in its First Session, UN Doc. E/CN.4/2004/44 (2004)." Available online: https://documents-dds-ny.un.org/doc/UNDOC/GEN/G04/120/29/PDF/G0412029. pdf?OpenElement (accessed on 14 July 2016).

15. United Nations Committee on Economic Social and Cultural Rights (UNCESCR). "An evaluation of the obligation to take steps to the 'Maximum of Available Resources' Under an Optional Protocol to the Covenant (2007), U.N. Doc. E/C.12/2007/1, adopted at the thirty-eighth session of the Committee on 10 May 2007." Available online: http://www2.ohchr.org/english/bodies/cescr/docs/statements/Obligationtotakesteps-2007.pdf (accessed 16 April 2016).

16. Lillian Chenwei. "Unpacking 'Progressive Realisation', its Relation to Resources, Minimum Core and Reasonableness, and some Methodological Considerations for Assessing Compliance." *De Jure* 46 (2013): 742–69.

17. See the categorisations set out in Gerard Quinn, and Theresia Degener. *Human Rights and Disability: The Current Use and Future Potential of United Nations Human Rights Instruments in the Context of Disability.* New York: Geneva: United Nations, 2002.

18. This section has largely been taken from Andrea Broderick. *The Long and Winding Road to Equality and Inclusion for Persons with Disabilities: The United Nations Convention on the Rights of Persons with Disabilities.* Antwerp: Intersentia, 2015 [5].

19. General Obligation 4(1) of the CRPD reads as follows: "States Parties undertake to ensure and promote the *full realization* of all human rights and fundamental freedoms for all persons with disabilities without discrimination of any kind on the basis of disability. To this end, States Parties undertake: a) To adopt all *appropriate* legislative, administrative and other measures for the implementation of the rights recognized in the present Convention." [emphasis added].

20. Office of the High Commissioner of Human Rights. "Signing of the Convention on the Rights of Persons with Disabilities and its Optional Protocol. Opening Address—High Level Dialogue: From Vision to Action: The Road to Implementation of the Convention." 30 March 2007. Available online: http://www.un.org/esa/socdev/enable/documents/Stat_Conv/High%20Commissioner%20PM%20speakingnoteshrsigningpanelFINAL.doc (accessed on 18 March 2016).

21. Fons Coomans. "Reviewing Implementation of Social and Economic Rights: An Assessment of the 'Reasonableness' Test as Developed by the South African Constitutional Court." *Heidelberg Journal of International Law* 65 (2005): 167–96.

22. See the statement by Ms. Louise Arbour. "High Commissioner for Human Rights to the third session of the Open-Ended WG OP ICESCR (Third session, 2006)." Available online: http://www.ohchr.org/EN/Issues/ESCR/OEWG/Pages/OpenEndedWGIndex.aspx (accessed on 15 July 2016).

23. Bruce Porter, and Sandra Liebenberg. "Consideration of Merits under the OP-ICESCR: Reasonableness Review under 8(4) and the Maximum of Available Resources Standard. Notes for Discussion at the Workshop on Strategic Litigation under the OP-ICESCR." Available online: https://docs.escr-net.org/usr_doc/Porter_and_Liebenberg,_Reasonableness.pdf (accessed on 16 July 2016).

24. Helen Keller, and Leena Grover. "General Comments of the Human Rights Committee and their Legitimacy." In *UN Human Rights Treaty Bodies: Law and Legitimacy.* Edited by Helen Keller and Geir Ulfstein. Cambridge: Cambridge University Press, 2012.

25. Ad-Hoc Committee on the CRPD. "Seventh Session of the Ad-Hoc Committee, volume 8(12)." 31 January 2006. Available online: www.un.org/esa/socdev/enable/rights/ahc7sum31jan.htm (accessed on 16 October 2014).

26. Gerard Quinn, and Theresia Degener. *Human Rights and Disability: The Current Use and Future Potential of United Nations Human Rights Instruments in the Context of Disability.* New York: Geneva: United Nations, 2002.

27. Peter Burnell, and Vicky Randall. "The international human rights regime is a fairly effective promotional regime but a relatively ineffective implementation regime." In *Politics in the Developing World,* 2nd ed. Oxford: Oxford University Press, 2008.

28. UN Committee on the Rights of Persons with Disabilities, Concluding Observations to Australia, UN Doc. CRPD/C/AUS/CO/1 (2013).

29. See generally, Eitan Felner. "New Frontier in Economic and Social Rights Advocacy? Turning Quantitative Data into a Tool for Human Rights Accountability." *International Journal on Human Rights* 5 (2008): 109–30.

30. Inclusion International. "The Implications of the Convention on the Rights of Persons with Disabilities (CRPD) for *Education for All*." Available online: http://inclusion-international.org/wp-content/uploads/2013/08/ImplicationsCRPD-dr2-X.pdf (accessed on 30 April 2016).
31. The Right to Education Project has developed over 200 indicators on the right to education according to the 4-A framework (availability, accessibility, acceptability, and adaptability), intended to be used as a tool to evaluate States' progress towards the full realisation of the right to education, to identify violations of the right to education, and to enable civil society to hold governments to account for their obligations regarding education. Available online: http://www.right-to-education.org/sites/right-to-education.org/files/resourceattachments/RTE_List_Right_to_Education_Indicators_May_2013.pdf (accessed on 17 July 2016).
32. See article 31(2) of the CRPD.
33. Sandra Liebenberg, and Beth Goldblatt. "The Interrelationship between Equality and Socio-Economic Rights under South Africa's Transformative Constitution." *South African Journal on Human Rights* 23 (2007): 335–61.
34. The UNCESCR has stated that non-discrimination and equality 'are essential to the exercise and enjoyment of economic, social and cultural rights.' UNCESCR, General Comment 20: Non-Discrimination in Economic, Social and Cultural Rights (Article 2, para. 2) (2009).
35. Susan J. Peters. "Inclusive Education: An EFA Strategy for All Children." Report on Inclusive Education. Washington, DC, USA: World Bank, November 2004.
36. Committee on the Rights of Persons with Disabilities, Concluding Observations to Argentina, U.N. Doc. CRPD/C/ARG/CO/1 (2012).
37. Sandra Liebenberg. "Adjudicating Social Rights under a Transformative Constitution." In *Social Rights Jurisprudence: Emerging Trends in International and Comparative Law*. Edited by Malcom Langford. Cambridge: Cambridge University Press, 2008.
38. See generally on this point, Oddný Mjöll Arnardóttir. "A Future of Multidimensional Disadvantage Equality." In *The UN Convention on the Rights of Persons with Disabilities: European and Scandinavian Perspectives*. Edited by Oddný Mjöll Arnardóttir and Gerard Quinn. Leiden: Martinus Nijhoff, 2009.
39. CRPD, Preamble, para. (h).
40. CRPD, General Principle 3(d). See also General Principle 3(a) of the Convention, which mandates respect for the inherent dignity, individual autonomy (including the freedom to make one's own choices) and independence of persons with disabilities.
41. Sandra Fredman rightly notes that "the right to equality cannot simply be collapsed into the right to dignity". Sandra Fredman. "Substantive Equality Revisited." Legal Research Paper Series, Paper No. 70/2014. October 2014. Available online: http://papers.ssrn.com/sol3/papers.cfm?abstract_id=2510287 (accessed on 17 July 2016).
42. For a summary of such criticisms, see Sandra Liebenberg. "The Value of Human Dignity in Interpreting Socio-Economic Rights." *South African Journal on Human Rights* 21 (2005): 1–31.
43. CRPD, Article 24(i).
44. CRPD, Article 13(1).
45. The capabilities approach was developed by Amartya Sen and refined by Martha Nussbaum. See Martha C. Nussbaum. "Capabilities and Human Rights." *Fordham Law Review* 66 (1997): 273–300. [CrossRef]
46. Caroline Harnacke. "Disability and Capability: Exploring the Usefulness of Martha Nussbaum's Capabilities Approach for the UN Disability Rights Convention." *Journal of Law, Medicine & Ethics* 41 (2013): 768–80. [CrossRef] [PubMed]
47. *Law v Canada (Minister of Employment and Immigration)* [1999] 1 S.C.R. 497, para. 53.
48. Charles G. Ngwena. "Human Right to Inclusive Education: Exploring a Double Discourse of Inclusive Education Using South Africa as a Case Study." *Netherlands Quarterly of Human Rights* 31 (2013): 473–504.
49. CRPD Committee. "Draft General Comment on Article 9—Accessibility." Available online: http://www.ohchr.org/EN/HRBodies/CRPD/Pages/DGCArticles12And9.aspx (accessed on 18 June 2016).
50. See Karl Hanson. "Strengthening legitimacy, effectiveness and efficiency of the UN Human Rights Treaty Body System." 20 October 2011. Available online: http://www2.ohchr.org/english/bodies/HRTD/docs/submissions201112/Academics/KarlHanson.pdf (accessed on 17 July 2016).
51. Suzanne Egan. "Strengthening the United Nations Human Rights Treaty Body System." *Human Rights Law Review* 13 (2013): 209–43. [CrossRef]

52. Gauthier de Beco. "Transition to Inclusive Education Systems according to the Convention on the Rights of Persons with Disabilities." *Nordic Journal of Human Rights* 34 (2016): 40–59. [CrossRef]
53. Gauthier de Beco. "Interplay between Human Rights and Development the Other Way Round: The Emerging Use of Quantitative Tools for Measuring the Progressive Realisation of Economic, Social and Cultural Rights." *Human Rights and International Legal Discourse* 4 (2010): 265–87.
54. Jos Philips. "Human Rights, the CRPD, and Priority-Setting." In *Disability and Human Rights: Legal, Ethical and Conceptual Implications of the Convention on the Rights of Persons with Disabilities.* Edited by Joel Anderson and Jos Philips. Utrecht: Netherlands Institute of Human Rights, 2012, pp. 150–51.
55. Helena Hofbauer, Ann Blyberg, and Warren Krafchik. "Dignity Counts: A Guide to Using Budget Analysis to Advance Human Rights, (Fundar, IBP, IHRIP)." 2004. Available online: www.internationalbudget.org/files/Dignity_Counts_english1.pdf (accessed on 16 July 2016).
56. Sandra Fredman. *Human Rights Transformed: Positive Rights and Positive Duties.* Oxford: Oxford University Press, 2008, p. 82.
57. Christopher B. Brown. "Incorporating Third-Party Benefits into the Cost-Benefit Calculus of Reasonable Accommodation." *Virginia Journal of Social Policy and the Law* 18 (2010–2011): 319–44.
58. See generally Sebastian Buckup. "The Price of Exclusion: The Economic Consequences of Excluding People with Disabilities from the World of Work." Employment Working Paper No. 43, International Labour Office, Geneva, 2009.
59. Janet Lord, and Rebecca Brown. "The Role of Reasonable Accommodation in Securing Substantive Equality for Persons with Disabilities: The UN Convention on the Rights of Persons with Disabilities." In *Critical Perspectives on Human Rights and Disability Policy.* Edited by Marcia H. Rioux, Lee Ann Basser and Melinda Jones. The Hague: Martinus Nijhoff, 2011.
60. Bruce Porter. "Reasonableness in the Optional Protocol to the ICESCR." Available online: http://www.socialrights.ca/documents/Reasonableness%20in%20the%20OP-ICESCR.pdf (accessed on 18 July 2016).

![laws logo]

Article

Legal Capacity and Access to Justice: The Right to Participation in the CRPD

Graduate School of Business and Law, RMIT University, 124 La Trobe St, Melbourne, VIC 3000, Australia;
penelope.weller@rmit.edu.au; Tel. +6-139-925-5710

Academic Editor: Anna Arstein-Kerslake
Received: 24 December 2015; Accepted: 15 February 2016; Published: 8 March 2016

Abstract: This article provides an applied analysis of Article 12 (Equal recognition before the law) of the Convention on the Rights of Persons with Disabilities (CRPD) and Article 13 (Access to justice) in the context of Article 6 (Women with disabilities). Recent literature on the CRPD has extended the analysis of Article 12 to consider its broader relevance for the interpretation of Article 13. The interaction between Article 12 and Article 13 is an emerging issue in CRPD debates. This article argues that the CRPD must be interpreted in light of current human rights theory. It provides a case study of the interaction between Article 12 and Article 13 based on the facts recited in the Court of Appeal case in the United Kingdom (*RP v Nottingham City Council* (2008)) and RP's petition to the European Court of Human Rights (*RP and Others v United Kingdom* (2012)). The analysis shows that CRPD principles could and should have been applied in RP's case. It concludes that current practices excluding people with disabilities from participation in legal proceedings are contrary to the CRPD.

Keywords: convention on the Rights of Persons with Disabilities; Article 12; Article 13; capacity; participation

1. Introduction

The Convention on the Rights of Persons with Disabilities (CRPD) continues to generate vigorous debate, particularly with respect to Article 12 (Equal recognition before the law) [1–18]. The Article 12 debate is characterized by a marked diversity of opinion and sometimes heated disagreement. In a contested intellectual environment, there is a danger that the contribution of the CRPD may be missed if the "philosophical and moral assumptions underpinning the formal structures of the law" remain unexamined [15]. As the scope and reach of Article 12 becomes more clearly defined, previously taken for granted structures in the law are thrown into sharp relief. This is especially so when Article 12 is considered in tandem with other articles in the CRPD. The purpose of this article is to consider the interaction between Article 12 (Equal recognition before the law) and Article 13 (Access to justice). The fundamental importance of the interaction between these two articles has been highlighted by Eilionoir Flynn, Lucy Series and Eilionoir Flynn and Anna Lawson [19–21]. Other CRPD scholars have commented on the application of Article 13 in the criminal law [14–18,22–25]. This article considers the application of Article 13 (Access to justice) in family law proceedings. Specifically, it considers the question of instructional capacity through an analysis of the factual situation in the English case of *RP v Nottingham City Council* (2008) and RP's petition to the European Court of Human Rights [26]. RP's case illuminates the way taken for granted attitudes, practices and processes in the law compound the discrimination experienced by people with disabilities. The effect of such practices is the exclusion of people with disabilities from participation in the law. Without participation, access to justice is limited and the right to equal recognition before the law is compromised. Considering RP's case in light of the CRPD provides an opportunity to illustrate how a "shift from substituted decision making to supported decision making" would enable RP's active participation in the legal process consistent

Laws 2016, *5*, 13   43   www.mdpi.com/journal/laws

with Article 13 (Access to Justice) ([26], para. 22). The argument advanced in this article is that RP's involvement in the legal proceedings could and should have been maintained. Rather than being excluded on the basis of a lack of mental capacity, RP should have been provided with appropriate information and support. In addition, institutional structures and processes should have been altered to accommodate her disability. The interpretation of Article 12 put forward by the Committee on the Rights of Persons with Disabilities asserts that determinations that a person "lacks mental capacity for the purposes of the law" are not permitted in a human rights compliant framework [27]. If the latter proposition is accepted, a profound shift in current practice is required.

RP's case is significant because it illustrates the process and consequence of exclusion from the law. RP was a 21-year-old young woman with a mild intellectual disability who gave birth to a premature infant with significant health problems. After a period of intensive hospital treatment, the health authority initiated formal care proceedings, seeking to place RP's child with a foster family. At that time, it was determined that RP lacked the capacity to instruct her appointed solicitor. A *guardian ad litem* or guardian solicitor was appointed to represent RP in the proceedings. RP and her family contested the subsequent placement [26].

The litigation surrounding RP provides a "case study" for the analysis of CRPD principles. Considered from a CRPD perspective, three CRPD articles are directly relevant to RP's situation: Article 6 (Women with disabilities) recognises the multiple discriminations faced by women and girls; Article 13 (Access to justice) requires state parties to facilitate the participation of people with disabilities in all legal proceedings; and Article 12 (Equal recognition before the law) asserts the right to recognition before the law [1]. The analysis of substitute decision making in CRPD General Comment 1 is also relevant for the analysis of RP's case [27]. It may be the case that had appropriate support been provided from the outset, RP may have been better assisted in the care of her child. With respect to the legal proceedings, had support been provided, RP could have understood the legal context, contested the evidence, expressed her point of view and challenged the decision to remove her child. This does not mean that the outcome of the care proceedings should have been different ([26], paras. 19–20). The point being made is that the grounds upon which a child is removed should be clear and untainted by discrimination and preconceived ideas about disability and motherhood. To this end, the CRPD requires the provision of support to enable the full involvement of people with disabilities in the processes of the law, including the modification of institutional practices that work to exclude people from participation in such processes. Ultimately, what is at stake is the democratic ideal of full participation in society for people with disabilities. As the work of Tom Tyler has shown, procedural justice and due process play a vital role in ensuring individual and community acceptance and confidence in legal decisions and processes [28–30]. Procedural justice informs contemporary approaches to justice and complements the human rights approach. The current practice of excluding people with disabilities from legal proceedings following a determination of instructional incapacity, as occurred in RP's case, no longer accords with the expectations of a modern community.

The argument for universal participation is advanced in the five parts of this article. Part 2 provides a brief sketch of the evolution of human rights thinking from the 20th to 21st centuries showing how international human rights law and critical disability theory entwine to illuminate the meaning and significance of the CRPD. Part 3 provides an extended account of RP's case. Part 4 provides an analysis of RP's situation in light of Article 12, showing that the assessment of instructional capacity in the first instance was not conducted according to law. In keeping with CRPD General Comment 1, the extended analysis in Part 5 concludes that tests for capacity are not compatible with the CRPD ([27], para. 25 (i)). In summary, this article illustrates how the principle of universal legal capacity can be pursued by showing how the CRPD ethos of social and legal participation could and should have been applied in RP's case.

2. Social and Legal Inclusion as a Human Right

Gerard Quinn argues that the CRPD requires scholars to re-conceptualise the philosophical and legal relationships thought to constitute citizenship, entitlement and the power and responsibilities of the state [15]. Quinn alludes to the conceptual developments in international human rights law that recognise human rights as entitlements adhering to socially, economically and spiritually contextualised human persons ([14]; [31], p. 31; [32], p. 274). In human rights documents, recognition of the human context is crystallised in the statement that "all human rights are universal, indivisible, interdependent and interrelated" [33]. Much of the human rights discourse since the World Congress in 1993, when the latter phrase was coined, has sought to articulate the interconnectedness of human rights and their relevance for the human condition ([34], p. 110). For example, Amartya Sen posits a contemporary analysis of justice as one that seeks the actual realisation of rights in society (understood as integrated rights) ([35], p. 9). The emergence of a complex, contextualised account of human rights is also evident in the medical understanding of the social determinants of health and the economic appreciation of development [36,37]. In human rights terms, these ideas manifest in the principle of substantive equality. Accordingly, "...the notion of equality in international law has (also) changed...with the conceptual shift from formal equality to substantive equality" ([27], para. 14). The disability rights movement has taken the theoretical analysis of interconnected human rights a step further by appreciating the intersections between human rights theory, feminism, critical theory, critical disability studies, and the notion of embodiment [14,22]. Disability theory responds to the documentation of the mechanisms and effects of discrimination, marginalisation, inequality and exclusion [38,39]. The direct involvement of people with disabilities in the drafting of the CRPD also underpins the human rights logic expressed in the CRPD [2]. The CRPD recognizes social and legal *exclusion* as the basis of discrimination against people with disability (author's emphasis). The CRPD is oriented toward social and legal inclusion and recognises social and legal inclusion as a tool for reintegration in society.

The emphasis in the CRPD on inclusion and participation is evident in the "social model of disability", the requirement of equal access and equality before the law, the inclusion of reasonable accommodation and the overarching concern with participation in society as a measure of social change ([38]; [40], p. 15). Recognition of the barriers experienced by people with disability has informed the new approach. In CRPD terms, inclusion is the key to the realisation of human rights for people with disabilities. CRPD principles point to the proposition that the starting point for all decisions or procedures in the law and elsewhere is the involvement of people with disabilities [14].

3. The Facts of RP's Case

This section provides a brief summary of the facts in RP's case based on the European Court of Human Rights (ECrtHR) judgment [26]. As is noted above, RP was a young woman of 21 years of age with a mild intellectual disability who gave birth to a 27-week-old premature baby ([26], para. 7). RP had not known she was pregnant and was not in a relationship with the father of the child ([26], para. 7). She lived with her family in modest circumstances. The family was "known" to the health authority. RP's baby had serious health problems requiring 24-hour intensive care. RP visited the hospital and participated in the care of her child but did not establish a good rapport with hospital staff ([26], para. 8). The staff reported that she "only" attended for 1–2 hours a day and seemed unable to complete basic care tasks ([26], para. 9). It appears that the health authority did not view other family members as suitable caregivers. It is not clear from the documentation whether the practical and emotional difficulties any young woman would face in RP's situation were considered. The local authority was concerned about RP's ability and motivation to care for her child, and conducted a "parenting assessment" ([26], para. 10). The baby was placed in temporary foster care. Over the following seven months, RP participated in parenting education and supported contact visits. Following another parenting assessment, the health authority instigated care proceedings for permanent foster placement, contrary to RP's (and her family's) wish to keep her child ([26], para. 11)

In anticipation of the care proceedings, it was arranged that RP be represented by a publically funded, independent solicitor. After their initial interaction, RP's solicitor raised serious concerns about RP's ability to understand the advice she was given ([26], para. 12). RP's "capacity to instruct" was assessed by a clinical psychologist, who advised the appointment of a *guardian ad litem* or litigation guardian. In English law, the appointment of a litigation guardian, pursuant to the Mental Capacity Act is the responsibility of the Official Solicitor ([41], s51(2)(e)). The role of the litigation guardian is to represent a person who lacks instructional capacity on a best interests basis ([26], para. 13). RP's original (independent) solicitor was appointed as her *guardian ad litem*.

The care proceedings resulted in the permanent placement of RP's child. RP appealed unsuccessfully in the UK courts. The Official Solicitor did not oppose the making of the care order. Acting in accordance with the best interest obligation, therefore, the litigation guardian did not put RP's case to the court nor contest the evidence ([20], p. 68). RP and her mother, father, and brother subsequently brought parallel applications before the ECrtHR, with the Equality and Human Rights Commission (United Kingdom) intervening [26]. RP argued, unsuccessfully, that her rights under Articles 6, 8, 13 and 14 of the European Convention on Human Rights (ECHR) had been breached [42]. While the ECrtHR accepted that RP had litigation capacity for its purposes, the court found that the earlier appointment of the guardian was appropriate; that further assessment of RP's capacity had been taken during proceedings; that there were appropriate and effective means in place to enable RP to challenge the involvement of the guardian; that it would not have been practical to review RP's capacity in the courts; that the solicitor had taken proper steps to make RP aware of the involvement of the Official Solicitor and the nature of the guardian's role; and that the guardian solicitor was not obliged to advance the argument desired by RP, or to ensure that her views were put to the court ([26], paras. 69–76; [43]). Curiously, the CRPD was mentioned in support of the court's findings but was not discussed at length [44].

4. CRPD Based Analysis

Article 13—Access to justice

1. States Parties shall ensure effective access to justice for persons with disabilities on an equal basis with others, including through the provision of procedural and age-appropriate accommodations, in order to facilitate their effective role as direct and indirect participants, including as witnesses, in all legal proceedings, including at investigative and other preliminary stages.

2. In order to help to ensure effective access to justice for persons with disabilities, States Parties shall promote appropriate training for those working in the field of administration of justice, including police and prison staff.

Article 13 (Access to justice) requires States Parties "to ensure effective access to justice for persons with disabilities on an equal basis with others" [1]. This is to be achieved "through the provision of procedural and age appropriate accommodations", applies to "all legal proceedings" and to both direct and indirect participatory roles ([1], Article 13(1)). As is noted above, RP was excluded from participation in the legal proceedings in the UK on the basis that she lacked instructional capacity. While Article 13 is silent about the notion of instructional capacity, CRPD General Comment 1indicates that it is correct to read Article 13 in tandem with Article 12 [4,5,27].

Article 12 invokes the proposition that people with disabilities should never be excluded from participation in legal proceedings on the basis of disability. According to General Comment 1, "(d)enial of legal capacity must not be based on personal traits such as gender, race, or disability, or have the purpose or effect of treating the person differently" ([27], para. 9). Moreover, while individuals may have different cognitive capabilities, a person's lack of mental capacity must never be the basis for a denial of legal capacity ([27], paras. 13–14). This means that both direct and indirect discrimination on the basis of disability are not permitted under the CRPD. Tests for mental capacity offend the principle of indirect discrimination because they will have a disproportionate impact on people with cognitive impairment ([27], para. 9). The principle of indirect discrimination, therefore, creates a conundrum for the operation of laws that rely on determinations of mental capacity. If capacity testing is unacceptable, how will the law operate? Answering this question requires a close examination of the text of Article 12.

4.1. Article 12(1)—Recognition as a Person before the Law

1. States Parties reaffirm that persons with disabilities have the right to recognition everywhere as persons before the law.

Article 12 is pivotal to the CRPD's conception of social and legal inclusion. Article 12(1) affirms the universal right to "recognition everywhere as persons before the law" without exception or limitation ([3], p.124).

4.2. Article 12(2) on an Equal Basis with Others

2. States Parties shall recognize that persons with disabilities enjoy legal capacity on an equal basis with others in all aspects of life.

Article 12(2) recognises that "persons with disabilities enjoy legal capacity on an equal basis with others in all aspects of life" [1]. Legal capacity refers to the dual concepts of legal standing (where the person who is recognised as a holder of rights) and legal agency (where the person is recognised as being able to "create, modify or end legal relationships" ([27], para. 12; [45], p. 23). A person with legal standing is entitled to the full protection of his or her rights by the legal system. Legal capacity therefore encompasses the right to be recognised as a person before the law and the subsequent right to have one's decisions legally recognised [3]. In CRPD terms, protection of the law is not sought through withdrawal from the law, but through active participation in legal processes. In short, the CRPD promotes a radical revision of the law. Its approach stands in contrast with laws that operate on the assumption that mental incapacity is a threshold requirement or necessary precondition of legal capacity.

Article 12(2) recognises that people with disabilities are frequently denied legal capacity on discriminatory grounds ([27], para. 8). Typically, legal capacity is denied on the basis that the person has a disability (the status approach), that the person makes an unpalatable decision (the outcome approach) or that the person's reasoning is faulty (the functional approach) ([27], para. 15). A key difficulty for the CRPD approach to universal legal capacity is that modern legal systems promote functional tests of capacity as enlightened, objective standards that are capable of equal application to all people ([27], para. 9). RP's case illustrates Amita Dhanda's substantive point that capacity assessments are typically overlaid with discriminatory attitudes and practices [2]. The first instance of discrimination in RP's case was the erroneous assessment of capacity.

4.3. The Assessment of Capacity in RP's Case

In English law, the relevant standard for capacity is found in Articles 2 and 3 of the Mental Capacity Act 2005 (UK) [41]. The standard for instructional capacity is found in the Court of Appeal decision of *Masterman-Lister* (*Masterman-Lister v Brutton & Co (Nos 1 and 2))* [46].

Article 2 (1) of the Mental Capacity Act states:

For the purposes of this Act, a person lacks capacity in relation to a matter if at the material time he is unable to make a decision for himself in relation to the matter because of an impairment of, or a disturbance in the functioning of, the mind or brain.

Article 3 (Inability to make decisions) of the Mental Capacity Act states:

(1) For the purposes of Section 2, a person is unable to make a decision for himself if he is unable—

  (a) to understand the information relevant to the decision,

  (b) to retain that information,

  (c) to use or weigh that information as part of the process of making the decision, or

  (d) to communicate his decision (whether by talking, using sign language or any other means).

(2) A person is not to be regarded as unable to understand the information relevant to a decision if he is able to understand an explanation of it given to him in a way that is appropriate to his circumstances (using simple language, visual aids or any other means).

(3) The fact that a person is able to retain the information relevant to a decision for a short period only does not prevent him from being regarded as able to make the decision.

Article 3 represents a codification of the common law of capacity as developed in the English case law in the second half of the twentieth century, and is a standard that has been adopted in most Anglo-American jurisdictions [47,48].

In Masterman-Lister (Masterman-Lister v Brutton & Co (Nos 1 and 2)), Lord Justice Chadwick considered how instructional capacity should be assessed. His Honour stated that capacity must be assessed contemporaneously and in relation to the relevant transaction or decision "What is required is the capacity to understand the nature of the transaction involved *when it is explained*" ([46], per Chadwick LJ at para. 58). His Honour continues:

> ...the test to be applied, it seems to me, is whether the party to legal proceedings is capable of understanding, with the assistance of such proper explanation from legal advisors and experts in other disciplines as the case may require, the issues on which his consent or decision is likely to be necessary in the course of proceedings. If he has capacity to understand that which he needs to understand in order to pursue or defend a claim, I can see no reason why the law whether substantive or procedure should require the imposition of a next friend or guardian ad litem...([46], per Chadwick LJ at para. 75).

According to Chadwick LJ, a person is considered able to understand the information relevant to the decision if he or she can understand an explanation about that information in broad terms and simple language. Moreover, he or she should not be regarded as unable to make a rational decision merely because it is not a decision that another person with ordinary prudence would make.

In RP's case, a clinical psychologist assessed her instructional capacity independent from the informational context. The psychologist's report concluded that RP had a significant learning disability, stating that:

> Because of the difficulties [RP] has in understanding, processing and recalling information, I believe that she will find it very difficult to understand the advice given by her solicitor. She will not be able to make informed decisions on the basis of this advice, particularly when this involved anticipating possible outcomes. It would be appropriate for the Official Solicitor to become involved ([26], para. 13).

This passage indicates that the clinical psychologist applied an incorrect legal test. Many individuals who are permitted to instruct solicitors have a general understanding of the objectives and purpose of legal proceedings, but would be unable to follow the detail of legal argument. To provide expert advice on such matters is the very purpose of seeking legal advice. The discriminatory basis of RP's assessment is evident. First, an assessment of capacity should never occur in isolation from the information that is relevant to the decision. Second, there should always be an opportunity for explanation. Finally, the psychologist placed the bar of understanding too high. What is required is an ability to understand the general nature of the transaction.

4.4. Substituting RP's Judgement

The consequence of the determination that RP lacked instructional capacity was the appointment of a substitute decision maker in the form of a *guardian ad litem*. Once the guardian was appointed, RP was considered to be a "protected party" and was barred from giving instructions ([26], para. 28). One of the major achievements of CRPD General Comment 1 is the clear definition of what constitutes substitute decision-making. Substitute decision-making occurs when:

(a)   The legal capacity of the person is removed;

(b)   A substitute decision maker is appointed by another person without the consent or approval of the person with a disability; and

(c)   The substitute decision-maker is required to make decisions on a best interest basis ([27], para. 27).

Substitute decision-making, as defined in the General Comment, is contrary to CRPD principles. In RP's case, the appointment of *guardian ad litem* was made without RP's knowledge or consent, because RP was never effectively informed that the appointment had been made. RP believed (mistakenly) that the solicitor was acting as an independent advocate, when, in fact, the solicitor had been appointed as the litigation guardian. The failure to effectively inform RP that she was subject to special arrangements lies at the heart of procedural justice deficit in the justice process.

4.5. Best Interests

The special arrangement also involved the substitution of RP's wishes with a best interest test. CRPD General Comment 1 makes it clear that "(T)he 'best interests' principle is not a safeguard which complies with Article 12 in relation to adults" ([27], para. 21). It states that "the 'will and preferences' paradigm must replace the 'best interests' paradigm to ensure that persons with disabilities enjoy the right to legal capacity on an equal basis with others" ([27], para. 21). RP was represented in the care proceeding by a litigation guardian on a "best interest" basis. Aside from the immediate observation that the CRPD does not support a best interest approach, the court's discussion of best interests reveals that in RP's case, RP's best interests were conflated with the best interests of her child. As is the norm in the Official Solicitor's scheme, RP's child was not represented in the proceedings. The matter of the child's representation is a separate issue that is beyond the scope of this article. However, in RP's case, the Official Solicitor appeared to interpret the responsibility of the litigation guardian as including consideration of the best interests of the child. It was assumed that it was in RP's best interests for the child's best interests to dictate the outcome of the proceedings. The conflation of best interest between mother and child reveals the role that an ideal standard of motherhood played in determining the outcome. That the legal actors involved were willing to interpret RP's most intimate responses to the experience of motherhood, in her absence and without consultation, and with full knowledge of her desire to mother the child, encapsulates the loss of dignity that is concomitant of the denial of legal capacity. Both the UK court and the ECrtHR accepted without question the appropriateness of the substitute decision-making arrangement.

4.6. Article 12(3)—The Obligation to Provide Support

3.   States Parties shall take appropriate measures to provide access by persons with disabilities to the support they may require in exercising their legal capacity.

The CRPD's answer to the traditional system of substitute decision-making is the introduction of "measures to support legal capacity". The CRPD requires all substitute decision-making arrangements to be replaced by supported decision-making. The requirement in Article 12(3) is expressed as the requirement that individuals with disabilities are entitled to "support...in exercising their legal capacity" [1] The CRPD debate has tended to focus on "supported decision-making" in its various forms rather than the idea of "support for legal capacity" which has a broader meaning [4]. Support for legal capacity should enable persons with a disability to exercise their legal capacity and should otherwise give effect to the decisions of people with disabilities. Measures of support for capacity encompass "informal and formal support arrangements of varying types and intensity" ([27], para. 17), with the overarching requirement that such arrangements are suitable for the person, desired by them and subject to appropriate safeguards in accordance with Article 12(4) ([27], para. 20).

In RP's case, the independent solicitor was appointed as her *guardian ad litem*. RP argued that she was never informed of the appointment. At the time, she believed that her solicitor continued to act on her behalf. RP claimed that no one explained the situation to her. She did not know that she could challenge the determination of capacity or challenge the appointment of the Official Solicitor. The Official Solicitor claimed that RP was informed of these matters by way of a standard letter that RP received in the post ([26], paras. 14–15). The letter set out the legal matters and the consequences of the determination that RP lacked instructional capacity. The letter was written in complex and technical language. It seems strange that such a letter was posted to a person who is known to have a learning disability, as a means of communication. In the absence of a verbal or plain language explanation, it seems unlikely that RP could have understood the information in that form.

It cannot be concluded that because RP did not understand the letter, she lacked the capacity to understand the information. Rather, it illustrates the importance of appropriate explanation and support. Without appropriate explanation, most people are unable to understand complex legal concepts. It is significant in the context of the letter that consideration of RP's functional literacy appears to be absent. Moreover, because RP continued to have some contact with her solicitor, she assumed the original instructing relationship continued. In the absence of a proper explanation of the changed relationship, RP was prevented from considering how best to proceed, or whether to seek additional assistance. She was not made aware that the scheme allowed for the appointment to be revoked if there was a challenge to the determination of capacity, if it were determined that the person had capacity, or it was determined that the person had regained capacity. Without such information and advice, RP was effectively prevented from triggering the "safeguards" that were embedded in the Official Solicitor scheme. The practices of the Official Solicitor rendered the rights embedded in the scheme illusory.

4.7. Article 12(4)—Safeguards

> 4. States Parties shall ensure that all measures that relate to the exercise of legal capacity provide for appropriate and effective safeguards to prevent abuse in accordance with international human rights law. Such safeguards shall ensure that measures relating to the exercise of legal capacity respect the rights, will and preferences of the person, are free of conflict of interest and undue influence, are proportional and tailored to the person's circumstances, apply for the shortest time possible and are subject to regular review by a competent, independent and impartial authority or judicial body. The safeguards shall be proportional to the degree to which such measures affect the person's rights and interests.

RP's case illustrates the importance of surrounding "measures that support capacity" with appropriate safeguards as outlined in Article 12(4). The question of how the safeguards requirement in 12(4) should be satisfied is yet to be fully addressed in the CRPD literature [3,4]. Article 12(4) safeguards require that measures supporting legal capacity are directed toward recognition of the person's "rights, wills and preferences". Article 12(4) therefore speaks to the quality of support relationships and mechanisms. It aims to ensure that interactions with the people with a disability are free "from fear aggression threat deception or manipulation" ([27], para. 22). It contemplates the introduction of both formal and informal arrangements to monitor such relationships.

A similar point was made in the submissions of the Equality and Human Rights Commission (United Kingdom) to the ECrtHR. The Commission submitted that:

...Articles 6, 8 or 14 could be breached if limitations were placed on a learning-disabled litigant's right of access to a court which were not strictly necessary, or if a litigation friend did not take sufficient positive steps to ensure that the specific needs and interests of such a parent were properly taken into account. In particular, it was important that strong procedural safeguards existed to ensure that the parent's views were properly, fully and fairly advanced before the court. In order for this to be the case, it was essential that decisions about the parent's litigation capacity should not be taken on the basis of a joint report part funded by an opposing party in family litigation; that the question of capacity be kept open, with a formal institutional/legal mechanism for it to be challenged by the learning-disabled person and reviewed if any evidence suggested it could be wrong or that the position had changed; and that the case put forward by the Official Solicitor or other litigation friend should be focused solely on the needs of the parent ([40], para. 60).

In RP's case, the Official Visitor scheme included processes of appeal and review. Such processes are a typical feature of many statutory schemes and are commonly referred to as safeguards. To what extent such mechanisms constitute effective safeguards, sufficient to satisfy 12(4), is a matter of evaluation. In RP's case, the safeguards in the Official Visitors scheme were rendered meaningless by the absence of appropriate decision-making support for RP.

4.8. Reasonable Accommodation

Article 2 (Definitions)

Reasonable accommodation means necessary and appropriate modification and adjustments not imposing a disproportionate or undue burden where needed in particular case, to ensure to persons with disabilities the enjoyment or exercise on an equal basis with others of all human rights and fundamental freedoms.

Articles 12(3) and 12(4) mandate special, positive measures for the support of legal capacity, governed by the requirement of "reasonable accommodation" [1] (Article 2 Definitions).

Considered in light of RP's case, the reasonable accommodation requirement imposes a positive obligation to provide specific measures that support RP's legal capacity and secure her participation in the legal proceedings [32]. Under the reasonable accommodation principle, RP would have been entitled to additional explanation, communication and support with respect to all legal decisions and processes. Maintaining RP's effective role in the legal proceedings could have been achieved by (i) providing an adequate explanation to RP of her legal circumstances and implications of the clinical psychologist's determination that RP lacked litigation capacity; (ii) ensuring that RP had the opportunity to challenge the determination; and (iii) ensuring that RP was properly represented by an independent solicitor or advocate.

Without limiting the range of possible solutions that might be found, the following suggestions address the practical implications of the obligation to provide support outlined in the previous paragraph. The first point could be achieved by ensuring that there was a "legal interpreter" or an advocate who would assist RP to understand her legal situation. The second point could be achieved by ensuring that an independent opinion was sought, and that the determination of capacity was reviewed by an independent authority or tested in a court of law. The third point could be achieved by enabling RP to appoint an independent solicitor who was willing to advocate on her behalf. The deciding factor should be the strategy preferred by RP.

5. Discussions

Tom Tyler's work emphasises the importance of considering the perspective of the person who is at the centre of the legal process [30]. Considered in light of the CRPD, procedural justice principles provide a framework for implementing Article 13 obligations. Understanding the philosophical underpinnings of the CRPD assists in appreciating the way in which Article 12 and 13 combine to extend the principle of universality to individuals with disability through the requirement for support and participation. In RP's case, the determination of incapacity resulted in her exclusion from the legal process. The absence of legal standing was interpreted as a requirement that RP be removed from participation in the proceedings. It was assumed that her current thoughts, opinion and aspirations were irrelevant. Article 12 indicates that the person's legal capacity must always be respected. The person must always be involved. If a person is not involved, the CRPD requirement of making decisions in accordance with the "rights, will and preferences" is difficult to meet. If they are not involved, only the person's past preferences are available for consideration, not their current views or their response to changing circumstances. In RP's case, once it was determined that she lacked instructional capacity, she was no longer viewed as a participant in the proceedings in any meaningful way. RP's preference for the child to be placed in her care was made known to the court, but not pursued. Her second preference, that the child be placed with her family, was dismissed from the outset. RP was never involved in active discussions about possible options and solutions. This dynamic suggests that as the adversarial format of all legal proceedings is modified by active negotiation between the parties or is imbued with mediation strategies, the disadvantage associated with exclusion from legal proceedings on the grounds of incapacity is increased.

The argument advanced in this article is that the CRPD should be interpreted in light of critical theory's challenge to the reification of disembodied "reason" or rational capacity as the defining characteristic of the human personality. The human person in modern philosophy is imbued with social, cultural and emotional experiences and relationships [49]. Accepting a proposition of relational autonomy allows for a reading of Article 12(2) that challenges the conclusion that only independent rational beings are entitled to participate in the law. Instead, the contextualised perception of each individual is recognised as part of subjective reality that must be incorporated into the legal landscape. In RP's case, the practical consequence of the determination of incapacity was that RP did not participate in the original legal proceedings. The European Court of Human Rights compounded the legal exclusion by basing its decision on an assessment of the outcome of the earlier proceedings, not on the processes that should have ensured RP's access to justice. A procedural justice focus would have altered the court's reasoning.

RP's case highlights a point of conceptual confusion associated with the notion of mental capacity. Threaded through disability related literature is a persistent inference that one's "mental capacity" is a fixed attribute that can be determined objectively without reference to the decision-making or informational context. This is out of step with the CRPD and with the modern law of capacity. Mental capacity must always be determined in the context of the provision of relevant information and in a way that takes into account the particular circumstances of the person. The CRPD recognises that "understanding" is never a stand-alone concept. It is influenced by a person's ability to receive and comprehend, in the sense of "make sense of", the information. For example, a person who is frightened or stressed may be unable to hear or comprehend basic instructions. A person may not comprehend information that is provided in an unfamiliar language. Information may be incomprehensible if it is related to knowledge or facts that are unknown. In short, mental capacity is always subjective, information driven and context dependent. A failure to comprehend does not indicate an inability to do so, but points to possible deficits in the information or its delivery.

Article 12 is important because it requires the law to engage with the subjective, contextual nature of decision-making. It requires support measures that are tailored to the needs of each individual. Above all, CRPD based decision-making requires the involvement of people with disabilities. A re-orientation toward support for legal capacity as required by the CRPD can be summarised as the shift toward the principles of support, participation and procedural justice. CRPD requirements cannot be met unless the person is present and involved. When support is understood in the light of the principle of participation, the basic proposition in modern law that people who lack the requisite understanding should not be permitted to participate in the law evaporates.

6. Conclusions

In RP's case, the interaction between Article 12 and Article 13 occurs in the context of Article 6 (Women with disabilities). Article 6 recognises that "women and girls with disabilities are subject to multiple discrimination" ([1], Article 6). It requires states parties to take measures to ensure the full and equal enjoyment by the name of all human rights and fundamental freedoms ([1], Article 6). RP is multiply disadvantaged. She is far from the ideal rational legal subject of classical liberal theory. Feminist legal scholarship has long observed that when "freedom" is inscribed as the inalienable and inherent right of a legally privileged, atomistic, individual citizen, the call to equality will inevitably challenge basic precepts in the law ([19], p. 22). RP's case underscores this observation. Eilionoir Flynn and Anna Artstein-Kerslake argue that the CRPD requires "a radical rebalancing of autonomy and protection" ([3], p. 127). This article has argued that the radical rebalancing required by the CRPD is one that secures the effective, voluntary participation of people with disabilities in the legal process. RP was not in need of protection in the traditional sense. She was in need of effective, accessible, honest, information. She was in need of support for her legal capacity. She was in need of support from her family, who were also excluded. Had the necessary information been provided to her, in a timely way, a more suitable legal outcome may have been reached, and the ongoing litigation avoided. In retrospect, it can be seen that the (erroneous) determination of instructional incapacity not only excluded RP from the legal proceedings, but reinforced the initial premise of the proceedings which was the assumption that RP was and always would be, an unsuitable mother. The determination of instructional incapacity foreshadowed and secured the pre-ordained outcome—that RP's child would be permanently placed with another family. From a CRPD perspective, if appropriate support had been provided, RP could have taken her place as an active participant in the legal proceedings. Ultimately, it is her right to legal capacity that underpins her right to access to justice on an equal basis with others.

Acknowledgments: This research was undertaken at RMIT University, Melbourne, Australia.

Conflicts of Interest: The author declares no conflict of interest.

Abbreviations

The following abbreviations are used in this manuscript:

CRPD   Convention of the Rights of Persons with Disabilities
ECHR   European Convention on Human Rights and Fundamental Freedoms
ECrtHR European Court of Human Rights

References and Notes

1.   CRPD: Adopted 13 December 2006, GA Res 61/106, UN Doc A/Res/61/106, Entered into Force 3 May 2008.
2.   Amita Dhanda. "Legal Capacity in the Disability Rights Convention: Stranglehold of the Past or Lodestar for the Future?" *Syracuse Journal of International Law & Commerce* 34 (2007): 429–62.
3.   Eilionóir Flynn, and Anna Arstein-Kerslake. "The Support Model of Legal Capacity: Fact Fiction or Fantasy?" *Berkeley Journal of International Law* 32 (2014): 124–43.
4.   Eilionóir Flynn, and Anna Arstein-Kerslake. "Legislating personhood: Realising the right to support in exercising legal capacity." *International Journal of Law in Context* 10 (2014): 81–104. [CrossRef]
5.   Anna Arstein-Kerslake, and Eilionóir Flynn. "The General Comment on Article 12 of the Convention on the Rights of Persons with Disabilities: A roadmap for equality before the law." *International Journal of Human Rights*, 2015. [CrossRef]

6.   Michael Bach, and Lana Kerzner. "A New Paradigm for Protecting Autonomy and the Right to Legal Capacity." *Law Commission of Ontario*, 2010. Available online: http://www.ontla.on.ca/library/repository/mon/24011/306184.pdf (accessed on 8 April 2014).

7.   Michael L. Perlin. *International Human Rights and Mental Disability Law: When the Silenced Are Heard*. Oxford and New York: Oxford University Press, 2011.

8.   Bernadette McSherry, and Penelope Weller, eds. *Rethinking Rights-Based Mental Health Laws*. Oxford and Portland: Hart Publishing, 2010.

9.   Janet E. Lord, David Suozzi, and Allyn L. Taylor. "Lessons from the Experience of U.N. Convention on the Rights of Persons with Disabilities: Addressing the Democratic Deficit in Global Health Governance." *Journal of Law Medicine & Ethics* 38 (2010): 564–79. [CrossRef] [PubMed]

10.   Genevra Richardson. "Mental capacity in the shadow of suicide: What can the law do?" *International Journal of Law in Context* 9 (2013): 87–105. [CrossRef]

11.   Amita Dhanda. "Universal legal capacity as a universal human right." In *Mental Health and Human Rights: Vision, Praxis, and Courage*. Edited by Michael Dudley, Derrick Silove and Fran Gale. Oxford: Oxford University Press, 2012, pp. 177–88.

12.   Lucy Series. "Relationships, autonomy and legal capacity: Mental Capacity and Support Paradigms." *International Journal of Psychiatry* 40 (2015): 80–89. [CrossRef] [PubMed]

13.   George Szmukler, Rowena Daw, and Felicity Callard. "Mental health law and the UN Convention on the rights of persons with disabilities." *International Journal of Law and Psychiatry* 17 (2013): 245–52. [CrossRef] [PubMed]

14.   Penelope Weller. "Reconsidering legal capacity: Radical critiques, governmentality and dividing practices." *Griffith Law Review* 23 (2014): 498–518. [CrossRef]

15.   Gerard Quinn. "Personhood & Legal Capacity: Perspectives on the Paradigm Shift of Article 12 CRPD." Paper presented at HPOD Conference, Harvard Law School, Cambridge, MA, USA, 20 February 2010. Available online: http://www.nuigalway.ie/cdlp/staff/gerard_quinn.html (accessed on 27 September 2012).

16.   Tina Minkowitz. "Rethinking criminal responsibility from a critical disability perspective: The abolition of insanity/incapacity acquittals and unfitness to plead, and beyond." *Griffith Law Review* 23 (2014): 434–66. [CrossRef]

17.   Jill Peay. "Mental incapacity and criminal liability: Redrawing the fault lines?" *International Journal of Law and Psychiatry* 40 (2015): 25–35. [CrossRef] [PubMed]

18.   Christopher Slobogin. "Eliminating mental disability as legal criterion in the deprivation of liberty cases: The impact of the Convention on the Rights of Persons with Disabilities on the insanity defence, civil commitment and competency law." *International Journal of Law and Psychiatry* 40 (2015): 36–42. [CrossRef] [PubMed]

19.   Eilionoir Flynn. *Disabled Justice? Access to Justice and the UN Convention on the Rights of Persons with Disabilities*. Surrey: Ashgate, 2015.

20.   Lucy Series. "Legal capacity and participation in litigation: Recent developments in the European Court of Human Rights." In *The European Yearbook of Disability Law*. Edited by Gerard Quinn, Lisa Waddington and Eilionoir Flynn. Mortsel: Intersentia, 2015, vol. 5, pp. 128–32.

21.   Anna Lawson, and Eilionoir Flynn. "Disability and Access to Justice in the European Union: Implications of the UN Convention on the Rights of Persons with Disabilities." In *The European Yearbook of Disability Law*. Edited by Gerard Quinn, Lisa Waddington and Eilionoir Flynn. Mortsel: Intersentia, 2013, vol. 4, p. 7.

22.   Linda Steele, and Stuart Thomas. "Disability at the periphery: Legal theory, disability and criminal law." *Griffith Law Review* 23 (2014): 357–69. [CrossRef]

23.   Eileen Baldry. "Disability at the margins: Limits of the law." *Griffith Law Review* 23 (2014): 370–88. [CrossRef]

24.   Claire Spivakovsky. "Making risk and dangerousness intelligible in intellectual disability." *Griffith Law Review* 23 (2014): 389–404. [CrossRef]

25.   Paul Harpur, and Heather Douglas. "Disability and domestic violence: Protecting survivors' human rights." *Griffith Law Review* 23 (2014): 405–33. [CrossRef]

26.   P v Nottingham City Council & the Official Solicitor [2008] EWCA Civ 462; RP v UK 38245/08 (2008) ECHR 1124; R.P. and Others v United Kingdom [2012] ECHR 1796.

27.   CRPD General Comment No. 1 Article 12: Equal Recognition before the law, CRPD/C/GC/1 11th Session, 31 March–11 April 2014.

28. Tom R. Tyler. *Why People Obey the Law*. Princeton: Princeton University Press, 2006.
29. Tom R. Tyler. "Justice Theory." In *Handbook of Theories of Social Psychology*. Edited by Paul A. M. Van Lange, Arie W. Kruglanski and E. Tory Higgins. London and New York: Sage Publications, 2011.
30. Steven L. Blader, and Tom R. Tyler. "Relational Models of Procedural Justice." In *The Oxford Handbook of Justice in the Workplace*. Edited by Russell Cropanzano and Maureen L. Ambrose. Oxford and New York: Oxford University Press, 2015, pp. 351–69.
31. Jack Donnelly. *Universal Human Rights in Theory and Practice*, 3rd ed. Ithica: Cornell University Press, 2013.
32. Janet E. Lord, and Rebecca Brown. "The role of reasonable accommodation in securing substantial equality for persons with disabilities: The UN Convention on the Rights of Persons with Disabilities." In *Critical Perspectives on Human Rights and Disability Law*. Edited by Marcia Rioux, Lee Ann Basser and Melinda Jones. Boston: Martinus Nijhoff, 2011.
33. Vienna Declaration and Programme of Action Adopted by the World Conference on Human Rights in Vienna on 25th of June 1993.
34. Wendy Brown. *States of Injury: Power and Freedom in Late Modernity*. Princeton: Princeton University Press, 1995.
35. Amartya Sen. *The Idea of Justice*. London: Penguin Books, 2010.
36. Jennifer Prah Ruger. *Health and Social Justice*. Oxford: Oxford University Press, 2009.
37. Jennifer Prah Ruger. "Toward a theory of a right to health: Capability and incompletely theorized agreements." *Yale Journal of Law and Human Rights* 18 (2006): 273–326.
38. Penelope Weller. *New Law and Ethics in Mental Health Advance Directives: The Convention on the Rights of Person with Disabilities and the Right to Choose*. Sussex and New York: Routledge, 2013.
39. Penelope Weller. "Lost in Translation: Human rights and mental health law." In *Rethinking Rights Based Mental Health Laws*. Edited by Bernadette McSherry and Penelope Weller. Oxford and Portland: Oregon, 2010.
40. Penelope Weller. "Towards a genealogy of coercive care." In *Coercive Care; Rights Law and Policy*. Edited by Bernadette McSherry and Ian Freckelton. Oxon and New York: Routledge, 2013.
41. Legislation. "Mental Capacity Act 2005 (England and Wales)." Available online: http://www.legislation.gov.uk/ (accessed on 23 December 2015).
42. European Convention on Human Rights: Convention for the Protection of Human Rights and Fundamental Freedoms, as amended by Protocols 11 and 14, supplemented by Protocols 1, 4, 6, 7, 12 and 13, November 4, 1950, Europ. T.S No 5 213 U.N.T.S, 221, Rome 4.XI (1950).
43. Lexology. "RP v UK Lexology." Available online: http://www.lexology.com/library/detail.aspx?g=f7b5b4e4-502a-43d2-9df9-f08eeb3c081f (accessed on 15 February 2015).
44. Cf *Stanev v Bulgaria* [2012] I ECrHR 46.
45. Bernadette M. McSherry. "Legal capacity under the convention on the rights of persons with disabilities." *Journal of Law and Medicine* 20 (2012): 22–27. [PubMed]
46. Masterman-Lister (Masterman-Lister v Brutton & Co (Nos 1 and 2)) [2002] EWCA Civ 1889; see also Masterman-Lister v Jewell and another [2003] EWCA Civ 70.
47. For Example Hunter and New England Area Health Service v A [2009] NSWSC 761.
48. Legislation. "Mental Health Act 2014 (Vic)." Available online: http://www.legislation.vic.gov.au (accessed on 23 December 2015).
49. Judith Butler. *Gender Trouble: Feminism and the Subversive Identity*. New York and London: Routledge, 1999.

laws

MDPI

Article

Assumptions of Decision-Making Capacity: The Role Supporter Attitudes Play in the Realisation of Article 12 for People with Severe or Profound Intellectual Disability

Joanne Watson

School of Health & Social Development, Faculty of Health, Deakin University, 221 Burwood Highway, Burwood, VIC 3125, Australia; joanne.watson@deakin.edu.au; Tel.: +613-9251-7189

Academic Editor: Anna Arstein-Kerslake
Received: 17 December 2015; Accepted: 15 February 2016; Published: 19 February 2016

Abstract: The United Nations Convention on the Rights of Persons with Disabilities (UNCRPD) was the first legally binding instrument explicitly focused on how human rights apply to people with disability. Amongst their obligations, consistent with the social model of disability, the Convention requires signatory nations to recognise that " ... persons with disabilities enjoy legal capacity on an equal basis with others in all aspects of life" and mandates signatory nations to develop " ... appropriate measures to provide access by persons with disability to the support they may require in exercising their legal capacity". The Convention promotes supported decision-making as one such measure. Although Australia ratified the UNCRPD in 2008, it retains an interpretative declaration in relation to Article 12 (2, 3, 4), allowing for the use of substituted decision-making in situations where a person is assessed as having no or limited decision-making capacity. Such an outcome is common for people with severe or profound intellectual disability because the assessments they are subjected to are focused on their cognition and generally fail to take into account the interdependent nature of human decision-making. This paper argues that Australia's interpretative declaration is not in the spirit of the Convention nor the social model of disability on which it is based. It starts from the premise that the intention of Article 12 is to be inclusive of all signatory nations' citizens, including those with severe or profound cognitive disability. From this premise, arises a practical need to understand how supported decision-making can be used with this group. Drawing from evidence from an empirical study with five people with severe or profound intellectual disability, this paper provides a rare glimpse on what supported decision-making can look like for people with severe or profound intellectual disability. Additionally, it describes the importance of supporters having positive assumptions of decision-making capacity as a factor affecting supported decision-making. This commentary aims to give a focus for practice and policy efforts for ensuring people with severe or profound cognitive disability receive appropriate support in decision-making, a clear obligation of signatory nations of the UNCRPD. A focus on changing supporter attitudes rather than placing the onus of change on people with disability is consistent with the social model of disability, a key driver of the UNCRPD.

Keywords: UNCPRD; supported decision-making; severe or profound cognitive disability; human rights; decision-making capacity

---

1. Introduction

The United Nations Convention on the Rights of Persons with Disabilities (UNCRPD) is not only the first human rights treaty of the twenty-first century, it is the first legally binding instrument that explicitly provides an explanation of how human rights can be applied to people with disability [1]. Although Australia ratified the Convention in 2008, it included an Interpretative Declaration specifically relating to Article 12. An interpretative declaration is, " ... a unilateral statement, however phrased or named, made by a State or an international organization, whereby that State or that organization purports to specify or clarify the meaning or scope of a treaty or of certain of its provisions" ([2], p. 21). Australia's Interpretative declaration relating to Article 12 states: "Australia declares its understanding that the Convention allows for fully supported or substituted decision-making arrangements, which provide for decisions to be made on behalf of a person, only where such arrangements are necessary, as a last resort and subject to safeguards" [3]. Substituted decision-making occurs where "guardians and administrators [are] appointed to make decisions in the 'best interests' of the person concerned" ([4], p. 26). Australia's interpretative declaration has the effect of enabling Australia to retain laws that use substituted decision-making in situations where a person is believed to have no or limited decision-making capacity, denying them their right to legal capacity. Because such an assessment outcome is common for people with severe or profound intellectual disability, Australia's declaration has the effect of excluding them from the protections promised under Article 12. It is important to note that at the time at which Australia created the Interpretative Declaration, the theory around supported decision-making and understanding of Article 12 was in its infancy. There is a clear need to incorporate contemporary understandings of supported decision-making, the social model of disability, and Article 12, into practice and legal reform particularly in relation to those with more severe cognitive disability.

The UNCRPD promotes supported decision making as the vehicle by which people with disabilities can exercise their legal capacity to the greatest extent possible [1]. Considering its clear relationship with supported decision-making it is important to operationally define legal capacity, as it is conceptualised in this paper. Legal capacity is a universal human attribute enshrined in law. It allows a person to be recognised as a person before the law [1]. Accepting the right to legal capacity as a given, this paper's focus is on the more practical construct of decision-making capacity. Decision-making capacity is conceptualised within the context of this paper as a person's ability to lead a self-directed life with support. It is acknowledged that while the term "decision-making capacity" is not considered synonymous with the notion of legal capacity, where a person is perceived to have decision-making capacity, they are more likely to have their right to legal capacity, under Article 12 realised.

From here on the term severe or profound intellectual/cognitive disability is used to describe those who are the focus of this paper. Over the last two decades, philosophies that have emerged within disability culture generally have discouraged the use of labels to describe people with intellectual disability for fear of their individuality being buried within stereotypes. Despite these views, there is a compelling argument for using specific language to signal the unique, and poorly understood, support needs of people with severe or profound cognitive disability. Although the use of a label does not take precedence over seeing the person first, an explicit acknowledgment of their needs is necessary if they are to receive the significant support they require to lead a self-determined life.

People with severe or profound intellectual disability require support in most aspects of their lives. They generally communicate informally using nonverbal behaviours such as facial expression, gesticulation, vocalisations, eye gaze and touch. They have difficulty understanding formal communication such as speech, sign, written text, pictures, or photos. In addition to communicating informally, many people with severe or profound intellectual disability communicate unintentionally. This means, they appear unaware that their actions can have an impact on their environment. This means that for effective information transfer communication partners infer meaning from the person's behaviours, an activity acknowledged in the intellectual disability related literature as an ambiguous and subjective task [5–7].

While research and practice guidance focused on Article 12 and supported decision-making for people with mild to moderate cognitive disability and mental illness is emerging [8–11], such guidance is clearly lacking for people with severe or profound cognitive disability. There are likely to be numerous reasons for this lack of empirical attention. Firstly, within an Australian context, while an interpretative declaration allowing for substitute decision-making for people with severe or profound cognitive disability is in place, there is no legislative incentive for researchers to work toward enhancing this group's capacity to lead self-directed lives. Moreover, there is less ambiguity around the intention of Article 12 for people with milder as opposed to more profound cognitive disability, making research with this group less attractive. Flynn and Arstein-Kerslake, examining the granting of personhood through the permitting or denying of legal capacity, have articulated this, describing people with severe/profound cognitive disability as the "hard cases" ([12], p. 98). Additionally, a lack of empirical attention maybe due to widely-held prejudices regarding people with severe or profound cognitive disability's ability and right to be supported to lead self-directed lives [13,14].

These beliefs regarding people with severe or profound cognitive disability's ability and right to be supported to lead self-directed lives maybe rooted in the premise that a person's ability to make and communicate decisions is characterised solely by a set of cognitive based pre-requisites, such as an ability to understand abstract notions of causality. These cognitive skills are seen as independent of environmental factors such as support from family and friends [15]. These beliefs are emphatically rejected within the social model of disability [16–18]. Clough ([18], p. 31) argues that this focus on individualised cognitive skills "fails to accord with the reality of human interdependence" Moreover, Kittay argues that although the phenomenon of human interdependence is considered acceptable within the non-disabled community, for people with the most profound disabilities different rules apply. Rather than being embraced, their dependency on others is exceptionalised as problematic and in order to be recognised as having a human right to lead a self-directed life, they are expected to measure up to standards of cognitive capacity not applied to the rest of the population [17].

Such a focus on cognitive as opposed to ecological barriers to self-determination is exemplified in the medical model of disability and is in direct conflict with the social model, firmly embedded within the UNCRPD. The social model of disability promotes that the barriers and enablers to self-determination exist well beyond an individual, and are constructed by the society in which a person lives. Such an ecological view of self-determination is consistent with a supported decision-making approach, and places the onus of change on supporters, rather than those being supported. Brayley reflects Kittay's views calling for a system of law that moves away from this focus on cognition, to one that universally recognises that a person's legal capacity (and consequently their recognition as a person) does not rest on their individual cognitive capability but on the quality of support available to help them to make decisions [19]. Beamer and Brooks articulated this view half a decade before the drafting of the UNCRPD stating that:

> The starting point is not a test of capacity, but the presumption that every human being is communicating all the time and that this communication will include preferences. Preferences can be built up into expressions of choice and these into formal decisions. From this perspective, where someone lands on a continuum of capacity is not half as important as the amount and type of support they get to build preferences into choices. ([20], p. 4)

There is little doubt that the cognitive approach to the granting of legal capacity underlies Australia's interpretative declaration in relation to Article 12. As described such an approach is reflective of the medical as opposed to the social model of disability. Considering the importance of the social model of disability within the drafting of the UNCRPD, it can be argued that while it continues to have an interpretative declaration with regard to Article 12 in place, Australia is contravening the Convention. McSherry further articulates this concern suggesting that while the universality of Article 12 is not recognised Australia is not acting within the spirit of the Convention [4]. Reinforcing these concerns, in 2014 the UN Committee on the Rights of Persons with Disabilities shared this view, articulating that it was "...concerned about the possibility of maintaining the regime of substitute decision-making, and that there is still no detailed and viable framework for supported decision-making in the exercise of legal capacity ... The Committee recommends that the State party [Australia] uses effectively the current inquiry process to take immediate steps to replace substitute decision-making with supported decision-making and provides a wide range of measures which respect the person's autonomy, will and preferences and is in full conformity with article 12 of the Convention" [21]. In response to the UN Committee's report, the Australian Law Reform Commission (ALRC) mirrored the Committee's concerns in its 2014 Inquiry and Report, *Equality, Capacity and Disability in Commonwealth Laws* [22]. In its report the Commission emphasised the universality of the right to lead a self-directed life, suggesting that the understanding articulated in the Australian Declaration does not comprehend the true intention of Article 12, which extends beyond the provision of supported decision-making to include measures that respect a person's autonomy, will and preferences. The notion of 'will and preference', which is particularly relevant to people with severe or profound cognitive disability is explicitly mentioned in Article 12 (4) of the UNCRPD, indicating the Article's clear intention to be inclusive of this group. In its report the ALRC pays explicit attention to the exclusionary impact this lack of understanding of the intention of Article 12, has on people with severe or profound cognitive disability [22].

2. Empirical Study Methodology

This paper draws on research with five people with severe or profound intellectual disability and their support networks [23,24]. Each participant and their support network participated in a supported decision-making process [25]. This process provided a lens through which to observe and characterise the phenomena of supported decision-making and identify practical strategies for the realisation of Article 12 for this group. An interpretative, multiple case study design was used, and interview, focus group, questionnaire and observation data were collected and analysed.

The process of gaining ethics approval for this study was complex. There is ample discussion in the literature regarding the vulnerability of people with severe to profound cognitive disabilities when participating in research [26,27]. The HREC that evaluated the research proposal had particular concerns relating to obtaining consent from research participants with cognitive disability. The researcher spent considerable time with the HREC discussing these concerns, particularly the ethical question around whether to exclude this group from the study and its associated benefits or obtain proxy consent from people who know them well. A decision was made to obtain proxy consent from those who knew the participants well, using the principles of supported decision-making embedded in the study itself. It is important to note that there is concern in the literature around the validity of proxy reporting with regard to the expression of personal preferences [28,29]. McVilly *et al.* (2000) stated, "overall research findings to date indicate a need for caution when interpreting proxy-based data" ([29], p. 60). Heeding these concerns, those providing proxy consent were required to adhere to the principle of assent, an important characterisation of supported decision-making methodology used in the study. That meant any consents obtained by proxy were required to be accompanied by nonverbal indications that the person was comfortable participating in the study, and as mandated by the National Human Medical Research Committee (NHMRC) any indication at any time over the course of the study of refusal to participate had to be respected [30].

3. Empirical Study Findings and Implications

3.1. Characterising Supported Decision-Making for People with Severe or Profound Cognitive Disability

There is no doubt that supported decision-making for people with severe or profound cognitive disability is likely to look different than for other members of the population, but it is also undeniable that decision-making is a mandated right for all citizens living in jurisdictions that are signatory to the UNCRPD. This begs the question of "what is decision-making" for this group, or perhaps more usefully framed, "what is supported decision-making?"

An analysis of the study's data provided a characterisation of supported decision-making for people with severe or profound intellectual disability, in terms of two distinct but interdependent roles. The data highlights the roles played by (a) the person with a disability (supported); and (b) the supporters in the supported decision-making process. The role of the person with a disability in this dynamic was to express will and preference, either intentionally or unintentionally, using a range of communication modalities, including behaviour, vocalisation, vocal pitch, muscle tone, facial expression, eye movement, and physiological reactions (e.g., changes in breathing patterns). The role of supporters within this dynamic is to respond to the expression of will and preference of those they support. Within this decision-making dynamic, supporter responsiveness, as opposed to focus people's expression of preference, is the component that is amenable to change through structured practice guidance, making the enablement of responsiveness a crucial strategy for supported decision-making.

3.2. Supporter Responsiveness

The act of supporter responsiveness is not well examined in the research literature, and therefore, is poorly understood. The data collected evidenced that supporter responsiveness to the expression of will and preference of those they support is a multi-faceted activity, made up of a number of tasks. These tasks include acknowledging, interpreting and acting on the expression of will and preference of those they support. The study has highlighted, that although each of these tasks are important, none of them in isolation, characterise responsiveness. Rather, supporter responsiveness was observed to be reliant on the implementation of these tasks collectively. To respond, firstly supporters acknowledged/noticed, as opposed to ignored, expressions of preference, secondly, they interpreted these expressions of preference, assigning meaning to them, and thirdly they acted on this meaning.

In addition to the previous characterization, key factors underlying supporter responsiveness to the will and preference of people with severe or profound intellectual disability within a supported decision-making context were identified and examined. These factors were clustered into five overarching domains, (1) focus person's attributes; (2) supporter attitudes and perceptions; (3) relational closeness; (4) functioning and make up of circles of support; and (5) characteristics of the service system. A discussion of each of these factors is beyond the scope of this paper, and will be reported elsewhere. The remainder of this paper will focus on one identified theme, the association between supporter responsiveness to expressions of will and preference and the views they hold regarding the ability of those they support to lead self-directed lives. This emphasis on supporter responsiveness to the expression of preference of those they support is consistent with the social model of disability (embedded within the UNCRPD), where the onus of change is not on the person with a disability, but rather, the environment of which they are a part.

3.3. Supporters' Views Regarding the Ability of Those They Support to Lead Self-Directed Lives

The literature highlights a widely held belief that concepts relating to self-determination and autonomy are irrelevant to people with cognitive disability, because they have limited ability to lead self-directed lives [31–35]. "Historically, people with an intellectual disability have been assumed to be incapable of exercising the sort of control over their own lives which others take for granted" ([32], p. 362). Jenkinson and Nelms made the point: "since by definition intellectual disability is characterized by significant impairments in adaptive behaviour, discretion, social competence, and comprehension of own self-interest, the temptation has been to presume total incompetence in decision-making" ([36], p. 199). Ward and Stewart, referring to people with intellectual disability, stated "it is often assumed that they are eternal children, unable to speak on their own behalf and therefore not competent to make their own decisions" ([34], p. 305). This negative perception of the ability of those they support to lead self-directed lives is particularly apparent for people with severe or profound cognitive disability. Wehmeyer, Agran and Hughes surveyed over a thousand teachers regarding their understanding of self-determination of their students. They reported that the severity of a student's disability influenced these teachers' perceptions of the self-determination of their students. Specifically, teachers working with students with severe or profound intellectual disability rated the capacity of their students to make decisions significantly lower than their colleagues working with students with milder intellectual disability [37].

The value of supporters having a positive perception of the ability of those they support to lead self-directed lives is reflected within the research literature. This literature provides evidence that people are more likely to lead self-determined lives, when those who support them have a positive view of their ability to lead self-directed lives [38,39]. Reviewing over one hundred articles, Harchik *et al.* (1993) concluded that people who are expected to express choice and preference are more likely to behave autonomously, be happy, and exhibit positive as opposed to negative behaviour [38]. Rawlings *et al.* (1995) conducted a participant observation study of four women with intellectual disability. They concluded that supporters who presume those they support can guide the decisions that are made about them are likely to be willing and able to "encourage, recognise and respond to expressions of choice" ([39], p. 143). In contrast, Antaki *et al.*, drawing from their analysis of interactions between staff and fifteen people with intellectual disability, report that the negative perceptions of the capacity of a person to guide their own decisions, is one factor responsible for reducing the opportunities people with intellectual disability have for decision-making [40]. The impact of supporters' assumptions regarding a person's ability to lead a self-directed life is not only reflected in the research literature relating to people with intellectual disability, but also that related to acquired brain injury (ABI). Drawing from two case studies and the research literature, Knox *et al.* (2013) discuss the impact of clinicians holding negative assumptions regarding decision-making for people with ABI. They suggest that negative assumptions held by rehabilitation professionals that people with ABI cannot participate in decisions is a factor that influences the self-determination of their patients [41].

The importance of positive perceptions of a person's ability to lead self-directed lives is not only reflected in the research literature, but in principles guiding contemporary law and policy. For example, the UNCRPD promotes an assumption of decision-making capacity [1], while the English and Welsh Mental Capacity Act 2005 (MCA), has as its first principle, a need for supporters to assume a person has decision-making capacity [42]. This focus on the need for a change in supporter attitudes, rather than a change in people with disability, is reflected in the social model of disability, solidly embedded within the UNCRPD.

Findings from my research further highlights the importance of supporters having positive perceptions of the ability of those they support to make decisions. Supporters who held such perceptions, predominantly demonstrated greater responsiveness to expressions of will and preference overall, than those who did not hold these beliefs. Considering the value of supporter responsiveness within a supported decision-making process, this finding is legally and practically important. It reinforces the value of inclusion of principles such as "a person must be assumed to have capacity", in legal frameworks such as the UNCRPD [1] and the English and Welsh Mental Capacity Act [42]. In practice, it points to a need for supporters having a belief in the universality of decision-making capacity, inclusive of those with severe or profound cognitive disability.

4. Conclusions

Australia's interpretative declaration regarding Article 12 of the UNCRPD, allowing for substituted decision-making, stems from a belief that some Australians, such as those with severe or profound cognitive disability, are not capable of having their will and preference reflected in the decisions made about them. This paper has challenged this view, providing a characterisation of supported decision-making for people with severe or profound cognitive disability.

Supported decision-making for people with severe to profound intellectual disability is an interdependent and complex process carried out between supporters and supported. Within this dynamic, both parties contribute differently. The person facing the decision contributes by expressing their will and preference, using a range of informal communication methods such as body language, facial expression, gesture, and physiological reactions (e.g., changed breathing patterns).

Supporters contribute to the process by responding to these expressions of will and preference, through acknowledging (as opposed to ignoring), interpreting and acting on this expression. Effective supporter responsiveness was found to be most likely when supporters had a positive view of the decision-making capacity of those they supported.

This paper calls for an emphasis on legislative, policy and practice guidance that aims to enhance supporters' understanding that a person's ability to lead a self-directed life is universal, as relevant to people with severe or profound cognitive disability as those with milder disability. The findings reported in this paper, point to the value of this emphasis in enhancing supporter responsiveness to a person's will and preference, an essential component of supported decision-making. Such a focus is consistent with the social model of disability, a construct that is core to the UNCRPD, where the onus of change is not on the person with a disability, but the environment of which they are a part. This environment includes the perceptions supporters hold regarding a person's ability to lead a self-directed life, and therefore have access to supported approaches to decision-making. Without this focus, the promises of Article 12, and the recommendations of the ALRC report, are likely to remain a pipe dream for people with severe or profound cognitive disability and their supporters.

Due to their complex lives decision-making is obviously challenging for people with more severe cognitive disability. However, if signatory nations to the UNCRPD are to live up to their obligations under Article 12, interpretative declarations, such as Australia's need to be abandoned, and significant attention needs to be paid to how best to support all citizens to have their preferences heard and reflected in the decisions that are made about their lives, both practically and within the context of law reform.

Acknowledgments: I acknowledge the guidance and support of Erin Wilson and Nick Hagiliassis who have supervised the PhD research upon which this paper is based. I acknowledge the Office of the Senior Practitioner and the Department of Human Services Victoria who partially funded the research from which this paper draws.

Conflicts of Interest: The author declares no conflict of interest.

Abbreviations

The following abbreviations are used in this manuscript:

UNCRPD	United Nations Convention on the Rights of Disability
SDM	Supported decision-making

References

1. UN General Assembly. "Convention on the rights of persons with disabilities." *A/RES/61/106*, 2006. Available online: http://www.un.org/Docs/asp/ws.asp?m=A/RES/61/106 (accessed on 4 December 2014).
2. International Law Commission. "Report of the International Law Commission Sixty-Third Session." 2011. Available online: http://legal.un.org/ilc/reports/2011/english/addendum.pdf (accessed on 3 December 2014).
3. United Nations Treaty Collection. "Convention on the Rights of Persons with Disabilities: Declarations and Reservations." 2007. Available online: https://treaties.un.org/Pages/ViewDetails.aspx?src=IND&mtdsg_no=IV-15&chapter=4&lang=en (accessed on 29 November 2014).
4. Bernadette Maree McSherry. "Legal capacity under the convention on the rights of persons with disabilities." *Journal of Law and Medicine* 20 (2012): 22–27. [PubMed]
5. Jill Bradshaw. "Complexity of staff communication and reported level of understanding skills in adults with intellectual disability." *Journal of Intellectual Disabiility Research* 45 (2001): 233–43. [CrossRef]
6. Nicola Grove, Karen Bunning, Jill Porter, and Cecilia Olsson. "See what I mean: Interpreting the meaning of communication by people with severe and profound intellectual disabilities." *Journal of Applied Research in Intellectual Disabilities* 12 (1999): 190–203. [CrossRef]
7. Karen Bunning. "Making sense of communication." In *Profound Intellectual and Multiple Disabilities: Nursing Complex Needs*. Edited by Jillian Pawlyn and Steven Carnaby. Oxford: Wiley-Blackwell, 2009.

8. Christine Bigby, Mary Whiteside, and Jacinta Douglas. *Supporting People with Cognitive Disabilities in Decision Making—Processes and Dilemmas*. Melbourne: Living with Disability Research Centre, La Trobe University, 2015.
9. Lucy Knox, Jacinta M. Douglas, and Christine Bigby. "'Even when I say we, it was a decision that I made': The experiences of adults with severe tbi and their partners in making decisions about life after injury." *Brain Injury* 28 (2014): 739.
10. Lucy Knox, Jacinta Douglas, and Christine Bigby. "Exploring tensions associated with supported decision making in adults with severe tbi." *Neurorehabilitation and Neural Repair* 26 (2012): 690.
11. Piers Gooding. "Supported decision-making: A rights-based disability concept and its implications for mental health law." *Psychiatry, Psychology and Law* 20 (2013): 431–51. [CrossRef]
12. Eilionoir Flynna, and Anna Arstein-Kerslakea. "Legislating personhood: Realising the right to support in exercising legal capacity." *International Journal of Law in Context* 10 (2014): 81–104. [CrossRef]
13. Jeff McMahan. *The Ethics of Killing: Problems at the Margins Of Life*. Oxford: Oxford University Press, 2002.
14. Peter Singer. *Practical Ethics*, 2nd ed. Cambridge: Cambridge University Press, 1993.
15. Hilary Johnson, Jo Watson, Teresa Iacono, Karen Bloomberg, and Denise West. "Assessing communication in people with severe-profound disabilities: Co-constructing competence." *Journal of Clinical Practice in Speech-Language Pathology* 14 (2012): 64–68.
16. James Hogg. "Complex needs and complex solutions: The challenge of profound intellectual and multiple disabilities." *Journal of Policy & Practice in Intellectual Disabilities* 4 (2007): 79–82. [CrossRef]
17. Eva Feder Kittay. "At the margins of moral personhood." *Ethics* 116 (2005): 100–31. [CrossRef] [PubMed]
18. Beverley Clough. "What about us? A case for legal recognition of interdependence in informal care relationships." *Journal of Social Welfare and Family Law* 36 (2014): 129–48. [CrossRef]
19. John Brayley. *Supported Decision Making in Australia: Presentation Notes*. Carlton: Office of the Public Advocate, 2009.
20. Stephanie Beamer, and Mark Brookes. *Making Decisions. Best Practice and New Ideas for Supporting People with High Support Needs to Make Decisions*. London: Values into Action, 2001.
21. Committee on the Rights of Persons with Disabilities. "Concluding Observations on the Initial Report of Australia, Adopted by the Committee at Its Tenth Session (2–13 September 2013)." Available online: http://www.refworld.org/docid/5280b5cb4.html (accessed on 8 December 2015).
22. Australian Law Reform Commission. "Equality, Capacity and Disability in Commonwealth Laws: Final Report." 2014. Available online: https://www.alrc.gov.au/publications/equality-capacity-disability-report-124 (accessed on 9 December 2015).
23. Joanne Watson, Erin Wilson, and Nick Hagiliassis. "Abstracts of the 3rd IASSIDD asia-pacific conference (Tokyo, Japan): 'Participation in decision making for people with severe-profound intellectual disability: What can it look like?'" *Journal of Policy & Practice in Intellectual Disabilities* 10 (2013): 102–86.
24. Jo Watson. "Supported decision making framework: A tool for people supporting those who communicate informally to live lives they prefer." In *Clinical and Fieldwork Placement in the Health Professions*. Edited by Karen Stagnitti, Adrian Schoo and Dianne Welch. Melbourne: Oxford University Press, 2010.
25. Joanne Watson, and Rhonda Joseph. *People with Severe to Profound Intellectual Disabilities Leading Lives They Prefer through Supported Decision Making: Listening to those Rarely Heard. A Guide for Supporters. A Training Package Developed by Scope*. Melbourne: Scope, 2011.
26. Teresa Iacono. "Ethical challenges and complexities of including people with intellectual disability as participants in research." *Journal of Intellectual & Developmental Disability* 31 (2006): 173–79. [CrossRef] [PubMed]
27. Paul S. Siegel, and Norman R. Ellis. "Note on the recruitment of subjects for mental retardation research." *American Journal of Mental Deficiency Research* 89 (1985): 431–33.
28. Helen I. Cannella, Mark F. O'Reilly, and Giulio E. Lancioni. "Choice and preference assessment research with people with severe to profound developmental disabilities: A review of the literature." *Research in Developmental Disabilities* 26 (2005): 1–15. [CrossRef] [PubMed]
29. Keith R. McVilly, Rosanne M. Burton-Smith, and John A. Davidson. "Concurrence between subject and proxy ratings of quality of life for people with and without intellectual disabilities." *Journal of Intellectual & Developmental Disability* 25 (2000): 19–39.
30. National Health and Medical Research Council. *National Statement on Ethical Conduct in Research Involving Humans*. Canberra: NHMRC, 1999.

31. Jo Jenkinson, Cheryl Copeland, Vicky Drivas, Helen Scoon, and Mei Ling Yap. "Decision-making by community residents with an intellectual disability." *Journal of Intellectual & Developmental Disability* 18 (1992): 1–8. [CrossRef]

32. Josephine C. Jenkinson. "Who shall decide? The relevance of theory and research to decision-making by people with an intellectual disability." *Disability, Handicap and Society* 8 (1993): 361–75. [CrossRef]

33. Michael L. Wehmeyer. "Self-determination and individuals with severe disabilities: Re-examining meanings and misinterpretations." *Research and Practice for Persons With Severe Disabilities* 30 (2005): 113–20. [CrossRef]

34. Tony Ward, and Claire Stewart. "Putting human rights into practice with people with an intellectual disability." *Journal of Developmental & Physical Disabilities* 20 (2008): 297–311. [CrossRef]

35. Michael L. Wehmeyer. "Self-determination and individuals with significant disabilities: Examining meanings and misinterpretations." *Journal of the Association for Persons with Severe Handicaps* 23 (1998): 5–16. [CrossRef]

36. Jo Jenkinson, and Robyn Nelms. "Patterns of decision-making behaviour by people with intellectual disability: An exploratory study." *Journal of Intellectual & Developmental Disability* 19 (1994): 99–109. [CrossRef]

37. Michael L. Wehmeyer, M. Martin Agran, and Carolyn Hughes. "A national survey of teachers' promotion of self-determination and student-directed learning." *Journal of Special Education* 34 (2000): 58–68. [CrossRef]

38. Alan E. Harchik, James A. Sherman, Jan B. Sheldon, and Diane J. Bannerman. "Choice and control new opportunities for people with developmental disabilities." *Annals of Clinical Psychiatry* 5 (1993): 151–61. [CrossRef] [PubMed]

39. Meredith Rawlings, Leanne Dowse, and Anthony Shaddock. "Increasing the involvement of people with an intellectual disability in choice making situations: A practical approach." *International Journal of Disability, Development and Education* 42 (1995): 137–53. [CrossRef]

40. Charles Antaki, Mick Finlay, and Chris Walton. "Choices for people with intellectual disabilities: Official discourse and everyday practice." *Journal of Policy & Practice in Intellectual Disabilities* 6 (2009): 260–66. [CrossRef]

41. Lucy Knox, Jacinta M. Douglas, and Christine Bigby. "Whose decision is it anyway? How clinicians support decision-making participation after acquired brain injury." *Disability and Rehabilitation* 35 (2013): 1926–32. [CrossRef] [PubMed]

42. Department of Health. "The Mental Capacity Act." In *9*. London: HMSO, 2005.

⚖ *laws*

MDPI

Article

Germany without Coercive Treatment in Psychiatry—A 15 Month Real World Experience

Martin Zinkler

Kliniken Lankreis Heidenheim gGmbH, Academic Teaching Hospital of Ulm University, Department of Psychiatry, Psychotherapy and Psychosomatic Medicine, Schlosshaustr. 100, 89522 Heidenheim, Germany; martin.zinkler@kliniken-heidenheim.de

Academic Editor: Anna Arstein-Kerslake
Received: 28 December 2015; Accepted: 14 March 2016; Published: 17 March 2016

Abstract: Coercive treatment with antipsychotic drugs was commonly used in German psychiatric institutions until it became a topic of substantial medical, legal and ethical controversy. In 2011 and 2012, several landmark decisions by Germany's Constitutional Court and Federal Supreme Court challenged this practice in all but life-threatening emergencies. In March 2013, the new legal provisions governing coercive treatment took effect allowing coercive medication under stricter criteria. While mainstream psychiatry in Germany resumed the use of coercive medication, although less frequently than before 2012, there are examples where clinicians put an even greater emphasis on consensual treatment and did not return to coercive treatment. Data from a case study in a local mental health service suggest that the use of coercive medication could be made obsolete.

Keywords: coercive treatment; human rights; psychiatry; Germany; constitutional court; UN convention

1. Introduction

Coercive use of antipsychotic medication is common in psychiatric institutions and usually affects people with severe mental illness [1,2]. Nevertheless, few studies into the rationale, frequency and effects of coercive medication have been conducted. While there is a remarkable absence of randomized trials on coercive antipsychotic treatment in hospitals, the use of community treatment orders has been studied in an experimental design in the UK and was found not to be effective in reducing relapse and readmission to hospital [3].

In 2011, Germany's Constitutional Court declared the regulations on coercive treatment in two German states (Rhineland-Palatine and Baden-Wurttemberg, 2 BvR 882/09 and 2 BvR 633/11) unlawful, which effectively stopped coercive antipsychotic treatment in these parts of Germany [4]. It was not the view of the Constitutional Court that coercive treatment per se was unconstitutional but rather that the criteria under which it could be given were far too wide. In 2012, Germany's Federal Supreme Court followed these rulings (XII ZB 99/12, XII ZB 130/12) [4] and extended the ban on coercive antipsychotic treatment across Germany, when it found the regulations governing coercive treatment in German guardianship law unconstitutional.

An outcry of protest, amongst others from Germany's professional association for psychiatry [5], led to changes in federal law allowing coercive treatment [6] under strict criteria (impaired capacity, prior attempts to reach consensual treatment, treatment is necessary to avert serious damage to the patient's health, least restrictive option, expected benefit exceeds the expected adverse effects).

Additional procedural safeguards were put in place, such as an assessment by a second opinion doctor and the option for the patient to go through an appeal process before treatment is commenced. In 2013, against fierce protest from users' organizations and a small minority within the psychiatric profession [4], these changes in guardianship law were passed by the German Bundestag.

Between the decisions by Germany's Federal Supreme Court in June 2012 and the amendments in guardianship law passed by the Bundestag in January 2013 Germany was left without a law governing coercive treatment in psychiatry in all but life-threatening emergencies. The legal hiatus applied to both people with and people without capacity to consent to the treatment. Doctors were left with section 34 of Germany's criminal code, which allows action in justified emergencies (Rechtfertigender Notstand) to avert an imminent danger (similar to self-defense).

However, this section is not regarded as a justification for treatment of mental or other illness, and will only be used in exceptional circumstances, for example rapid tranquillization in a hospital emergency department, when the delay incurred to make a formal application and to call a judge would infer serious health risks.

The debate in public and in parliament [7] revealed an absence of data on the rationale, frequency, form and effect of coercive treatment in Germany's psychiatric hospitals. In small studies, coercive treatment is reported in 2%–8% of inpatients of psychiatric hospitals [8]. There is some data however, on the use of detention in hospitals and on the use of mechanical restraint (being strapped to a bed frame), physical restraint (being held down by staff), and seclusion (being locked in a small room). These vary considerably from hospital to hospital (between 2% and 10% of inpatients) [9] and between German states [10], suggesting perhaps that the use of coercion reflects the institutional culture rather than a variation in patient behavior for example between rural Bavaria and urban Hamburg.

At the same time on an international stage, combating human rights abuses in mental health care was identified as the "single most important priority for global mental health" ([11], p. 362). The 2015 first report of Germany by the UN Committee on the Rights of Persons with Disabilities [12] expressed serious concerns on Germany's compliance with the UN Convention and called on German authorities to acknowledge torture, inhuman and degrading treatment in psychiatric institutions and to end substitute decision making in German Guardianship proceedings.

Nevertheless, the legal void created by the court decisions did not prompt a huge interest in the research community to study this unique opportunity. Some observations were made and will be described in this paper.

2. Methods

A benchmark project [10] established in 1994 involves a network of psychiatric hospitals voluntarily submitting their data on the use of coercion in their institutions. These data will be reviewed against data on the use of coercive treatment in a group of hospitals in Bavaria since 2014 [13]. Furthermore, in an attempt to shed some light on institutional cultures some more detailed data will be presented from one institution with an uncommon approach to violence and coercion in mental health care. These data will highlight areas for further research and consideration of standard clinical practice.

In this paper a narrow definition of coercion is used. Included are: physical restraint (holding someone down), mechanical restraint (strapping someone to a bed frame), seclusion (locking someone in a room) and coercive medication (medication being administered against the declared will and/or with physical force).

3. Results

3.1. Data on Coercion in Mental Health Institutions in Germany

Prior to the Constitutional Court decisions of 2011, coercive medication could be administered to those patients being detained in psychiatric institutions under German mental health laws without an additional judicial procedure. As long as an individual was detained in hospital by a court of law, he or she could be treated against his or her will. The decision on involuntary medication was left to the treating physician.

Soon after the Constitutional Court rulings, some psychiatrists reported an increase in violence and other coercive measures in their hospitals as they felt unable to control their patients' disruptive behavior when these patients objected to treatment with antipsychotic medication. Flammer and Steinert looked at the network data and concluded that with the court rulings of 2011 and the ban on coercive antipsychotic medication, other forms of coercion were used more frequently in a defined group of patients, those with psychotic disorders, and presumably in situations where coercive medication was not permitted anymore [14]. They also reported significantly more violent incidents in patients with a diagnosis of psychosis (+44%).

Recently, data from a group of psychiatric institutions in Bavaria suggested that coercive medication under the new 2013 rules is used for 0.5% of inpatients [13]. This may well represent a less frequent use compared to pre-2011 data indicating coercive medication in 2%–8% of inpatients [8], as the new rules from 2013 introduced stricter criteria and additional safeguards regarding its use: a separate judicial procedure, a second opinion given by a doctor who is independent from the institution where the patient is detained and procedural requirements involving a separate court hearing.

3.2. Data from Heidenheim Mental Health Service

In a case study on a smaller level but over a longer time period, observations in a psychiatric department of a general hospital in South-West Germany allow for a more detailed narrative. The Heidenheim Department of Psychiatry serves a population of 130,000 in a small town and rural part of Baden-Wurttemberg. Against the mainstream of German psychiatry, coercive antipsychotic medication was not reintroduced with the new law in 2013, but remained obsolete since the 2011 court rulings.

Before 2011, coercive medication was used in 2–5 cases per year, thereby affecting up to 0.4% of inpatients. Compared to the data of the pre 2011 studies quoted above [8], this appears low and may well represent the therapeutic culture of this institution. The department, from its beginnings in 1995 operated an open-doors policy. There are no locked wards, voluntary and detained patients are being treated on open wards. All members of staff are trained in de-escalation, the department is a member of the above mentioned network of hospitals aiming to reduce coercion in mental health care. The department does not use seclusion rooms to contain disruptive behavior.

The hospital keeps detailed records of violent behavior of inpatients, of the use of coercion (according to the network definitions) and the use of antipsychotic medication. Violent incidents are defined as incidents where disruptive behavior by a patient leads to painful or harmful physical contact with another patient or member of staff (for example: when a cup is thrown and hits a wall, this is not a violent incident. If the cup hits a person, this will be counted. Threatening language is not counted; kicking, beating, pulling hair are counted).

For the data on antipsychotic medication, defined daily doses (DDDs) according to the WHO Collaborating Centre for Drug Statistics Methodology are used. This accounts for the different dose ranges of various antipsychotics. Some antipsychotics are used in a dose range between 2–12 mg, others between 100–900 mg. From the amount of each antipsychotic used within one year by a hospital department, defined daily doses can be calculated and added up. This allows a quantification of the use of medication of a certain group (antibiotics, antidepressants, antipsychotics, *etc.*) within a defined period.

Contrary to assumptions made by mainstream psychiatry and within the hospital network, the frequency of violent behavior (Table 1) and the frequency of other forms of coercion (mechanical restraint, Table 1) did not increase in Heidenheim once coercive use of antipsychotic medication was abandoned. During this period however, a shift in the therapeutic culture led to a reduction in the use of antipsychotic medication of more than 40% (Figure 1).

Table 1. Violent incidents and mechanical restraint in Heidenheim Psychiatric Department 2009–2015.

	Violent Incidents	Percentage of Inpatients Subject to Mechanical Restraint
2009	30	3.2
2010	49	3.1
2011	38	4.5
2012	21	5.2
2013	14	5.4
2014	31	4.8
2015	19	2.9

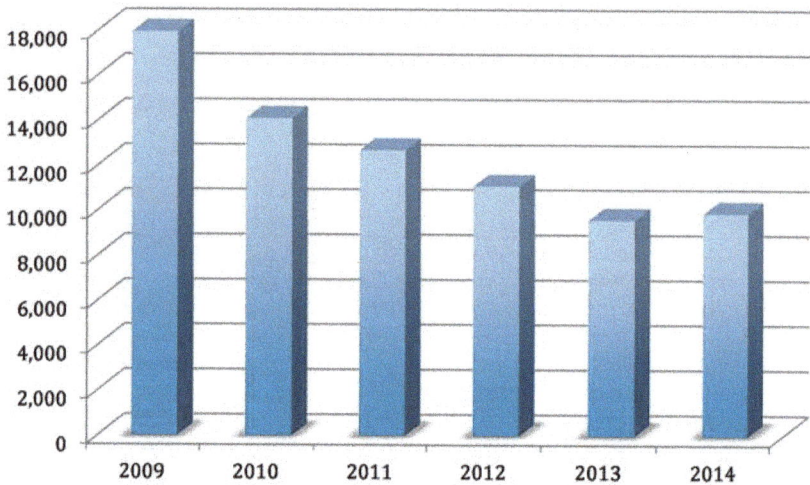

Figure 1. Defined Daily Doses of antipsychotic medication in Heidenheim Psychiatric Department 2009–2014.

It appears unlikely that these data result from a different mix of diagnoses treated in this hospital, as the population served by the institution, the number of inpatients (between 1250 and 1300 admissions per year) and the distribution of recorded diagnoses has largely remained the same during the period from 2009 to 2015.

4. Conclusions

Constitutional court rulings in Germany sparked a lively debate on the use of coercion in psychiatric institutions. Welcomed by users' organizations, the court rulings stipulated additional efforts in the field of human rights and mental health care. Germany's largest professional organization for psychiatry and psychotherapy responded with the formulation of an ethical position on autonomy and coercion in mental health care [15].

National and local data during the legal void between 2011 and 2013 and thereafter suggest that giving up coercive medication is not straightforward and problems arise when one form of coercive treatment (coercive medication) is stopped but other forms of coercion (restraint) and violence in psychiatric institutions increase. This was observed in several mental health services.

The data from one mental health service in south-west Germany go against this trend. In this service, giving up coercive medication did not coincide with an increase in another form of coercion (restraint or seclusion). Also, the service did not observe an increase in violent behavior and managed to reduce the use of antipsychotic medication substantially. On a cautious note, the data from a small-town/rural area may not be representative for mental health services in urban areas. Yet, the data cover a time period of several years and may well offer an opportunity to study complex interventions aimed at reducing coercion and violence in mental health care and to formulate best-practice models.

A further limitation to the research is that compulsory treatment was abolished, but compulsory detention was not. It may well be the case that while people were not legally coerced, they were well aware that if they wanted to get out, they would have to follow medical advice. Case reports about what happened in clinical situations without the option of coercive medication provide an insight into the institutional culture of this service [4].

From a human rights perspective, the German experience of the brief hiatus in the legal sanction of coercive medication from 2011 (in some parts of Germany, from June 2012 across Germany) to 2013 was largely disappointing. Little research was conducted until the new law was passed. There are however promising experiences, albeit on a small scale, which suggest that a reduction in the use of coercive treatment is possible under strict legal regulation.

An important barrier to accessing mental health services in high income countries is the stigma involved with mental illness and mental health services. Efforts to reduce stigma have been largely unsuccessful [16]. Stigma may be an obstacle in reporting human rights abuses ([11], p. 371). One might argue that reducing coercion in mental health services will help to reduce the stigma of mental illness and mental institutions. A mental health system treating everyone with care, dignity and respect would eventually earn respect from all corners of the community.

Conflicts of Interest: The author declares no conflict of interest.

References

1. Manuela Jarrett, Len Bowers, and Alan Simpson. "Coerced medication in psychiatric inpatient care: Literature review." *Journal of Advanced Nursing* 64 (2008): 538–48. [CrossRef] [PubMed]
2. Richard Bentall. "Too much coercion in mental health services." *The Guardian*, 1 February 2013. Available online: www.theguardian.com/commentisfree/2013/feb/01/mental-health-services-coercion (accessed on 5 December 2015).
3. Tom Burns, Jorun Rugkåsa, Andrew Molodynski, John Dawson, Ksenija Yeeles, Maria Vazquez-Montes, Merryn Voysey, Julia Sinclair, and Stefan Priebe. "Community treatment orders for patients with psychosis (OCTET): A randomised controlled trial." *Lancet* 381 (2013): 1627–33. [CrossRef]
4. Martin Zinkler, and Jose-Marie Koussemou. "Germany's Federal Constitutional Court rules against compulsory medication—Three case reports." *Recht & Psychiatrie* 31 (2013): 76–79.
5. Deutsche Gesellschaft für Psychiatrie, Psychotherapie und Nervenheilkunde. "Stellungnahme zum Urteil des Bundesverfassungsgerichts vom 23.03.2011 zur Zwangsbehandlung im Maßregelvollzug 16.01.2012." Available online: www.dgppn.de/en/presse/stellungnahmen/detailansicht/article//zum-urteil-d-1.html (accessed on 5 December 2015).
6. Deutscher Bundestag. "17. Wahlperiode Drucksache 17/12086." Available online: http://dip21.bundestag.de/dip21/btd/17/120/1712086.pdf (accessed on 5 December 2015).
7. Deutscher Bundestag. "17. Wahlperiode Drucksache 17/12090." Available online: http://dip21.bundestag.de/dip21/btd/17/120/1712090.pdf (accessed on 5 December 2015).
8. Tilman Steinert, and Thomas W. Kallert. "Involuntary medication in psychiatry." *Psychiatrische Praxis* 33 (2006): 160–69. [PubMed]
9. Tilman Steinert, Veronika Martin, Manfred Baur, Ulrich Bohnet, Rita Goebel, Gottfried Hermelink, Rita Kronstorfer, Wolfgang Kuster, Beate Martinez-Funk, Martin Roser, Albrecht Schwink, and Wolfram Voigtländer. "Diagnosis-related frequencies of compulsory measures in 10 German psychiatric hospitals and correlates with hospital characteristics." *Social Psychiatry and Psychiatric Epidemiology* 42 (2007): 140–45. [CrossRef] [PubMed]
10. Tilman Steinert, Martin Zinkler, Hans-Peter Elsässer-Gaißmaier, Axel Starrach, Sandra Hoppstock, and Erich Flammer. "Long-Term Tendencies in the Use of Seclusion and Restraint in Five Psychiatric Hospitals in Germany." *Psychiatrische Praxis* 42 (2015): 377–83. [PubMed]

11. Vikram Patel, Arthur Kleinman, and Benedetto Saraceno. "Protecting the Human Rights of People with Mental Illness: A Call to Action for Global Mental Health." In *Mental Health and Human Rights*. Edited by Michael Dudley, Derrick Silove and Fran Gale. Oxford: Oxford University Press, 2012.

12. United Nations Committee on the Rights of Persons with Disabilities, Thirteenth Session. "Concluding observations on the initial report of Germany. UN document CRPD/C/DEU/CO/1." 25 March–17 April 2015. Available online: http://daccess-dds-ny.un.org/doc/UNDOC/GEN/G15/096/31/PDF/G1509631.pdf?OpenElement (accessed on 5 December 2015).

13. Margot Albus, Peter Brieger, and Wolfgang Schreiber. "Compulsory treatment with psychotropic drugs—Effects of the 2013 legislation amendment on treatment in psychiatric hospitals in Bavaria." *Recht & Psychiatrie* 33 (2015): 193–97.

14. Erich Flammer, and Tilman Steinert. "Impact of the Temporaneous Lack of Legal Basis for Involuntary Treatment on the Frequency of Aggressive Incidents, Seclusion and Restraint among Patients with Chronic Schizophrenic Disorders." *Psychiatrische Praxis* 42 (2015): 260–66. [PubMed]

15. Deutsche Gesellschaft für Psychiatrie, Psychotherapie und Nervenheilkunde. "Achtung der Selbstbestimmung und Anwendung von Zwang bei der Behandlung von psychisch erkrankten Menschen." Available online: www.dgppn.de/de/presse/stellungnahmen/detailansicht/article//achtung-der.html (accessed on 17 January 2016).

16. Michael Smith. "Anti-stigma campaigns: Time to change." *The British Journal of Psychiatry* 202 (2013): s49–50. [CrossRef] [PubMed]

Article

Strengthening the Voice of Persons with Mental Health Problems in Legal Capacity Proceedings

Marie Fallon-Kund [1,2,*] **and Jerome Bickenbach** [2]

1   Department of Health Sciences and Health Policy, Faculty of Humanities and Social Sciences, University of Lucerne, Frohburgstrasse, 6002 Lucerne, Switzerland
2   Swiss Paraplegic Research, Guido A Zächstrasse 2, 6207 Nottwil, Switzerland; jerome.bickenbach@paraplegie.ch
*   Correspondence: marie.fallon-kund@paraplegie.ch; Tel.: +41-419-396-578

Academic Editor: Anna Arstein-Kerslake
Received: 24 February 2016; Accepted: 24 June 2016; Published: 29 June 2016

Abstract: Despite the standards set out by the United Nations Convention on the Rights of Persons with Disabilities (CRPD), states are reluctant to put an end to substitute decision-making regimes all at once. Persons with mental health problems are particularly affected by such regimes that are instituted by independent authorities through legal capacity proceedings. In order to allow the person to express their will and preferences throughout the proceedings, the right to be heard is of primary importance for the person concerned. The objective of this paper is to review the essential support mechanisms as well as procedural accommodations for the implementation of an equal and effective right to be heard for persons with mental health problems. Fulfilling the right to be heard in legal capacity proceedings is a step towards more individualized regimes that promote the autonomy of the person.

Keywords: mental health; legal capacity proceedings; right to be heard

---

1. Introduction

This paper addresses the gap between current practices regarding legal capacity as well as substitute decision-making and the standards set out by the United Nations Convention on the Rights of Persons with Disabilities (CRPD), from a procedural point of view. Most, if not all, state parties to the CRPD still legally allow for the possibility to restrict a person's legal capacity and appoint a third person who is able to take decisions in the "best interests" of the person concerned regarding property, finances or other personal matters (such as housing) ([1]; [2], p. 25). Such legal capacity proceedings are also known as proceedings regarding guardianship, curatorship, and protection of adults. According to the first general comment of the CRPD Committee, interpreting Article 12 of the Convention, guardianship constitutes substitute decision-making and must be abolished ([3], paras. 9, 29).

Throughout legal capacity or guardianship proceedings a person's capacity is generally assessed or the assessment made by a medical doctor evaluated. Although capacity assessments might be necessary in certain cases of compulsory intervention as "the recognition of equal human dignity may sometimes require limits on the right to self-determination" [4], these assessments as well as involuntary treatment proceedings, that are usually regulated in separate mental health laws, are not the primary focus of the study.

Indeed, this article specifically focuses on the right to be heard for persons with mental health problems in legal capacity proceedings. A variety of terms are used for people with mental health problems or psychosocial disabilities. According to the European Agency for Fundamental Rights and in the absence of a common terminology, we will refer to them as "persons with mental health problems" ([5], p. 10).

We start by referring to increasing critical commentary on the interpretation of Article 12 by the CRPD Committee and by highlighting the discrepancies between the CRPD Committee and national practices regarding legal capacity. We focus on how authorities appoint external decision-makers and look at previous studies that show a lack of participation on the part of persons concerned in proceedings. Then we set out what is understood as the right to be heard and its significance from the person's perspective. We further analyze what would be required for the implementation of an equal and effective right to be heard and look at whether the identified components are legally provided across a sample of eight countries in Europe. We argue that if a person is effectively heard in legal capacity proceedings, there is an increased probability that the competent authority will adopt least restrictive, individualized measures and thus promote the autonomy of persons concerned. These procedural issues, as noted in Article 13 of the CRPD, are non-negligible in light of current practices and the powers conferred to authorities dealing with the legal capacity proceedings. These authorities are legal or administrative bodies composed of a single decision-maker or multidisciplinary panel.

2. Background

The purpose of the Convention on the Rights of Persons with Disabilities is to promote, protect and ensure the full and equal enjoyment of all human rights and fundamental freedoms by all persons with disabilities, and to promote respect for their inherent dignity. The Convention applies to persons who have long-term physical, mental, intellectual or sensory impairments, which in interaction with various barriers may hinder their full and effective participation in society on an equal basis with others. Adopting a human rights perspective on mental health, the Convention places a particular emphasis on individual autonomy and freedom to make one's own choices. Furthermore, the CRPD underlines the importance of support for and inclusion of adults in decisions affecting them ([6], Article 1).

Article 12 of the CRPD on the right to equal recognition before the law is pivotal in this regard as its second paragraph establishes a right to the enjoyment of legal capacity for persons with disabilities on an equal basis with others. Legal capacity has generally been defined as consisting of two components: legal standing—the right to be a holder of rights and duties—and legal agency—the right to act upon these rights and to have them recognized by law [7]. Article 12.3 further states that all persons should be given access to support in order to exercise the right to legal capacity, i.e., supported decision-making regimes must be available to all. This is confirmed by the interpretation of Article 12 given by the first general comment of the CRPD Committee. The Committee also underscored that legal capacity and mental capacity are distinct concepts: mental capacity refers to the decision-making skills of a person, which naturally vary from one person to another and may be different for a given person depending on many factors, including environmental and social factors; but legal capacity does not vary and is a human right ([3], paras. 9, 29). Finally, the Committee states that "persons with cognitive or psychosocial disabilities have been, and still are, disproportionately affected by substitute decision-making regimes and denial of legal capacity" and explicitly calls for the abolishment of guardianship and other forms of substitute decision-making regimes ([3], paras. 9, 29).

Recently, the professional mental health community, as well as legal practitioners and academics have come out in opposition to this strong interpretation of Article 12 [8–11]. These comments acknowledge that the CRPD is exemplary in many respects and underline the importance of promoting the human rights of persons with disabilities and opposing paternalistic forms of substitute decision-making that ignore the views of persons with disabilities. However, it is increasingly being argued that the ambiguities of the CRPD, especially in light of General Comment 1, are highly problematic for progress towards the rights of persons with disabilities. In addition, it is argued that this Comment failed to give a balanced interpretation of article 12.

Even though some states parties have modified their legal capacity laws, they have been reluctant to discontinue guardianship and other substitute decision-making regimes all at once. Indeed, upon ratification of the Convention, several states made declarations or reservations with regard to Article 12 of the CRPD. These states expressed their intention to follow the Convention in a way that allows for restrictions of legal capacity in certain circumstances, for example in cases where protective measures "are necessary, as a last resort and subject to safeguards" [12]. Complying with the standards as interpreted by the CRPD Committee is thus proving to be a challenge at the national level. Currently, no jurisdiction in the world can claim to be fully compliant with Article 12 of the CRPD, and countries still regulate proceedings instituting substitute decision-making regimes [1,2], which allow a decision-maker to make decisions for the person based upon what is believed to be in "the best interests" of the person concerned, even if opposed to the person's will and preferences ([3], paras. 27–28). This despite the clear language of article 12.4:

> States Parties shall ensure that all measures that relate to the exercise of legal capacity
> provide for appropriate and effective safeguards to prevent abuse in accordance with
> international human rights law. Such safeguards shall ensure that measures relating to the
> exercise of legal capacity respect the rights, will and preferences of the person (...)

Article 12.4 is clear that the state cannot proceed in a manner that is against a person's will and preferences. The general comment further strengthens this by insisting that that the 'will and preference' test must replace the 'best interests' test to ensure that persons with disabilities enjoy the right to legal capacity on an equal basis with others ([3], paras. 27–28).

It is argued that "the first thing that a political authority should do is to put in the supports that enable individuals to make decisions, rather than take away this opportunity and do the easier thing of letting another person make the decision for them" ([13], p. 90). This opportunity is often removed in legal capacity proceedings conducted by independent authorities, generally judicial authorities such as courts or tribunals. Procedural rights operate as safeguards throughout these proceedings, and this is where Article 13 of the CRPD comes into play. It establishes a right to an equal and effective access to justice for persons with disabilities, which includes being able to participate in the proceedings. An equal participation means that no distinction, exclusion or restriction on the basis of disability which has the purpose or effect of impairing or nullifying participation may occur ([6], Article 2). An effective role as a direct or indirect participant in legal proceedings might require the provision of procedural and age-appropriate accommodations as referred to in article 13. These accommodations are necessary and appropriate adjustments made by the authorities in the justice system to treat a person as a subject of rights and not as an object of protection ([14], p. 95). However, accommodations should not impose a disproportionate or undue burden on the authorities ([6], Article 2). Implementing an equal and effective right to be heard would provide persons with support in order to allow them to express their will and preferences in legal capacity proceedings. Read in conjunction with Article 12, persons with mental health problems should thus be guaranteed the necessary support and accommodations in order to participate in proceedings, including legal capacity proceedings ([15], p. 103).

Legal proceedings on mental health issues are often not perceived to be fully inclusive of the person concerned. Previous studies demonstrate a lack of participation and empowerment of persons with mental health problems in judicial decision-making processes as well as too much decision-making power granted to legal authorities, which perhaps places excessive emphasis on protection and not enough on the autonomy of the person concerned ([16], p. 10; [17], p. 168). Authorities are reported as lacking awareness of the importance of the roles of power and powerlessness and focusing on the illness rather than the person ([18], p. 43; [19], p. 138). Finally, authorities are thought to perform their activities as formal routine and face-to-face interviews between the person with the mental health problems and the legal authority are exceptional [20]. A kind of mutual alienation is thereby created between competent authorities and the persons involved ([21]; [22], p. 578). Although most of these studies concern legal proceedings on involuntary psychiatric admission or treatment, the findings can be compared to what would prevail in proceedings on legal capacity as these deal with similar questions regarding a person's decision-making capacity.

Discrepancies can thus be noted between the legal standards set out in the CRPD and the current situation. While the paradigm shift from substituted to supported decision-making has not been implemented in states parties, in this paper we depart from the current state of procedural practices to consider how the participation of persons with mental health problems might be strengthened by a more rigorous enforcement of the right to be heard. Also, we ask whether this right can contribute to promoting autonomy, or in other words, whether the essence of individual autonomy can be preserved by minimizing decisions taken on behalf of persons with mental health problems.

3. Right to Be Heard

The right to be heard has had recognition at the international level. Although the entry into force of the CRPD superseded other instruments such as the 1991 United Nations Principles for the Protection of Persons with Mental Illness and the 1999 Council of Europe, Committee of Ministers Recommendation No R(99)4 on Principles concerning the Legal Protection of Incapable Adults, these instruments outlined various procedural safeguards for mental health related proceedings, such as the "right to attend, participate and be heard personally in any hearing" [23] or "the right to be heard in person in any proceedings which could affect his or her legal capacity" [24]. These instruments have had a major impact on legal capacity laws and proceedings across Europe.

More recent human rights developments regarding the right to be heard can be found throughout case law of the European Court of Human Rights (ECtHR) as referred to within this article. However, we start by establishing what we understand as the right to be heard and its significance from the perspective of the person concerned by legal capacity proceedings.

3.1. Main Characteristics of the Right to Be Heard

The right to be heard and express one's views relates to the active inclusion of the person throughout proceedings and is essential for effective participation ([25], p. 11). It implies that the person needs to be allowed to express her concerns and experience that what is said is taken into consideration in the decision-making process ([18], pp. 34, 37; [22], p. 574; [26]). Rather than the expression of concerns, within the scope of this article and in alignment with the CRPD, we understand the expression of a person's will and preferences related to the matters discussed in legal capacity proceedings as constitutive of the right to be heard. It requires competent authorities to personally meet with adults with mental health problems who are the subject of a case and to talk with them rather than about them ([14], p. 49). The person is thus part of the proceedings and able to influence its results through the articulation of their will and preferences. It does not mean, however, that the outcome of the proceedings will align with the will of the person, as the competent authorities are the ones taking the decisions.

The right to be heard needs to be distinguished from the right to be informed or consulted. Informing the person does not actively involve her in a decision-making process and is purely an act of providing someone with facts or information. Consulting goes a step further than informing as the person is actively asked for information or advice. Nevertheless, the facts or information provided by the person do not need to be taken into account, and so consultation can be carried out "purely for the politically correct but ultimately vacuous purpose of legitimizing decisions" [27].

3.2. Significance of the Right to Be Heard

Being heard and given the opportunity to participate in legal capacity proceedings is of significant importance for the persons whose rights are affected by the proceedings. Indeed, legal authorities provide people with information about their standing both in the eyes of the law and in society more generally ([28], pp. 443–44). Perhaps no type of hearing more directly threatens a person's equal membership of society than proceedings in which legal capacity is at issue. These proceedings touch upon the very essence of personhood and are key to accessing meaningful participation in society as they deal with a person's decision-making capacity. As stressed by the European Court of Human Rights, "an individual's legal capacity is decisive for the exercise of all the rights and freedoms" [29,30]. Moreover, without the participation of the person with mental health problems in decisions affecting them, the outcomes seem to be granted as largesse rather than obtained as of right [15]. Throughout its case law, the ECtHR underlines the importance of personal contact in legal capacity proceedings, given the fact that that the person is both the interested party and the main object of the court's examination [29,31]. As a consequence, the Court stresses, "that strict scrutiny (of the decision-making process) is called for where measures that have such adverse effect on an individual's personal autonomy, as deprivation of legal capacity has, are at stake" [32,33].

In addition, people are often most strongly affected by the procedures used to reach the outcomes, or by the judicial process itself, rather than the outcomes themselves [28]. If persons feel that they are able to participate in proceedings, that they are being treated with dignity and respect, and if they view the authorities as trustworthy, then they are more likely to accept the court's decisions ([22], p. 573; [28], p. 439). Being heard and feeling that what is said is taken into account by independent authorities, moreover, facilitates the acceptance of what might at times be highly intrusive outcomes.

4. Components of an Equal and Effective Right to Be Heard

In what follows, we assume for the sake of the argument that everyone is capable of expressing their will and preferences in some way, even where that expression is not easily understood and support and accommodations are needed to facilitate this expression [34,35]. Similarly, the ECtHR argued that "the fact that an individual has to be placed under guardianship because he lacks the ability to administer his affairs does not mean that he is incapable of expressing a view on his situation" [36]. We review some of the main components required for the implementation of an equal and effective right to be heard for persons with mental health problems, components that would facilitate the expression of the person's will and preferences. We then apply these components to a sample of national laws in Europe in order to compare the actual state of statutory provision in order to assess whether these provisions provide are feasible framework, given the current state of national practices.

4.1. Identification of Components

The components, as represented in Table 1, have been selected based on statutory indicators provided by the European Agency for Fundamental Rights on the right to be heard for children ([25], p. 14). Given that children may also need support and accommodation, these components were selected because they seem relevant to legal capacity proceedings involving persons with mental health problems. The selection and specification of the components was done based on a review of the literature on participation in legal proceedings and the right to be heard as well as case law [14,15,37]. The result is a non-exhaustive list of support mechanisms and procedural accommodations, some of which are general and apply to all citizens, while others are specific for persons with mental health problems ([14], p. 45).

Table 1. Framework for an equal and effective right to be heard.

Concept		Component
	1.	Right to be heard
	2.	Exclusion criteria do not depend on mental capacity
	3.	Right to representation
Equal and effective right to be heard	4.	Person of trust
	5.	Most favorable setting
	6.	Multidisciplinary authority
	7.	Mandatory training

4.1.1. Fulfilling the Right to Be Heard and Exclusion Criteria

First, we look at whether the right to be heard is statutorily provided and whether it contains exceptions. The European Court held that persons are entitled to public oral hearings unless exceptional circumstances justify dispensing with the hearing [38]. As mentioned earlier, the ECtHR emphasizes the importance of personal contact with the person concerned by the legal capacity proceedings [29,31–33,39,40]. Exceptional circumstances have been accepted in cases where proceedings concerned exclusively legal or highly technical questions [38]. The Convention on the Rights of the Child (CRC) in turn provides that a child who is capable of forming his or her own views should be provided the opportunity to be heard [41]. This provision does not depend on the decision-making skills of the child. By analogy, exceptions to the right to be heard in legal capacity proceedings must not depend on the mental capacity of the person if equality is the aim. This would constitute a functional approach, which attempts to assess mental capacity and deny legal capacity accordingly. As stated in the general comment, the functional approach may result in the determination that a person's decision-making skills are deficient, which leads to a denial of his or her legal capacity:

> It is often based on whether a person can understand the nature and consequences of a decision and/or whether he or she can use or weigh the relevant information. This approach is flawed for two key reasons: (a) it is discriminatorily applied to people with disabilities; and (b) it presumes to be able to accurately assess the inner-workings of the human mind and, when the person does not pass the assessment, it then denies him or her a core human right—the right to equal recognition before the law ([5], para. 15).

Applied to the right to be heard, such an exclusion from a hearing based on a person's decision-making skills would discriminatorily exclude persons with mental health problems from the right to be heard. A contrario, the waiving of the right to appear and be heard must be established in an unequivocal manner and be attended by minimum safeguards commensurate to its importance [42]. For similar reasons persons should not be forced to attend hearings if they reach an informed decision not to.

4.1.2. Support Mechanisms: Right to Representation and Person of Trust

Secondly, support mechanisms and procedural accommodations might be required in order to practically achieve equality and effectiveness and balance out prevalent power relations in legal capacity proceedings. According to the first general comment of the CRPD Committee Comment, support in the exercise of legal capacity in relation to access to justice can take various forms, including recognition of diverse communication methods, allowing video testimony in certain situations, procedural accommodations, the provision of professional sign language interpretation, and other assistive methods ([3], para. 39). Regarding the right to be heard, we can distinguish between support mechanisms at the individual level and procedural accommodations made at the court level. By support mechanisms, we refer to the support of other persons during the proceedings, which can for example take the form of assistance or representation by counsel or by a person of trust accompanying the person throughout the proceedings and beyond.

In a recent judgment, the ECtHR emphasized that in cases of persons with mental health problems, there is an obligation "to ensure afforded, independent representation" in order to fulfill the right of an effective access to a court [43]. Indeed, without adequate representation, the right to equal and effective participation in legal proceedings is likely to be void, especially in matters related to the practice of guardians "as these can be particularly complex, intrusive or far-reaching" [44]. This goes hand in hand with the right to information of the person and a sense of understanding as good preparation with the person will contribute to effective participation and will allow counsel to stand alongside the person and not in their place ([19], p. 136; [28], p. 495; [39]; [45], p. 97). Effective assistance by counsel thus comprehends the representation of the will and preferences of the client [46].

Assistance from a person of trust, freely chosen by the person with mental health problems, can enhance the person's understanding of the proceedings, and make it more likely that the will of the person will be expressed. A person of trust can come from the person's social network or from independent advocacy services. Care must be taken, however, to clearly distinguish the role of the person of trust from that of counsel. Indeed, no undue burden should be put on persons in close relationships with the person with mental health problems ([47], pp. 141–42), and legal representation should remain a mandate of the counsel. Nevertheless, the involvement of a person of trust increases the consideration given to the family, friends, and support people including the appreciation of the social network of persons standing before the legal authorities [48,49]. As such, it allows the competent authorities also to take into account the perspectives of others affected by the decisions ([45], p. 100).

4.1.3. Procedural Accommodations: Most Favorable Setting, Multidisciplinary Authority and Training

Procedural accommodations, in the sense of necessary and appropriate adjustments in the justice system, can also take various forms. One possibility is to adapt the setting of the hearing to accommodate the person's needs. Another way is to adapt the composition of the competent authorities deciding about legal capacity, by using multidisciplinary panels. This adaptation facilitates a collaborative exchange between members from different disciplines or walks of life. This may also defuse some of the implicit power relations, where, for example too much weight was given to the medical doctor's opinion and not enough to the input from social workers who deal with the persons on a day-to-day basis ([19], p. 138; [45], p. 89). Another procedural accommodation involves explicitly training those working in the administration of justice to involve the person concerned in the proceedings. In Article 13, the CRPD refers to the promotion of appropriate training for those working in the field of administration of justice. Such training would allow, not just the panels of deciding authorities, but also counsels and persons acting as guardians, "to be better informed about the communication needs of clients with mental disabilities and the characteristics associated with different mental disabilities" [44,50]. In addition, an appropriate training might contribute to avoid the temptation to substitute the judgment of those working in the field of administration of justice for the person's judgment [50]. Finally, procedural accommodations can also be to set up less formal proceedings with regular breaks ([14], pp. 4, 55). Although these accommodations might greatly improve how these proceedings are conducted from a human rights perspective, without observational studies, it is difficult to say whether this would be the result.

4.2. Application across Europe

We now apply this framework to countries in Europe to determine which components are already statutorily provided. We selected Belgium (BE), the Czech Republic (CZ), England and Wales (E&W), Finland (FI), Germany (DE), the Netherlands (NL), Spain (ES), and Switzerland (CH) as these countries represent a good geographical coverage and a variety of legal traditions. All of these countries are bound by the evolving standards of the ECtHR. We also took care to include countries that have recently made modifications to their legislation and those that have not. It should be noted that only the Netherlands and Finland have failed to ratify the CRPD, although for both countries they have signed and expressed their intention to comply with its standards.

Table 2 sets out the results of the assessment by component and country. It starts by mentioning the main sources used and the year of the latest revision relevant for this study. The legal provisions expressing the right to be heard in legal capacity proceedings and the other components were found in procedural laws of the eight countries. For the Czech Republic and Switzerland, the right to be heard is set out in the substantial legislation on legal capacity while for Finland it is provided for in both substantial and procedural legislation [51–54]. In England and Wales, it is the 2007 Court of Protection Rules that provides guidance on this matter.

4.2.1. Fulfilling the Right to Be Heard

Overall, the regulations refer to a right to be heard in legal capacity proceedings, although this can be given different formulations. Either the person literally has "the right to be heard" (Switzerland) or the right "to exercise his or her right to be heard" (Finland), the court "shall hear" the person (Finland, Germany), the person "will be heard" (Spain), is "convoked to be heard" (Belgium), is given an opportunity to "share his opinion" (Netherlands) or "must have been seen" and his "statement heard" or "his opinion obtained" (Czech Republic). In England and Wales the court "may hear" the person, so the right to be heard is not mandatory [51,55–62].

Table 2. Results of the assessment per component and per country.

Framework	BE	CZ	E&W	FI	DE	NL	ES	CH
Source	Judicial Code 2014	Civil Code 2014	Court of Protection Rules 2007	Guardianship Services Act 1999	Act on Proceedings in Family Matters 2009	Code of Civil Procedure 1994	Code of Civil Procedure 2015	Civil Code 2013
Fulfilling the right to be heard	√	√	×	√	√	√	√	√
Exclusion criteria do not depend on mental capacity	√	√	√	×	√	√	×	√
Right to representation	√	√	√	√	√	√	√	√
Person of trust	√	√	×	×	√	×	×	×
Most favorable setting	√	√	×	√	√	√	×	×
Multidisciplinary authority	×	×	×	×	×	×	×	√
Provision of training	×	×	×	×	×	×	×	×

4.2.2. Exclusion Criteria and Dependency on Mental Capacity

All countries provide for exceptions to the right to be heard. The Czech Civil Code states that the person must be seen unless it is "impossible due to an insurmountable obstacle" [61]. The Spanish Code of Civil Procedure states that the person will be heard if she has enough mental capacity [58]. In Finland, a person without full legal capacity shall exercise the right to be heard if he or she has attained eighteen years of age and is able to understand the significance of the matter [52–54]. In turn, the German Act on Procedures in Family Matters specifically states that "in matters concerning custodianship, the person concerned has the capacity to participate in the proceedings without consideration of his capacity to contract" [57]. Capacity to participate is here separated from mental and legal capacity.

The Belgian Judicial Code states that the person's opinion does not need to be asked in matters related to legal capacity if the person is considered unable to share his or her opinion [59]. This exception is not based on the inability to have an opinion but on the inability to share it. Other exceptions are mainly related to a proportionality criterion or health reasons. In the Netherlands and Switzerland for example, if a matter related to legal capacity is considered secondary or complementary, the hearing does not need to take place, as this would be out of proportion [56,60]. The same reasoning applies to the Finnish exception of the right to be heard, where no hearing needs to take place if the petition is at once rejected as ill-founded [51]. In Belgium, Germany, and Finland, legal authorities can also depart from the right to be heard if there is a risk of detriment to the health of the person, if the hearing is impossible because of the condition of the person, or if it would cause her undue inconvenience [51,57,59].

Consistent with ECtHR case law, exclusions to the right to be heard based on health reasons are mostly determined by the opinion of a medical expert [31]. This is intended to guarantee that this inability is based on an objective assessment. The ECtHR has questioned, however, the quality of medical evidence used in domestic legal capacity cases ([15], p. 117; [31,32]). The CRPD implicitly raises a concern about an overreliance on medical evidence for these determinations ([15], p. 118). It is often all too easy to allege that an adult cannot understand the procedure in order to bypass his or her right to be heard ([14], p. 53; [63], p. 43; [64]). There might, moreover, be a potential conflict of interest if the medical doctor assessing the person's ability to participate in the proceedings is the same doctor who assesses legal capacity. The medical doctor then risks being both judge and party to the proceedings, which violates the right to a fair trial by an independent authority.

4.2.3. Right to Representation

In most countries, a right to representation is statutorily provided. This contrasts with previous findings in other countries where minimal access to counsel is rarely mandated statutorily (or even judicially). However, and although provided for in law, access to counsel is rarely implemented in legal capacity proceedings [64]. Furthermore, the right to representation in legal capacity proceedings is often conferred to public authorities, such as in the Czech Republic, England and Wales, Finland, Germany, Spain, and Switzerland [53,56–58,61,62]. This raises questions with regard to the independency of the representation. Accordingly, the CRPD Committee expressed its concerns with regard to the "the designation of public defenders that treat the person concerned as if they lacked legal capacity" asking whether these are not "patronizing measures" undermining effective support in the decision-making process [65].

4.2.4. Person of Trust

Several countries allow for persons of trust to accompany the person concerned into legal capacity proceedings while in Finnish courts more generally, family members can be appointed as support persons in main hearings ([14], pp. 60–61; [53], Section 21). Only Belgium, the Czech Republic and Germany however specifically refer to the possible participation of a person who the concerned person trusts in their legislation ([57], Section 274 (4) 1; [59], Section 1243; [66]).

4.2.5. Most Favorable Setting

Five out of the eight countries regulate the possibility of letting the hearing take place at a more favorable setting for the person than the courtroom. In Belgium and the Netherlands, the judge can go to the place where the person resides or where he finds himself, and the German law also states that the hearing can take place in the person's usual environment [57,59,60].

In Finland, the hearing of the person can be arranged outside the main hearing of the court if the person cannot appear in court without considerable inconvenience. In addition, given the sometimes long distances to courtrooms in Finland, the possibility of video hearings is also legally provided for, while the Czech law says that the person can elect the way of communicating his opinion ([14], p. 58; [61], Section 56).

4.2.6. Multidisciplinary Authority

Only Switzerland has a multidisciplinary system, instituted when its modified legal capacity legislation entered into force in 2013. The competent legal authority is composed of one legal member able to guarantee a correct application of the law, and, depending on the litigated matter, two other persons who must have the required psychological, social, pedagogical, accounting, actuarial, or medical competencies. The decisions need to be made by at least three members, but the regions can fix a higher number depending on the case ([56], Article 440). Such a system was implemented because of the perceived increasing complexity of psychosocial problems involved in the "protection of adults" and pursuant to the requirement that individualized measures be instituted [67]. The Swiss system allows authorities to obtain a comprehensive understanding of the case. Finally, and although not multidisciplinary, the English Court of Protection and the German Custodianship Court are specialized legal authorities in the sense that they only deal with capacity related cases while authorities in the other countries also deal with other legal matters.

4.2.7. Provision of Training

So far, none of the countries specifically regulate the promotion of training for persons working in the field of the administration of justice and involved in legal capacity proceedings.

4.3. Preliminary Conclusion

The application of our framework to a sample of countries in Europe shows that the overall compliance with the statutory components of an equal and effective right to be heard is rather deficient. A limitation here, however, is that we do not assess the concrete implementation of statutory provisions such as the right to representation, on one hand, nor practices such as legal authorities who displace themselves to the person despite the lack of legal provisions, on the other hand. Nonetheless, recently modified legal capacity laws seem to be moving towards more participation of the person with mental health problems in legal capacity proceedings. This is exemplified by the Swiss interdisciplinary legal authorities and by the Belgian, Czech, and German provisions regarding a person of trust. Therefore, it reinforces the idea that the selected components have the potential to be effectively implemented and promote an equal and effective right to be heard for persons with mental health problems. How this can contribute to the autonomy of the persons involved in the legal capacity proceedings is briefly discussed in the final section.

5. Conclusions

This article did not go into the question of how authorities can legitimize decisions deviating from a person's will and preferences but rather provided a framework for the implementation of an equal and effective right to be heard, a right we argued was particularly significant for the person involved in legal capacity proceedings. As a further step in promoting the autonomy of the person, we would also need to look at the significance of the right to be heard from the perspective of competent authorities. Arguably, an effective hearing on legal capacity would require authorities to base their decision about legal capacity from different perspectives, going beyond the medical certificate to other evidence and documents in person's file.

In previous years, results of court applications regarding legal capacity have been inflexible and followed an "all or nothing" approach ([47], p. 139). Persons were either placed under plenary guardianship regimes or not provided with any kind of protective measures at all. Competent authorities were said to "rubberstamp the conclusions of the clinical experts", and attorneys often seemed to "act in concert with the judge and clinical experts" [68]. Today, the freedom to make one's own choices is given particular significance across international human rights instruments, most especially the CRPD. This entails that there is a need to individualize the procedures used to make legal capacity determinations, which, we have argued, can only be realized if an effective hearing takes place.

The implementation of the proposed framework allows authorities to hear what a person's will and preferences are in relation to the discussed matters. In short, a person's mental capacity cannot be used solely to exclude her from a hearing. However, if considered necessary and to ensure that the person is provided equal standing before the law, supportive, as well as procedural accommodations need to be provided, such as trained multidisciplinary authorities and more favorable settings. Only in this way can the person's will and preferences be communicated and entail measures tailored to the circumstances of each individual.

Individualized measures would be least restrictive of autonomy in as much as decision-making capacity is preserved in all areas that do not require any type of protection or support. A proper implementation of the proposed framework would thus contribute to closing the gap between the current situation in countries and the standards set out by the CRPD, and to overcome the assumption that, because of mental health problems, people lack will and preferences. In addition, these measures lead to a fundamental rethinking of the foundations of guardianship proceedings ([15], p. 128). As small steps pave the ways to change, an equal and effective hearing is one step in a gradualist approach towards promotion of the autonomy of persons concerned by legal capacity proceedings.

Acknowledgments: The research was supported by the European Union Seventh Framework Program [FP7/2007-2013] under the project Mental Health Training through Research Network in Europe (MARATONE), Marie Curie Actions—Initial Training Network, Grant Agreement Number 316795. In addition, the authors thank the anonymous reviewers for their helpful suggestions and acknowledge the feedback of Carly M. Toepke and Ivana Ivandic.

Author Contributions: Marie Fallon-Kund and Jerome Bickenbach designed the research and Marie Fallon-Kund analyzed the data. Both authors took part in writing the paper.

Conflicts of Interest: The authors declare no conflict of interest. The founding sponsors had no role in the design of the study; in the collection, analyses, or interpretation of data; in the writing of the manuscript, and in the decision to publish the results.

Abbreviations

The following abbreviations are used in this manuscript:

CRC	Convention on the Rights of the Child
ECtHR	European Court of Human Rights
UNCRPD	United Nations Convention on the Rights of Persons with Disabilities

References and Notes

1. European Agency of Fundamental Rights (FRA). *Implementing the United Nations Convention on the Rights of Persons with Disabilities (CRPD).* Luxemburg: Publication Office of the European Union, 2015, p. 9.
2. European Commission. "Commission Staff Working Document. Accompanying the Communication from the Commission to the European Parliament, the Council, the European Economic Social Committee and the Committee of the Regions. European Disability Strategy 2010–2020: A Renewed Commitment to a Barrier-Free Europe." 2010. Available online: http://eur-lex.europa.eu/legal-content/EN/TXT/PDF/?uri= CELEX:52010SC1324&from=EN (accessed on 10 February 2016).
3. UN Committee on the Rights of Persons with Disabilities. *General Comment No. 1 (2014).* Geneva: UN Committee on the Rights of Persons with Disabilities, 2014.
4. Jillian Craigie. "Against a singular understanding of legal capacity: Criminal responsibility and the Convention on the Rights of Persons with Disabilities." *International Journal of Law and Psychiatry* 40 (2015): 6–14. [CrossRef] [PubMed]
5. European Agency of Fundamental Rights (FRA). *Legal Capacity of Persons with Intellectual Disabilities and Persons with Mental Health Problems.* Luxemburg: Publication Office of the European Union, 2013.
6. UN General Assembly. "Convention on the rights of persons with disabilities (A/RES/61/106)." 2006. Available online: http://www.un.org/disabilities/convention/conventionfull.shtml (accessed on 10 February 2016).
7. International Disability Alliance. "Legal Opinion on Article 12 of the CRPD." 2008. Available online: http://www.internationaldisabilityalliance.org/en/ida-position-papers-and-statements (accessed on 10 February 2016).
8. Paul S. Appelbaum. "Protecting the Rights of Persons with Disabilities: An International Convention and Its Problems." *Psychiatric Services* 67 (2016): 366–68. [CrossRef] [PubMed]
9. John Dawson. "A realistic approach to assessing mental health laws' compliance with the UNCRPD." *International Journal of Law and Psychiatry* 40 (2015): 70–79. [CrossRef] [PubMed]
10. Jos Dute. "Should Substituted Decision-Making Be Abolished?" *European Journal of Health Law* 22 (2015): 315–20. [CrossRef] [PubMed]
11. Melvyn Colin Freeman, Kavitha Kolappa, Jose Miguel Caldas de Almeida, Arthur Kleinman, Nino Makhashvili, Sifiso Phakathi, Benedetto Saraceno, and Graham Thornicroft. "Reversing hard won victories in the name of human rights: a critique of the General Comment on Article 12 of the UN Convention on the Rights of Persons with Disabilities." *Lancet Psychiatry* 2 (2015): 844–50. [CrossRef]
12. United Nations Treaty Collection. "Convention on the Rights of Persons with Disabilities: Declarations and Reservations." 2007. Available online: https://treaties.un.org/Pages/ViewDetails.aspx?src=TREATY& mtdsg_no=IV-15-a&chapter=4&lang=en (accessed on 10 February 2016).
13. Gerard Quinn. "Interview: Promoting a paradigm shift: ERT talks with Gabor Gombos and Gerard Quinn about the UN CRPD and its optional protocol." *The Equal Rights Review* 2 (2008): 90.

14. AJUPID. "Comparison of legal systems in access to justice for persons with intellectual disabilities in the following countries: Bulgaria, Finland, France, Hungary, Ireland." 2015. Available online: http://www.ajupid.eu/images/research/AJuPID%20FINAL%20RESEARCH%20REPORT%20MAY%202015.pdf (accessed on 10 February 2016).

15. Lucy Series. "Legal Capacity and Participation in Litigation: Recent Developments in the European Court of Human Rights." In *European Yearbook of Disability Law*. Edited by Lisa Waddington, Gerard Quinn and Eilionóir Flynn. Antwerp: Intersentia, 2015, vol. 5, pp. 103–28.

16. Patrick Fassbind. "20 mois après l'introduction du nouveau droit de protection: Attentes et réalité—Bilan et perspectives." Paper presented at La protection de l'enfant et de l'adulte en pleine mutation—Expériences pratiques des 20 derniers mois, Bienne, Switzerland, 2–3 September 2014. Available online: http://www.kokes.ch/assets/pdf/fr/aktuell/2014_R_7_Fassbind_F.pdf (accessed on 10 February 2016).

17. Terry Carney, and David Tait. *The Adult Guardianship Experiment: Tribunals and Popular Justice*. Sydney: Federation Press, 1997.

18. European Agency of Fundamental Rights (FRA). *Involuntary Placement and Involuntary Treatment of Persons with Mental Health Problems*. Luxemburg: Publication Office of the European Union, 2012.

19. Terry Carney, Fleur Beaupert, Julia Perry, and David Tait. "Advocacy and Participation in Mental Health Cases: Realisable Rights or Pipe-Dreams?" *Law in Context* 26 (2008): 125–47.

20. Thomas W. Kallert. "Coercive Treatment in Psychiatry. A Human Rights Issue?" In *Mental Health and Human Rights: Vision, Praxis, and Courage*. Edited by Michael Dudley, Derrick Silove and Fran Gale. Oxford: Oxford University Press, 2012, p. 343.

21. Danny H. Sullivan, and Paul E. Mullen. "Mental Health and Human Rights in Secure Settings." In *Mental Health and Human Rights: Vision, Praxis, and Courage*. Edited by Michael Dudley, Derrick Silove and Fran Gale. Oxford: Oxford University Press, 2012, p. 289.

22. Brian G. McKenna, Alexander I. Simpson, John H. Coverdale, and Tannis M. Laidlaw. "An analysis of procedural justice during psychiatric hospital admission." *International Journal of Law and Psychiatry* 24 (2001): 573–81. [CrossRef]

23. UN General Assembly. "The protection of persons with mental illness and the improvement of mental health care (A/RES/46/119)." 1991. Available online: http://www.un.org/documents/ga/res/46/a46r119.htm (accessed on 10 February 2016).

24. Council of Europe, Committee of Ministers. "Recommendation No R (99) 4 on Principles concerning the Legal Protection of Incapable Adults." 1999. Available online: http://www.coe.int/t/dg3/healthbioethic/texts_and_documents/Rec(99)4E.pdf (accessed on 10 February 2016).

25. European Agency of Fundamental Rights (FRA). *Child-Friendly Justice—Perspectives and Experiences of Professionals on Children's Participation in Civil and Criminal Judicial Proceedings in 10 EU Member States*. Luxemburg: Publication Office of the European Union, 2015.

26. Council of Europe, Committee of Ministers. "Recommendation Rec(2004)10 of the Committee of Ministers to member states concerning the protection of the human rights and dignity of persons with mental disorder (Article 20 (1) (i))." 2004. Available online: https://wcd.coe.int/ViewDoc.jsp?id=775685 (accessed on 10 February 2016).

27. Oliver Lewis, and Nell Munro. "The Right to Participation of People with Mental Disabilities in Legal and Policy Reforms." In *Mental Health and Human Rights: Vision, Praxis, and Courage*. Edited by Michael Dudley, Derrick Silove and Fran Gale. Oxford: Oxford University Press, 2012, p. 585.

28. Tom R. Tyler. "The Psychological Consequences of Judicial Procedures: Implications or Civil Commitment." *Southern Methodist University Law Review* 46 (1992): 433–48.

29. ECtHR, Shtukaturov v. Russia, 44009/05 (2008) §§ 71–72.

30. ECtHR, Stanev v. Bulgaria, 36760/06 (2012) partly dissenting opinion of judge Kalaydjieva.

31. ECtHR, Lashin v. Russia, 33117/02 (2013) § 82.

32. ECtHR, M.S. v. Croatia, 36337/10 (2013) § 97.

33. ECtHR, X and Y v. Croatia, 5193/09 (2011) § 84, § 109.

34. Eilionóir Flynn, and Anna Arstein-Kerslake. "Legislating personhood: Realising the right to support in exercising legal capacity." *International Journal of Law in Context* 10 (2014): 81–104. [CrossRef]

35. Gerard Quinn. "Personhood and legal capacity. Perspectives on the paradigm shift of article 12 CRPD." Paper presented at HPOD Conference, Harvard Law School, Cambridge, MA, USA, February 2010. Available online: http://www.nuigalway.ie/cdlp/staff/gerard_quinn.html (accessed on 10 February 2016).

36. ECtHR, DD v. Lithuania, 13469/06 (2012) § 118.

37. Terry Carney. "Involuntary mental health treatment laws: The 'rights' and the wrongs of competing models?" In *Rethinking Rights-Based Mental Health Laws*. Edited by Bernadette McSherry and Penelope Weller. Oxford: Hart Publishing, 2010, p. 265.

38. ECtHR, Koottummel v. Austria, 49616/06 (2009) §§ 18–21.

39. ECtHR, Salontaji-Drobnjak v. Serbia, 36500/05 (2009) § 127.

40. ECtHR, Sýkora v. the Czech Republic, 23419/07 (2012) § 107.

41. UN General Assembly. "Convention on the rights of the child (A/RES/44/25, 1989, Article 12)." Available online: http://www.ohchr.org/Documents/ProfessionalInterest/crc.pdf (accessed on 10 February 2016).

42. ECtHR, Poitrimol v. France, 14032/88 (1993) § 31.

43. ECtHR, Ivinovic v. Croatia, 13006/13 (2014) § 37.

44. Peter Bartlett, Oliver Lewis, and Oliver Thorold. *Mental Disability and the European Convention on Human Rights*. Leiden and Boston: Martinus Nijhoff Publishers, 2006, pp. 235–52.

45. Penelope J. Weller. "Taking a reflexive turn: Non-adversarial justice and mental health review tribunals." *Monash University Law Review* 37 (2011): 81.

46. Michael L. Perlin. "'I Might Need a Good Lawyer, Could Be Your Funeral, My Trial': Global Clinical Legal Education and the Right to Counsel in Civil Commitment Cases." *Washington University Journal of Law and Policy* 28 (2008): 247–48.

47. Shih-Ning Then. "Evolution and Innovation in Guardianship Laws: Assisted Decision-Making." *Sydney Law Review* 35 (2013): 133–66.

48. Piers Gooding. "Supported decision-making: A rights-based disability concept and its implications for mental health law." *Psychiatry, Psychology and Law* 20 (2013): 431–51. [CrossRef]

49. Terry Carney, David Tait, Julia Perry, Alikki Vernon, and Fleur Beaupert. *Australian Mental Health Tribunals: Space for Fairness, Freedom, Protection and Treatment.* Sydney: Themis Press, 2011.

50. David A. Green. "I'm OK-You're OK: Educating Lawyers to Maintain a Normal Client-Lawyer Relationship with a Client with a Mental Disability." *Journal of the Legal Profession* 28 (2003): 65–92.

51. Guardianship Services Act 1999 (Finland), Section 74.

52. Administrative Judicial Procedure Act 1996 (Finland), Sections 17–18.

53. Administrative Procedure Act 2003 (Finland), Section 14.

54. Code of Judicial Procedure (Finland), chapter 12, Section 1.

55. Constitution (Switzerland), Article 29.

56. Civil Code 2013 (Switzerland), Articles 447–49.

57. Act on Proceedings in Family Matters and in Matters of Non-contentious Jurisdiction 2009 (Germany), Sections 275–78, 319.

58. Code of Civil Procedure (Spain), Articles 758–59.

59. Judicial Code 2014 (Belgium), Articles 1243–44, 1250.

60. Code of Civil Procedure (the Netherlands), Articles 802, 809.

61. Civil Code 2014 (Czech Republic), Sections 56, 460, 471.

62. Court of Protection Rules 2007 (England and Wales), Sections 9, 143.

63. MDAC. "Guardianship and Human Rights in Serbia." 2006. Available online: http://www.mdac.info/sites/mdac.info/files/English_Guardianship_and_Human_Rights_in_Serbia.pdf (accessed on 10 February 2016).

64. Michael L. Perlin. "International Human Rights and Comparative Mental Disability Law: The Universal Factors." *Syracuse Journal of International Law and Commerce* 34 (2007): 333–57.

65. Committee on the Rights of Persons with Disabilities. "Concluding Observations on the Initial Report of China, Adopted by the Committee at its eighth session (17–28 September 2012) § 23." Available online: http://tbinternet.ohchr.org/_layouts/treatybodyexternal/Download.aspx?symbolno=CRPD%2fC%2fCHN%2fCO%2f1%2fCorr.1&Lang=en (accessed on 10 February 2016).

66. Code of Civil Procedure 2014 (Czech Republic), §§ 22–23.

67. Conseil fédéral Suisse. "Message concernant la révision du code civil suisse (Protection de l'adulte, droit des personnes et droit de la filiation)." Available online: https://www.admin.ch/opc/fr/federal-gazette/2006/6635.pdf (accessed on 10 February 2016).
68. Bruce J. Winick. "Therapeutic Jurisprudence and the Treatment of People with Mental Illness in Eastern Europe: Construing International Human Rights Law." *New York Law School Journal of International and Comparative Law* 21 (2002): 537–72.

laws

| MDPI |

Article

Are Cutbacks to Personal Assistance Violating Sweden's Obligations under the UN Convention on the Rights of Persons with Disabilities?

Ciara Brennan [1,*], Rannveig Traustadóttir [1], Peter Anderberg [2] and James Rice [1,3]

[1] Centre for Disability Studies, Faculty of Social and Human Sciences, University of Iceland, Sturlugata, 101 Reykjavík, Iceland; rannvt@hi.is (R.T.); james@hi.is (J.R.)

[2] Department of Health, Blekinge Institute of Technology, SE-371 79 Karlskrona, Sweden; peter.anderberg@bth.se

[3] Department of Anthropology, University of Iceland, Oddi 332, Sæmundargötu 2, 101 Reykjavík, Iceland

* Correspondence: csb1@hi.is; Tel.: +354-526-4523

Academic Editor: Anna Arstein-Kerslake
Received: 17 February 2016; Accepted: 5 May 2016; Published: 16 May 2016

Abstract: Article 19 of the UN Convention on the Rights of Persons with Disabilities requires states to ensure that disabled people can choose where and with whom they live with access to a range of services including personal assistance. Based on qualitative research of the implementation of Article 19 in Nordic countries, this paper focuses on Sweden, which was at the forefront of implementing personal assistance law and policy and has been the inspiration for many European countries. Instead of strengthening access to personal assistance, this study found that since the Swedish government ratified the Convention in 2008, there has been an increase in the numbers of people losing state-funded personal assistance and an increase in rejected applications. This paper examines the reasons for the deterioration of eligibility criteria for accessing personal assistance in Sweden. The findings shed light on how legal and administrative interpretations of "basic needs" are shifting from a social to a medical understanding. They also highlight a shift from collaborative policy making towards conflict, where courts have become the battleground for defining eligibility criteria. Drawing on the findings, we ask if Sweden is violating its obligations under the Convention.

Keywords: independent living; personal assistance; Sweden; the United Nations Convention on the Rights of Persons with Disabilities

1. Introduction

The United Nations Convention on the Rights of Persons with Disabilities[1] opened for signatures in March 2007 and entered into force in May 2008. The Convention "embodies a 'paradigm shift', from the charitable and the medical approaches to disability to one which is firmly rooted in human rights" [1]. Article 19, in particular, "expresses the paradigm shift by outlining a series of tangible obligations to achieve independent living (something assumed for most people) and inclusion in the community" ([2], p. 22). Under the heading "Living independently and being included in the community" it requires states to ensure that "persons with disabilities have access to a range of in-home, residential and other community support services including personal assistance necessary to support living and inclusion in the community". The paradigm shift also requires the involvement of disabled people's organizations (DPOs) [3]. To comply with Articles 33.3 and 4.3, states need to involve organizations representing disabled people when bringing law and policy in line with the obligations

---

[1] Hereafter referred to as the CRPD or the Convention.

in Article 19—"some of which have immediate effect and others which are subject to "progressive achievement" over time" ([2], p. 24). Yet, "even where progressive achievement is the case, states are under an obligation to show that they are taking steps to the maximum of their available resources to implement this right" ([4], p. 31). Contrary to this, regressive measures are ones "that directly or indirectly leads to backwards steps being taken" with regard to obligations under international law ([5], p. 28).

The Convention aims to strengthen access to support services, including personal assistance in all state parties that ratify the CRPD including countries that already have such policies in place. Contrary to this, Sweden, which is often regarded as the "golden standard" of personal assistance law and policy in Europe [6], has in recent years, narrowed eligibility for personal assistance and has seen a sharp increase in the numbers of people losing state-funded personal assistance. In 2007, the year the Swedish government signed the Convention, 56 persons had their state-funded personal assistance removed [7]. This number increased significantly in the following years. The number of persons who lost their personal assistance peaked in 2012, when 284 people lost their assistance. The latest figures from 2015 show that 145 lost state funded personal assistance [7]. Furthermore, the proportion of first time applicants being denied personal assistance has increased. In 2007, the same year that the Sweden signed the Convention, 34.5% of applications were rejected. The latest figures from 2015 show that rejected applications have risen to 68.8% [7].

This paper examines why and how these cutbacks have occurred following the ratification of a UN Convention that requires access to personal assistance services and should strengthen the right to live independently in the community. The paper is based on a qualitative research project carried out between 2011 and 2014, which examined the implementation of Article 19 of the Convention in Iceland, Norway and Sweden [8,9]. The qualitative project involved in-depth semi-structured interviews with leaders of the independent living movement and government officials who oversee the implementation of the policy changes in Sweden. The findings of the qualitative fieldwork lead us to undertake an extensive review of laws, policies and literature on personal assistance in Sweden. This paper focuses on the findings of this extensive review and aims to shed light on the deterioration of personal assistance policy and discuss it in relation to Sweden's obligations under the CRPD. Section 2 describes the methods used in the study. Section 3 outlines the development of the international independent living movement and personal assistance, and their connection to the CRPD principles. Section 4 introduces Swedish personal assistance law and policy, examines the government's justifications for the review of this law and describes the changes that have occurred in recent years as a result of court rulings and the bureaucratic reinterpretation of "basic needs" and eligibility criteria. In Section 5, we discuss the changes to Swedish personal assistance law and policy and conclude by asking if Sweden is violating its commitments under the Convention.

2. Methods

This is one in a series of articles written as part of a larger project that aimed to examine the development and the implementation of Article 19 of the CRPD, with a focus on the Nordic countries. The overall objective of the project was to chart progress towards independent living and personal assistance. We aimed to provide an in-depth and critical understanding of the meaning of independent living and personal assistance. Qualitative research was conducted in Iceland, Norway and Sweden. Of these three countries Sweden was of particular interest because it is commonly considered to have the most advanced and extensive personal assistance law and policy in Europe [6]. In this article, we focus on Sweden where the qualitative research comprised two stages: fieldwork and an in-depth review of policy, law and literature on Swedish personal assistance. This paper focuses on the latter stage of the research. The review of Swedish law, policy and literature was informed by qualitative fieldwork that carried out in Sweden between January and May 2013. In-depth, semi-structured interviews were carried out with 19 leading figures in the Swedish independent living movement. Follow-up interviews were conducted with four policy makers and government officials who were responsible for reviewing and implementing changes to Swedish personal assistance policy. Fieldwork was carried out by the first author of this paper.

The constant comparative method of grounded theory was used to collect and analyze the qualitative data [10]. This involves analyzing the data, creating analytical memos during the data collection process and searching for central themes "and to continue looking (and interviewing) until the new information obtained does not further provide insight" [11]. We began with a broad set of questions about personal assistance and Article 19, but these became more focused as themes began to emerge. For example, analysis of interviews in Sweden indicated that many participants who were entitled to personal assistance feared that they would lose hours or their personal assistance would be removed altogether. Furthermore, government officials were in the process of reviewing and implementing new measures that narrowed the eligibility criteria for personal assistance. The findings of the qualitative fieldwork lead us to undertake an in-depth review of law, policy and literature on personal assistance in Sweden. All public policy papers since the ratification of the CRPD were reviewed as part of this stage of the research. This included a major policy paper, which analyzed court cases and interpreted the rulings to define "basic needs" for personal assistance [12]. There court cases have directly affected the assessment process for determining if and to what extent an individual is entitled to personal assistance. We examined these policy reviews and court cases in relation to the human rights commitments made by the Swedish government when it ratified the CRPD. Furthermore, we analyzed documents about the development and the history of independent living and personal assistance in Sweden. The findings of this review are outlined and discussed in this paper.

3. The Independent Living Movement and the UN Convention on the Rights of Persons with Disabilities

Personal assistance is rooted in disability rights activism. It began as a political struggle, which was initiated by a group of disabled students on the campus of the University of California, Berkeley in the late 1960s [13]. Independent living principles promote user-led services that enhance participation in society and equality with other citizens. Independence does not mean doing everything by oneself or living in isolation from others [14–17]. Jenny Morris [18] described independent living as:

> ...a means to an end: it is a way of people accessing their human and civil rights. Disabled people have the same human and civil rights as non-disabled people but we are different from non-disabled people in that we have additional requirements, such as mobility needs, communication assistance, personal assistance, and so on ([18], p. 428).

Independent living organizations (ILOs) have advocated for the goals and principles of the movement to be implemented in law and policy. ILOs are a distinct kind of disabled people's organization that focus on independent living, choice and control over services and participation in society. They are established primarily by disabled people, with a few exceptions of organizations that were founded by parents on behalf of their disabled sons or daughters. ILOs offer peer support, peer counseling and developed user-led services. Many ILOs have formed non-profit personal assistance user co-operatives which offer management and administration services in exchange for a small portion of the personal assistance payment.

Article 19 of the CRPD is a landmark for the international network of independent living organizations, which have struggled to have personal assistance recognized as a human rights issue. These organizations have been at the forefront of developing personal assistance services since the 1960s. Many of the key goals of independent living organizations are reflected in the general principles of the Convention, outlined in Article 3, which include freedom to make one's own choices, independence of persons, full and effective participation in society and equality of opportunity. The international disability community had a great deal of influence on the drafting of the CRPD as is reflected in the fact that there were 400 representatives of NGOs and disabled people's organizations in the drafting committee [19]. The important role of civil society continues to be recognized in the

Convention itself, which requires that "persons with disabilities should have the opportunity to be actively involved in decision-making processes about policies and programs, including those directly concerning them" (preamble o). Under the heading "National implementation and monitoring", Article 33.3 of the Convention recognises that "civil society, in particular persons with disabilities and their representative organisations, shall be involved and participate fully in the monitoring process". Furthermore, Article 4.3 requires that:

> In the development and implementation of legislation and policies to implement the present Convention, and in other decision-making processes concerning issues relating to persons with disabilities, states parties shall closely consult with and actively involve persons with disabilities, including children with disabilities, through their representative organisations [20].

Personal assistance is a cornerstone of the independent living movement. It is a catalyst for participation in society for persons who require a significant amount of support in their daily lives. The Convention does not contain a specific definition of "personal assistance". However, high level human rights organizations reflect definitions that were developed by the independent living movement. For example, a thematic study of independent living by the Council of Europe Commissioner for Human Rights [4] acknowledges that "persons with disabilities must have control over the support provided and be the ones who hire, employ, supervise, evaluate and dismiss their assistants". This reflects an earlier definition by Adolf Ratzka, a leader of both the Swedish and the European independent living movements. He explained that

> "Personal" assistance means that users exercise the maximum control over how services are organised and custom-design their services according to their individual needs, capabilities, life circumstances and aspirations. In particular, personal assistance requires that the individual user decides: who is to work, with which tasks, at which times, where and how. Thus, the individual user must be able to recruit, train, schedule, supervise, and, if necessary, fire his or her own assistants. Simply put, "personal assistance", means that the user is the boss [17].

These definitions emphasize the control that users should have over their personal assistance scheme. There is an emphasis on user-leadership. However, in his definition of personal assistance, Adolf Ratzka also acknowledges that "users with learning or mental disabilities will need support from third persons with these functions" [17].

4. Independent Living and Personal Assistance in Sweden

Independent living organizations were the strongest advocates for the implementation of personal assistance law and policy in Sweden. The first Scandinavian conference on Independent Living was held in Stockholm in 1984 and was organized by Adolf Ratzka alongside leaders from the movement in the United States [17]. The Stockholm Centre for Independent Living (STIL) was established that same year. STIL comprised a non-profit user co-operative and offered peer support to members on how to become employers of personal assistants. The Gothenburg co-operative for independent living was founded in 1989. Other centers for independent living emerged in the early 1990s. In most countries, ILOs were developed primarily by and for persons with physical impairments [13]. However, in Sweden, ILOs diversified to reflect the heterogeneity of persons who wanted to access to personal assistance services. For example, the JAG association was established in 1992, followed by a non-profit user co-operative in 1994. The JAG organization pioneered a model of personal assistance[2] for individuals who require support from a third party to co-ordinate the scheme

---

2   Often called the "JAG model".

on their behalf. The model is based on the premise that all people, regardless of impairment can self-determine if they have the appropriate individual support [21]. Non-profit user co-operatives spread throughout Sweden in the 1990s. In 1993, the Gothenburg Independent living co-operative and STIL established the Institute on Independent Living (ILI) which has "trained over 600 persons on how to manage the transition from being object of the local government's home help services to becoming good employers of their personal assistants and how to start up similar cooperatives" [22].

Swedish personal assistance providers are not limited to user co-operatives. In fact, user co-operatives only accounted for 9.2% of personal assistance providers in 2015, while for-profit companies were 54% of providers [7]. This is a result of calls for a market-driven approach to personal assistance, whereby individuals receive direct payments instead of services from the state and have a choice between a range of for-profit and non-profit providers [23,24]. This approach appealed to the center-right coalition government that was in power between 1991 and 1994. There was an increase in private providers during the 1990s in areas such as health care, primary school education and social services [24]. This continued after the election of another center-right coalition in 2006. The Act on System of Choice in the Public Sector [25] applies to health and social services (excluding services for children). The Act strengthens a "system of choice" in welfare, which "means a procedure where the individual is entitled to choose the supplier to perform the service and with which a contracting authority has approved and concluded a contract" (Article 1). The market of private providers was one of the most contentious issues when developing and implementing a law for personal assistance. There was significant political opposition against the private market using public funds to provide services [23]. This tension persists. For example, a report entitled "Measures to Combat Fraud and Misconduct with Assistance Allowance" [26] argued that there are strong economic incentives for companies to increase the number of hours for their customers in order to maximize profits.

Due to the fast growing numbers of personal assistance users, there have been increased attempts to regulate the market for personal assistance providers. The year 2009 was the first time personal assistance providers, including user- co-operatives had to apply for authorization to offer services. In 2015, 1109 assistance providing agencies were registered with the Health and Social Care Inspectorate (Inspektionen för vård och omsorg (IVO)) [7,27]. While many of these companies claim to abide by independent living principles, they are not necessarily led by disabled persons or their family members. Therefore, when we refer to ILOs, we are specifying those that are run primarily by disabled people and those that are run by relatives on behalf on their disabled family member. It was these ILOs that were instrumental in the development of personal assistance law and policy.

4.1. Swedish Personal Assistance Law and Policy

Personal assistance is one of ten rights outlined in the Act Concerning Support and Service for Persons with Certain Functional Impairments [28]. Other rights covered in the legislation include, relief service in the home, short-term respite stays, specially serviced housing for adults or other specially adapted housing for adults and daily activities for people of working age who are not employed in the open labor market [6]. The goals of LSS include "equality in living conditions", "full participation in the life of the community", "to live as others do" and "self-determination and privacy". Personal assistance applies to persons with "major and lasting functional impairments" who require assistance with five "basic needs": (1) personal hygiene; (2) meals; (3) dressing and undressing; (4) communication with others; and (5) help that requires extensive knowledge about the person with a functional impairment [28]. If a person qualifies for personal assistance, the number of hours of assistance per week should be calculated based on how much assistance they require due to these five needs.

The majority of personal assistance is funded and administered at national level. Askheim *et al.* ([29], p. 14) point out that personal assistance was implemented in Sweden in the early 1990s during a recession and therefore the "handing over of the main financial responsibility to the state could...be seen as a strategy for 'protecting' vulnerable groups against financial cutbacks in municipalities". An applicant for personal assistance must be assessed as requiring more than 20 h per week in order to qualify for state-funded personal assistance at the Social Insurance Agency (Försäkringskassan). If an applicant is assessed as needing less than 20 h they can apply for municipal personal assistance. People who have personal assistance are supposed to be reassessed every two years. Hence, people may have to move from the national to the municipal system upon reassessment of their needs if they fall below the 20 h threshold required for receiving state-funded assistance. People who lost state-funded personal assistance due to reassessment, received, on average a 25% reduction in their hours (from 72 to 54 h per week) when they transferred from state to municipal system [30]. This is problematic because there is a difference between national and local government policies and municipal policies vary. This problem was identified by the UN Committee on the Rights of Persons with Disabilities ([31], p. 2), which noted in their general comment to the Swedish government that "there is a serious gap between the policies followed by the state party and those followed by the municipalities with respect to the implementation of the Convention".

4.2. Civil Society's Influence on Law and Policy

Swedish personal assistance illustrates how the demands of ILOs are articulated in law and policy. The legislation is the "envy of many representatives of the international independent living movement" ([6], p. 2). There is a deeply rooted tradition of popular movements in Sweden that put pressure on pressure on the government and they are important consultative partners, showing how services are arranged in practice [32]. There were several ways in which Swedish independent living organizations influenced law and policy. For example, members of ILOs took part in a personal assistance pilot project in six local governments throughout Stockholm in 1987 [22]. They led the way in demonstrating the viability and desirability of personal assistance as an alternative to traditional, segregated services [8]. Members of the movement lobbied and met with politicians and succeed in finding political allies in government. There was a breakthrough when a close political allie of the independent living movement became the Deputy Prime Minister of Sweden in 1991. In 2012, Adolf Ratzka [23] wrote that "in retrospect, the reform, which added to the state budget what were once municipal expenditures, must be viewed as the result of Bengt Westerberg's strong personal commitment to the issue". Furthermore, members of the Swedish independent living movement were successful in their calls for national-level funding of personal assistance. Disabled people argued that "to be able to live in any municipality with the same quality of life...the responsibility for financing must be as centralized as possible" [33].

Sweden was not the only European country to implement personal assistance law and policy. However, it had the most extensive provisions in terms of who was entitled. This is due to the strong advocacy and pressure from independent living organizations. For instance, members of the JAG association met with politicians and ran an intense campaign to include persons who could not direct personal assistance for themselves to be included in the legislation [34]. As a result, personal assistance is available to children and adults with intellectual and physical disabilities, autism and acquired brain injuries.

While many principles of the independent living movement were reflected in the goals of the Swedish legislation, some issues divided the independent living movement and the government. Consumer choice of personal assistance providers, including private companies was one of the more controversial issues in the lead up to the law and policy reform. Sections of the independent living movement campaigned for direct payments instead of services, and for a wide choice of personal assistance providers. They faced opposition from, for instance, the municipal workers union and the communist party [23]. On the other hand, consumer choice appealed to the center right coalition government that was in power between 1991 and 1994, when personal assistance law and policy was developed and implemented. Calls for direct payments and consumer choice between many for-profit and non-profit providers prevailed and resulted in an unregulated market of personal assistance providers until 2009.

4.3. Justifications for Law and Policy Reviews

The goals of the Swedish law and policy for personal assistance demonstrate a social understanding of disability and bear a striking resemblance to some of the general principles of the Convention [35]. How can it be that the government is reviewing personal assistance law and policy with the aim to restrict access to this service immediately following the ratification of the CRPD which clearly strengthens access to personal assistance?

Our analysis indicates that a major reason for the reviews was due to an unprecedented rise in demand for personal assistance, which far exceeded the government's initial expectations when the law was implemented. In 1994, it was estimated that 7000 people would receive assistance, for an average of 40 h per week. In 2014, more than 16,000 persons received assistance, for an average of 126 h per week [36]. The crucial difference between personal assistance and other services is that it is demand-driven [23]. Furthermore, there was no limit on the amount of money the government would allocate towards the personal assistance budget. Hence, the cost of personal assistance grew beyond expectations.

Concerns arose that a significant proportion of personal assistance payments were not being used for what the legislation intended. A report, published in 2012 entitled "Measures to Combat Fraud and Misconduct with Assistance Allowance" produced by an Inquiry on State Assistance argued that a significant proportion of state funds for personal assistance are a result of over-use, fraud or cheating during the assessment process [26]. The report suggested that these problems were a result of the strong economic incentive to seek the maximum number of hours and the weak monitoring and controls in place at the Social Insurance Agency. Furthermore, there were concerns about municipalities overusing state-funded personal assistance. Some reports have suggested that municipalities grant too many hours of personal assistance, thereby passing the costs on to the state instead of providing municipal services, which they would have to pay for if the person needed less than 20 hours of assistance per week [26,36].

The government claims that a stricter definition of "basic needs" is required for clearer rules and guidelines to increase safety, uniformity and consistency of the assessment process [12]. It justified a review of the original goals of the legislation, claiming that they were too ambiguous. For instance, the Social Insurance Inspectorate (Inspektionen för socialförsäkringen) ([36], p. 4) suggested that key concepts underpinning the legislation, such as participation and independence were not defined in the law or legislative history. Another area of concern is the potential for personal assistance providers, in particular, for-profit companies, to misuse the direct payment system to make large profits from state funds.

4.4. Reinterpreting "Basic Needs"

Since the government ratified the Convention in 2008, several measures have been taken to clarify what it means to "need" personal assistance. The five "basic needs" outlined in the LSS have undergone intense scrutiny. Prior to this review process, civil society organizations representing disabled people collaborated with the government and influenced the policy making process. Disabled people's organizations and ILOs in particular, were instrumental in the original development of personal assistance law and policy. However, the relationship between the government and civil society organizations deteriorated during policy and legal reviews. In 2010, the National Board of Health and Welfare reported that representatives from the disability movement withdrew from a reference group in protest to proposals for a new assessment process, claiming that, among other things, it was too intrusive [37]. As a result, ILOs and other disabled people's organizations are on the margins or excluded from the policy review process. Instead of the previous collaborative process of policy making, the courts have become the main authorities in the review of "basic needs" for personal assistance. Interpretations of the courts were regarded as problematic by the UN Committee on the Rights of Persons with Disabilities ([31], p. 2). In their concluding observations to Sweden, the Committee said it was:

...concerned that the Convention has not been integrated into Swedish law and is therefore left to the interpretation of authorities and courts. The Convention articles cannot serve as guidelines in court rulings, as they are not explicitly included in the texts of the national law [31].

The Social Insurance Agency was authorized by the government to develop tools and methods that would lead to a more consistent and fair assessment process [38]. The Agency did so by closely scrutinizing the interpretation of "basic needs" in court rulings. In 2011, a report by the Social Insurance Agency aimed to determine what does and what does not constitute a "basic need" for personal assistance. It did so by reviewing thirty-five judgments that were made by administrative and county courts between July 2009 and September 2010 [12]. In all of these cases, only three of five "basic needs" were considered by the courts: dressing and undressing, meals, and personal hygiene. The other two needs, assistance with communication and help that requires extensive knowledge about the person, were not considered in any of the rulings. In the majority of these rulings, judges reference an earlier ruling by the Supreme Administrative Court[3] [12] in 2009. The court ruled that only needs that are considered to be of a very private nature, of a demanding and complex nature and of very personal character ([12], p. 8) were necessary to qualify for personal assistance. For instance, the need to prepare and pick up food with a knife and fork was not of a sensitive nature and therefore should not be considered the assessment of "basic needs" ([12], p. 8).

The court cases referenced in the report went into detail about the nature of the person's impairments and the support they required. Some of the "basic needs" judged to qualify an individual for personal assistance were: assistance to wipe oneself after using the toilet[4] and the need for constant supervision during meals, difficulty chewing and swallowing and a tendency to vomit[5]. The report described one particular case involving a woman who was described as having weakness and numbness on one side of her body and a visual impairment as a result of a stroke. Only three of the five "basic needs" were considered in the case. In relation to the first need, help with dressing and undressing, it was noted that she could not put on her bra, pull up her pants and required assistance with zippers, buttons on jackets and with her shoes. The second need, meals, it was stated that she could not make a sandwich, peel potatoes, gut fish, or pour a milk carton. The third need, personal hygiene, it was noted that she depended on assistance to transfer to the toilet and to the shower chair and that it took a very long time for her to wash the "healthy" side of her body. The court ruled that she did not satisfy the "basic needs" for personal assistance. It was suggested that her needs could be met by the social welfare committee and by her husband ([12], p. 27).

4.5. Medicalisation of Needs

The shift from a medical, towards a social understanding of disability is a key element of the CRPD. The recent reviews of Swedish personal assistance law and policy have focused on defining who is eligible based on impairment and medical classification. In its ruling on 25 June 2015, the Supreme Administrative Court concluded that the fifth "basic need" (assistance from another person who has detailed knowledge of the user) only applies to persons "with mental disabilities". Following this ruling, a report by the Social Insurance Agency [39] noted that there was no uniform definition of mental disability, and this, therefore, would have to be clarified. In December 2015, the Social Insurance Agency published a report [40] defining mental disability as reduced mental function. Their definition drew on the World Health Organisation's International Classification of Functioning, Disability and Health (ICF). If a person claims that they need assistance from another person who has detailed knowledge of the user, they must first prove that they have a mental disability by producing a

---

[3]   The ruling by the Supreme Administrative Court is referenced in the report as "RÅ 2009 ref. 57".
[4]   Appeal in Sundsvall (Case No. 3845-08).
[5]   Appeal in Jönköping (Case No. 48-10).

medical certificate. Although the implications of this ruling remain to be seen, the Social Insurance Agency [39] has acknowledged that persons who do not meet their definition of mental disability will lose assistance upon reassessment of their "basic needs". This example demonstrates a shift to a medical understanding of the need for personal assistance. In 2015, the Social Insurance Inspectorate was commissioned by the government to produce a report "to provide an analysis and define shortcomings in legislation and its application" [36]. The report by the Social Insurance Inspectorate suggests that:

> ...one way to make the assessment more transparent would be to start from the International Classification of Functioning, Disability and Health (ICF) and convert the assessment based on ICF to the number of hours that would be reasonable to grant to the person. Also, regulations about which medical professions that should be allowed to issue medical certificates regarding functional ability need to be considered ([36], p. 5).

The Government's strategy for the Social Insurance Agency in 2016 outlines its goals for personal assistance benefits. The government instructs the Agency to help break the trend of the hours for assistance benefit by ensuring uniform application of the law, combating overuse and to promote medical investigations and to ensure that the medical investigation is of high quality [41].

4.6. Civil Society, the CRPD and the Cutbacks

The cutbacks are continuing despite concerns from the UN Committee on the Rights of Persons with Disabilities report in 2014 [31]. In its concluding observations to Sweden, it made the following comment:

> The Committee is concerned that state-funded personal assistance has been withdrawn for a number of people since 2010 due to a revised interpretation of "basic needs" and "other personal needs", and that persons who still receive assistance have experienced sharp cutbacks, the reasons for which are unknown or only seemingly justified ([31], p. 6).

This raises the question of why the CRPD has not prevented the deterioration of personal assistance law and policy in Sweden. The qualitative research carried out for the wider project, conducted in Sweden in 2013, we found very little evidence that the CRPD was being used by ILOs in the years following ratification. Some leaders of independent living organizations complained that all of their energy was spent on challenging and opposing further deterioration of the law, resulting in insufficient time to develop strategies to advance the CRPD in Sweden. Recently, however, there is evidence to suggest that the CRPD is being used by ILOs as a tool to fight the revised interpretations of law and policy. One example is an organization called "Med lagen som verktyg" (MLSV) ("With the Law as a Tool" in English). The organization was established in 2015. It aims to defend and advance human rights for people with disabilities and counter disability-based discrimination in Sweden [42]. This is the first collective effort by the Swedish independent living movement to challenge the deterioration of the law and policy by using the CRPD. Another example is the Independent Living Institutes (ILI) development of a website which features an online service for reporting disability based discrimination and provides a database with information about personal assistance service providers in Sweden [42]. This is an example of capacity building and dissemination of information regarding the policy changes. Articles and papers on the website highlight the value of personal assistance, which is strikingly different to the focus of the government reports. These examples reflect the resistance against the policy reviews and the current conflict between the independent living movement and the government. This is in contrast to the previous collaboration in the policy process and is far from the requirements of the CRPD to include disabled people and their organizations in policies and practices influencing their lives.

5. Discussion

Changes to Swedish personal assistance law and policy demonstrate the precariousness and fragility of rights. People who have had personal assistance for several years, now risk losing it, not because their needs or their impairments have changed, but because of new interpretations of the law and new administrative approaches to assessing needs.

At the beginning of this paper, we asked if Sweden is violating its commitments under the Convention. The Council of Europe's Commissioner for Human Rights [4] Thomas Hammarberg, who is Swedish, wrote an issue paper on the implementation of Article 19. In it, he highlighted the importance of collecting historical data in order to measure trends over time, including progression or regression. Measuring an "increase or decrease in types and size of entitlements, and...the number of beneficiaries of support services in the community" over time is one of the indicators for monitoring the extent to which Article 19 of the CRPD is violated ([4], p. 52). Extensive statistical information and data have been available in Sweden since personal assistance was outlined in legislation in 1993. Hence, an abundance of statistics, historical documentation and policy papers documenting the Swedish experience of personal assistance provide valuable information on progress or regression over time. In this final section, we discuss changes in personal assistance law and policy and consider if Sweden is in breach of its obligations under the CRPD.

5.1. From a Social to a Medical Understanding of Disability

The goals of the Swedish law for personal assistance bear a striking resemblance to some of the general principles of the CRPD including full and effective participation in society and equality of opportunity. Likewise, the goals of LSS include "equality in living conditions", "full participation in the life of the community", "to live as others do" and "self-determination and privacy" [28]. These goals reflect the influence of independent living organizations in the formulation and implementation of personal assistance law and policy. ILOs collaborated actively in developing a social, rights-based understanding of personal assistance by emphasizing its value for individual users, their family members and the wider society. However, when civil society organizations withdrew from a reference group working on the policy reviews the Social Insurance Agency and the courts became the main authorities when interpreting "basic needs" for personal assistance [37]. Major policy decisions, which ultimately lead to cutbacks, were made in the absence of key representatives from DPOs. We would argue that this compromises Sweden's obligation to involve disabled people and their representative organizations in decision making processes relating to law and policy for personal assistance.

Court rulings and reviews of eligibility criteria have shifted from the original goals of the law towards a medical understanding of disability, which focuses on deficit rather than equality and participation in society. The Social Insurance Agency used the World Health Organisation's International Classification of Functioning, Disability and Health (ICF) to define mental disability as reduced mental function [40]. This is a limited and selective interpretation of the ICF, which addresses four areas: (1) bodily functions; (2) bodily structures; (3) activity and participation; and (4) environmental factors [43]. The Swedish Social Insurance Agency has focused mainly on the first two areas and appears to have much less emphasis on the second two, despite the fact that they are clearly more in line with the CRPD's understanding of disability. This selective use of the ICF does not take its broader frame into consideration when applying it to measure entitlements to personal assistance. In this context it is also noteworthy that General comment (number 5) by the UN Committee on Economic, Social and Cultural Rights (ESCR) outlines "the right to physical and mental health also implies the right to have access to, and to benefit from, those medical and social services—including orthopedic devices—which enable persons with disabilities to become independent, prevent further disabilities and support their social integration" [44]. Whichever measurements are used to allocate personal assistance, the aim should be to enhance the applicant's independence and social participation. However, currently, it appears that in Sweden measurements are employed to restrict and limit access to personal assistance based on narrow medical considerations and this is a clear sign of regression in implementing Article 19.

5.2. Confrontation in Courts

This paper has highlighted the shift from a collaborative approach to policy making, towards a confrontational reaction to the policy reviews. Instead of collaboration, the courts have become the main authority when interpreting the law and have emerged as a battleground for determining rights. This is particularly problematic considering that the UN Committee on the Rights of Persons with Disability ([31], p. 2) highlighted that the Convention "has not been integrated into Swedish law and is therefore left to the interpretation of authorities and courts". If the struggle for personal assistance is moved to the courts, then it is of utmost importance that judges and lawyers are well-informed about the CRPD and the social understanding of disability.

The court rulings and the subsequent reports by the Social Insurance Agency reveal the high levels of surveillance and scrutiny an individual is subjected to when she or he challenges the assessment of their "basic need" for personal assistance. The 2011 report by the Social Insurance Agency which assessed the court rulings, provided details about the age, gender, the municipality in which the person resided and when into detail about the nature of their impairment. Ironically, privacy is one of the goals of the legislation [28]. As a result, Sweden may be in violation of its obligation under Article 22 of the CRPD, which requires that states "shall protect the privacy of personal, health and rehabilitation information of persons with disabilities on an equal basis with others".

5.3. Over-Use or High Demand?

In many ways, personal assistance policy is a victim of its own success. A tension has arisen whereby, on one hand, the disabled people's movement sees the increase in personal assistance as a success because more and more people are able to live in the community, lead independent lives and participate in society. The government, on the other hand, views the unexpected increase and rising costs of personal assistance as out of control and a sign of fraud or over-use. Personal assistance is different from other services because it is demand-driven, rather than supply-driven [23]. The independent living movement has measured its success in relation to the desirability and demand for personal assistance. Its success was reflected in the diverse groups that joined the campaign to have access to personal assistance services.

The principles of choice, control and individual autonomy that underpin personal assistance appealed to the center-right coalition government that was in power in the early 1990s [23]. Personal assistance has also been presented as a cost-saving service because of the minimal role of the state in administrating services and employing staff. This cost saving, however, was largely dependent on people transitioning from a costly state service, such as residential care, to personal assistance and did not take into consideration persons who were living with their families, receiving unpaid, informal care from family members, relatives and others. The demand for personal assistance far exceeded the government's initial expectations when the law came into force in 1994. Government reports portray personal assistance law and policy as a problem in need of fixing, without considering the societal and individual value. Even the titles of reports make personal assistance sound like a problem; for instance, the report entitled "Assistance Benefit—Shortcomings in Legislation and Application" [36]. The Swedish government sees the increase as the consequence of overuse, both in numbers of individual users and hours that the individual personal assistance user is allowed. As a result, the eligibility criterion for accessing personal assistance has become a matter of public debate and intense bureaucratic scrutiny.

5.4. Targeting Individuals rather than for-Profit Providers

The state has legitimate concerns regarding the regulation of the market of assistance providers. Some effort has been made to weed out rogue companies. Cases of fraud and overuse of personal assistance payments has strengthened the government's argument for regulation of personal assistance providing agencies. However, most of the cutbacks have been directed at individuals, rather than the service providers. Private providers continue to profit from state funds, while there is a sharp rise in the numbers of persons losing their state-funded personal assistance. The distinction between for-profit personal assistance providers and non-profit co-operatives that are part of ILOs run by and for disabled people or their relatives is important when discussing state obligations under the CRPD. It was the ILOs and user co-operatives that pioneered personal assistance services in Sweden. It is these ILOs that developed the independent living movement and independent living principles in Sweden. Hence, they are particularly well positioned to guide the policy making process and monitor the implementation of Article 19.

6. Conclusions

In countries that already have incorporated personal assistance into law and policy, such as Sweden, the CRPD should have strengthened this service. Sweden has been at the forefront of advocating for and developing wide ranging rights to personal assistance in Europe since the 1980s and has served as an inspiration to other countries. Due to this, in our study of the implementation of Article 19 in three Nordic countries, we assumed that Sweden would be the "star" country. Instead we found that since Sweden ratified the CRPD in 2008 many disabled people have lost their personal assistance at a state-level or had their first application rejected.

This situation is disturbing to those advocating for human rights under the CRPD and can be an important lesson for other countries. Sweden is not the only European country to exercise cutbacks to personal assistance and services that support independent living. Other examples are found in the UK and the Netherlands [45]. As a result, some disability activists and disability scholars are cautious about the positive impact that the CRPD will have in practice [3,46]. There are concerns that the CRPD came into force shortly before a recession and austerity measures in Europe, which threatened the future and the sustainability of independent living and personal assistance in countries that implemented relatively extensive policies prior to the Convention. Clearly, states have the right to take regressive measures if there are "strong justifications" for doing so ([47], p. 16). While it could be argued that the unprecedented cost is a strong justification, in the case of Sweden, it is noteworthy that personal assistance law and policy were introduced during a recession in the 1990s [29]. Another interesting point is that the Swedish economy was less affected than other European countries in the recession that began after 2008. Furthermore, a contradiction arises whereby companies profiteer from personal assistance provision, while, at the same time, measures are taken to control costs by reinterpreting basic needs of individual users.

How can it be that a country with extensive legal rights to personal assistance prior to ratifying the CRPD has, upon ratification, cut back rights that are clearly articulated in the Convention? We have attempted to answer this question in this paper. Regressive action is not prohibited under international law which begs the question if these cut backs are justifiable under the limited principles that governing regression. Our conclusion is that the reinterpretation of the criteria for accessing personal assistance constitutes regression beyond what can be justified and, thus, violates the progressive achievement called for in the CRPD. As a result, we conclude that Sweden is in violation its obligations under the CRPD.

Acknowledgments: This work was supported by the FP7 Marie Curie Initial Training Network (ITN) DREAM, Disability Rights Expanding Accessible Markets (DREAM). Project ID: 265057.

Author Contributions: Ciara Brennan and Rannveig Traustadóttir conceived and designed the overall research with input from Peter Anderberg and James Rice. All four authors took part in conceptualising the article. Ciara Brennan was an Early Stage Researcher (ESR) for a Marie Curie Training Network entitled Disability Rights Expanding Accessible Markets (DREAM) and is a Ph.D. candidate at the University of Iceland. This article is a part of her PhD dissertation. She conducted the qualitative fieldwork in Iceland, Norway and Sweden and the data analysis under the supervision and advice of the co-authors. Ciara Brennan also carried out the policy analysis and literature review and took the main responsibility for the writing. During the writing process her co-authors read and commented on drafts of the paper. Rannveig Traustadóttir took active part in advising during the writing process and contributed to the writing of parts of the article. Peter Anderberg provided key materials and data, and his expert knowledge on Swedish personal assistance and independent living that facilitated data collection, analysis and writing. James Rice took part in conceptualising the article and read and commented on drafts during the writing process.

Conflicts of Interest: The authors declare no conflict of interest.

References and Notes

1. Office of the High Commissioner for Human Rights. "Priority issues and recommendations for the high-level meeting of the general assembly on disability and development and its outcome document: Inclusion of the rights of persons with disabilities in the post-2015 agenda." 2013. Available online: http://goo.gl/Id4ZOx (accessed on 12 December 2015).

2. Gerard Quinn, and Suzanne Doyle. *Getting a Life. Living Independent and Being Included in the Community. Legal Analysis of the Current Use of Structural Funds to Contribute to the Achievement of Article 19 of the UN Convention on the Rights of Persons with Disabilities.* Geneva: Office of the United Nations Commissioner for Human Rights Regional Office for Europe, 2012.

3. Rosemary Kayess, and Phillip French. "Out of darkness into light? Introducing the convention on the rights of persons with disabilities." *Oxford Journals Human Rights Law Review* 8 (2008): 1–34. [CrossRef]

4. Council of Europe Commissioner for Human Rights. "The right of people with disabilities to live independently in the community." 2012. Available online: https://wcd.coe.int/ViewDoc.jsp?id=1917847 (accessed on 10 January 2014).

5. United Nations Office of the High Commissioner for Human Rights. *Economic, Social and Cultural Rights: Handbook for National Human Rights Institutions.* Geneva: United Nations, 2005.

6. Peter Anderberg. "Aned country report on the implementation of policies supporting independent living for disabled people." 2009. Available online: http://www.disability-europe.net/content/aned/media/SE-6-Request-07%20ANED%20Task%205%20Independent%20Living%20Report%20Sweden_to%20publish_to%20EC.pdf (accessed on 5 April 2014).

7. Assistanskoll. "Statistics on personal assistance [statistik om personlig assistans]." 2015. Available online: http://assistanskoll.se/assistans-statistik.php (accessed on 16 December 2015).

8. Ciara Brennan. "Article 19 and the nordic experience of independent living and personal assistance." In *A Research Companion to Disability Law.* Edited by Peter Blanck, Eilionoir Flynn and Gerard Quinn. Farnham: Ashgate, 2016.

9. Ciara Brennan, Rannveig Traustadóttir, Peter Anderberg, and James Rice. "Negotiating independence, choice and autonomy: Experiences of parents who co-ordinate personal assistance on behalf of their adult son or daughter." *Disability and Society*, 2016, forthcoming.

10. Kathy Charmaz. *Constructing Grounded Theory.* London: Sage, 2006.

11. John W. Creswell. "Qualitative inquiry and research design." In *Choosing among Five Approaches*, 2nd ed. Thousand Oaks: Sage, 2007.

12. Social Insurance Agency. *Decisions Overview—Personal Assistance [Rättsfallsöversikt—Personlig Assistans].* Stockholm: Social Insurance Agency, 2011.

13. Gerben DeJong. "Defining and implementing the independent living concept. Developing, implementing, and evaluating self-help rehabilitation programs." In *Independent Living for Physically Disabled People.* Edited by Nancy Crewe and Irving Zola. New York: Jossey Bass, 1983.

14. Simon Brisenden. "Independent living and the medical model of disability." *Disability, Handicap and Society* 1 (1986): 173–78. [CrossRef]

15. Jenny Morris. "Community care or independent living?" *Critical Social Policy* 14 (1994): 24–45. [CrossRef]

16. John Glasby, and Rosemary Littlechild. *Social Work and Direct Payments.* Bristol: The Policy Press, 2010.

17. Adolf Ratzka. "Introduction to direct payments for personal assistance." 1996. Available online: http://www.independentliving.org/docs4/directpay.html (accessed on 18 March 2013).
18. Jenny Morris. "Independnet living and community care: A disempowering framework." *Disability and Society* 19 (2004): 427–42. [CrossRef]
19. Arlene S. Kanter. "The law: What's disability studies got to do with it or an introduction to disability legal studies." *Columbia Human Rights Law Review* 42 (2011): 403–79.
20. United Nations. "Convention on the Rights of Persons with Disabilities. Article 4.3." 2007. Available online: http://www.un.org/disabilities/convention/conventionfull.shtml (accessed on 11 January 2013).
21. JAG. *The Price of Freedom of Choice, Self-Determination and Integrity. A Cost Analysis of Different forms of Support and Service to People with Extensive Functional Impairments.* Stockholm: JAG, 2006.
22. Adolf Ratzka. "STIL, the stockholm co-operative for independent living." 1996. Available online: http://www.independentliving.org/docs3/stileng.html (accessed on 13 March 2016).
23. Adolf Ratzka. "The independent living movement paved the way: Origins of personal assistance in Sweden." 2012. Available online: http://www.independentliving.org/docs7/Independent-Living-movement-paved-way.html (accessed on 6 February 2016).
24. Paula Blomqvist. "The choice revolution: Privatization of swedish welfare services in the 1990s." *Social Policy and Administration* 38 (2004): 139–55. [CrossRef]
25. "The Act on System of Choice in the Public Sector." Reference number 2008: 962. Available online: http://goo.gl/0fXjv0 (accessed on 10 May 2016).
26. Inquiry on Assistance Compensation Costs. "Åtgärder mot fusk och felaktigheter med assistansersättning (Measures to combat fraud and misconduct with assistance allowance)." 2012. Available online: http://regeringen.se/content/1/c6/18/63/04/7bc4f4f9.pdf (accessed on 14 January 2015).
27. Health and Social Care Inspectorate. "Personal assistance [personlig assistans]." 2015. Available online: http://www.ivo.se/tillstand-och-register/lss-tillstand/personlig-assistans/ (accessed on 30 January 2016).
28. The Swedish Act concerning Support and Service for Persons with Certain Functional Impairments (LSS), Reference number 1993:387 [Lag om stöd och service till vissa funktionshindrade]Lag (1993:387)
29. Ole Petter Askheim, Hans Bengtsson, and Bjarne Richter Bjelke. "Personal assistance in a scandinavian context: Similarities, differences and developmental traits." *Scandinavian Journal of Disability Research* 16 (2014): 3–18. [CrossRef]
30. National Board of Health and Welfare. "Mapping and analysis of certain activities under lss [kartläggning och analys av vissa insatser enligt lss—Tilläggsuppdrag avseende insatsen personlig assistans]." 2015. Available online: http://www.socialstyrelsen.se/publikationer2015/2015-9-3 (accessed on 18 January 2016).
31. Committee on the Rights of Persons with Disabilities. "Concluding observations on the initial report of Sweden crpd/c/swe/co/1." 2014. Available online: http://goo.gl/1xqFpi (accessed on 12 September 2015).
32. Ulla Clevnert, and Lennarth Johansson. "Personal assistance in sweden." *Journal of Aging and Social Policy* 19 (2007): 65–80. [CrossRef] [PubMed]
33. Adolf Ratzka. "Personal assistance and attendant care in sweden. A consumer perspective." 1996. Available online: http://www.independentliving.org/docs1/ar1986spr.html (accessed on 3 January 2016).
34. JAG. *The "Jag Model"—Persnoal Assistance with Self-Determination.* Stockholm: JAG, 2011.
35. Rannveig Traustadóttir. "Disability studies, the social model and legal developments." In *The United Nations Convention on the Rights of Persons with Disabilities. European and Scandinavian Perspetives.* Edited by Gerard Quinn and Oddny Mjoll Anardóttir. Boston: Martinus Nijhoff, 2009.
36. Social Insurance Inspectorate. *Assistance Allowance: Shortcomings in the Law and Application [Assistansersättningenbrister i Lagstiftning och Tillämpning].* Stockholm: Social Insurance Inspectorate, 2015.
37. National Board of Health and Welfare. "Assessment of need for personal assistance." 2010. Available online: http://www.socialstyrelsen.se/nyheter/2010januaritillseptember/assistans (accessed on 22 January 2016).
38. Social Insurance Agency. *Response to Government Mandate. Reply Regarding Assistance.* Stockholm: Forsakringskassan, 2011.
39. Social Insurance Agency. "Questions and answers. Social insurance agency's interpretation of the judgment by the supreme administrative court concerning assistance [Frågor och svar försäkringskassans tolkning av dom från högsta förvaltningsdomstolen gällande assistansersättning]." 2015. Available online: https://goo.gl/8Hv747 (accessed on 23 January 2016).

40. Social Insurance Agency. "Mental disability in the assessment of basic needs [psykisk funktionsnedsättning vid bedömning av grundläggande behov]." 2015. Available online: https://goo.gl/FI3ffm (accessed on 8 February 2016).

41. Government of Sweden [Regeringen]. "Government's appropriation for the financial year 2016, for the social insurance agency [regleringsbrev för budgetåret 2016 avseende försäkringskassan]." Available online: http://www.esv.se/Verktyg--stod/Statsliggaren/Regleringsbrev/?RBID=17015 (accessed on 12 February 2016).

42. Independent Living Institute. "Using the law as a tool—Project of the independent living institute (ili) med lagen som verktyg—Projektansökan av independent living institute (ili)." 2014. Available online: http://www.independentliving.org/docs14/lagen-som-verktyg-projekt.html (accessed on 9 February 2016).

43. Jerome Bickenbach. "Monitoring the united nation's convention on the rights of persons with disabilities: Data and the international classification of functioning, disability and health." *BMC Public Health* 11 (2011): 1. Available online: http://www.ncbi.nlm.nih.gov/pmc/articles/PMC3104221/ (accessed on 20 December 2015). [CrossRef] [PubMed]

44. United Nations Enable. "Article 21—Right to health and rehabilitation." 2005. Available online: http://www.un.org/esa/socdev/enable/rights/ahcstata21refjurisprudence.htm (accessed on 21 April 2016).

45. ANED. "Dotcom the online tool of the commission." Available online: http://www.disability-europe.net/dotcom (accessed on 21 April 2016).

46. Michael Oliver, and Colin Barnes. *The New Politics of Disablment*. Leeds: Palgrave Macmillan, 2012.

47. Office of the United Nations High Commissioner for Human Rights. *Frequently Asked Questions on Economic, Social and Cultural Rights*. Geneva: Office of the United Nations High Commissioner for Human Rights, 2008.

laws

MDPI

Article

Uneasy Bedfellows: Social Justice and Neo-Liberal Practice in the Housing Market

Andrew Martel

Faculty of Architecture, Building and Planning, University of Melbourne, Melbourne VIC 3010, Australia; aamartel@unimelb.edu.au; Tel: +61-390-356-537

Academic Editor: Frank Pasquale
Received: 19 April 2016; Accepted: 7 June 2016; Published: 13 June 2016

Abstract: The Australian state has ratified the Convention on the Rights of Persons with Disabilities (CRPD), which emphasizes a social justice-based, personalized service delivery model. The upcoming National Disability Insurance Scheme (NDIS) reflects this model and aims to facilitate people living with a disability being able to access services while housed within the private residential market, a move away from a state-based combined residential/service care model. However, in Australia's neo-liberal housing market government intervention tends to shy away from policies that overtly impose restrictions on private firms. Therefore, in the absence of a subsidy from the state, the CRPD is of limited use in encouraging private developers to improve the appropriateness of its new built stock for people with a disability. A more persuasive approach is to highlight the size, diversity, and economic power of the disability-friendly housing consumer market when housing provision is separated from disability care delivery. This paper examines the feasibility of sustaining innovation in the volume builder housing market by aligning accessibility promoting changes to the existing innovation channels within Australian firms, suggesting that the NDIS concentrate on assisting the housing industry transition to a make-to-order model from the current make-to-forecast one.

Keywords: housing; NDIS; innovation; disability

---

1. Introduction: A Person-Centred Approach to Disability Service Delivery

The 2006 United Nations Convention on the Rights of Persons with a Disability (CRPD) advocates a person-centred approach to the provision of services for people with disabilities. This approach seeks to move service provision away from a mindset where disability is perceived to be a largely medical problem to be solved by the state, to one where the state intervenes to overcome obstacles to an individual participating in civil society as fully as their unique circumstances allow. Central to this position is the language of social justice. Ideas of independence, freedom, choice and control, are prominent in person-centred service discourse, as are the related notions of citizenship, autonomy, agency and community participation [1,2]. In respect to the built environment, this is manifested in the CRPD in several of the 50 articles. Article 9 'Accessibility' addresses the issue of access to the physical environment, transport, and public buildings and infrastructure. Article 19, 'Living Independently and Being Included in the Community', states the right to live in the community with access to public facilities as well as in-home support, while Article 28, 'Adequate Standard of Living and Social Protection', states in part the right to 'an adequate standard of living for themselves and their families, including adequate food, clothing and housing, and to the continuous improvement of living conditions' ([3], p. 20). Although couched largely in language that encourages the state to ensure the public realm does not exclude people with disabilities, the Convention includes promoting private sector participation, if not full responsibility, around the right to choose to live independently in the community. This raises a feature of person-centred discourse and policy noted by both advocates and critics of the approach, that although social justice is the overt frame through which the method is articulated, there is a parallel rationale of delivery that favours a neo-liberal free market approach, employing the framework of economic rationalism that 'small government' is best and that privatized services are more efficient, and ultimately more cost effective [1,4]. It has been described as a model that encourages the 'marketization of solutions' and a 'commercialisation of care' ([5], p. 642).

In keeping with the spirit of the CRPD, the National Disability Insurance Scheme (NDIS), the upcoming national restructuring of Australia's disability sector based on individualised service delivery, has both a strong social justice rhetoric in its policy outlines and aims, and a person-centred, market based delivery mechanism. While this is true for all areas of service provision covered by the NDIS, this paper has a focus on housing outcomes under the scheme. It has been estimated that when fully operational from 2017, the NDIS will have 410,000 participants, 255,000 of them aged between 25 and 64 who will require appropriate accommodation. Estimates of the current unmet need for affordable housing for eligible NDIS participants range from 83,000 to 122,000 [6]. A 2012 survey reported that around 100,000 people with disabilities (over 25) were living with their parents [7]. Publicly available discussion papers and presentations to date have emphasized the desire of the NDIS to use its capital allocation (between 3% and 4% of the total costs, or approximately $700 million a year) as a catalyst to leverage a much larger contribution and involvement by the private housing development sector [8]. The stated intention was not to allocate funds for construction of more government institutions to house people with disabilities, but to promote independent community living wherever possible ([8], p. 13). Central to this is the separation of housing provision from service provision. The following sections of this paper explore the feasibility of a voluntary increased involvement of the private housing sector in providing housing suitable for people with disabilities. After setting out the main characteristics of Australia's housing sector, the paper describes the principal modes of production and innovation that occur in the construction industry, highlighting a system of multiple inter-relationships and actors, and the large drag on innovation that uncertainty plays, particularly in the residential housing market. The paper concludes with a discussion of how the NDIS may be able to use its leverage to address the issue of uncertainty and promote more market-led competition.

2. Characteristics of the Australian Housing Sector

In order to assess the likely success of a move to increase private housing market engagement with the disability housing sector, it is necessary to examine some of the defining characteristics of Australia's housing market and review the performance of the current housing stock in relation to people with disabilities. Most fundamentally, Australia is a property owning, market based society with a strong cultural bias towards private home ownership. As a consequence, the vast majority of housing stock in Australia is delivered by the private sector at nearly every stage in the process from financing to design, construction, and sales. Government involvement is limited to ensuring a basic level of building control and safety through the Building Code of Australia, and at a local level setting planning regulations and controls. As a federal system of government, Australia has no central authority responsible for housing and responsibility sits at state and local government level. Even then, Australia's regulatory system regarding housing is considerably less intrusive than many other countries [9]. Despite periodic concern with housing affordability, this system has served the mainstream housing market in Australia well since the 1950s. A notable exception to the market provision of housing however, has been in the disability housing sector. Responsibility for housing and caring for people with disabilities has long been considered a core area of government or state-based provision, notwithstanding a slow progression towards de-institutionalisation over the last several decades [10,11]. To date, the private sector has had very little engagement with the disability sector, as the actual housing of people has been undertaken within the public housing sector, or within institutional settings. Regulations regarding accessibility and the provision of suitable facilities in public buildings and spaces, such as Australian Standard 1428 (AS1428.1–2009 Design for access and mobility, General requirements for access, New building work), are exempted in the case of private dwellings and so have had little influence of mass private housing market in Australia.

As a consequence, the current performance of Australia's housing stock for people with disabilities is very poor. Whether considering appropriateness for residents with mobility, vision or hearing impairment, or a cognitive disability, todays housing stock continues to be built with little or no forethought despite a full one-fifth of the Australian population, 4.2 million people in 2012, having a disability, with 3.8 million of those having:

> "A specific limitation or restriction that meant they were limited in the core activities of self-care, mobility or communication, or restricted in schooling or employment ... and one in five people with disability (19% or 813,900 people) reported a mental or behavioural disorder as the long-term health condition causing them the most problems. This included 5.6% with intellectual and developmental disorders, 3.8% with depression and mood affective disorders and 2.1% with dementia and Alzheimer's disease" [12].

3. Production and Innovation in the Construction Industry

The construction industry is a manufacturing one. It makes products (commodities) for consumption. In general terms, production strategies may be categorised into four types which differ primarily in where and when consumer choice enters the production stream. The strategies are termed Concept-to-order, Design-to-order, Make-to-order, and Make-to-forecast [13]. Concept-to-order and Design-to-order strategies are associated with 'complex systems' manufacturing where the final product is both highly technical and highly individual in nature, in building terms something akin to the Sydney Opera House or a state-of-the-art new hospital. Make-to-forecast is synonymous with mass production, where new products are designed in expectation of consumer demand rather than due to specific requests from consumers. The recent boom in investment apartments in central Melbourne is an example of this production method. Make-to-order is associated with a flexible production system that nevertheless can operate at high volume. It is sometimes referred to as lean production (particularly with reference to the car industry), and also as a mass customisation process. Volume housing production presents as the closest building industry version of lean production, although mass housing production has had such a close relationship with land development that historically development gain, rather than productivity gain, has been the principal motivation for profit making [13,14]. This is problematic for the strategy envisioned by the NDIS of consumer-based innovation, as the development gain profit motive favours make-to-forecast methods over make-to-order ones. That is, the potential benefits to producers of having a more attractive final dwelling, in terms of accessibility or universal design features for example, is undermined in terms of profit by the simplicity of capturing land value uplift.

Multiple definitions of innovation exist in the construction literature, but the definition of Freeman cited by Slaughter [15] captures the essence, that innovation is the 'actual use of a non-trivial change and improvement in a process, product, or system that is novel to the institution developing the change' ([15], p. 226). In developed countries, different governing strategies have a significant impact of how building innovation is supported. Australia, in common with the USA, UK, and Canada, operates in what has been described as a market-driven system, where it is assumed that innovation occurs due to the opportunities created by competitive forces in the marketplace, reflecting the dominance of neo-liberal policy settings in the construction industry ([14], p. 190). On the surface, this should complement the consumer-driven approach advocated by the NDIS. However, several complicating issues exist. The Australian federated government system has several implications for the effectiveness of a consumer-driven policy. Responsibility for construction rests at a state level, and is split between several agencies. Multiple interest groups and peak bodies exist, including the Property Council of Australia, the Urban Development Institute of Australia, the Master Builders association, and the Housing Industry of Australia, often advocating conflicting positions. As a consequence, no unified industrial representation at a Federal level exists to support innovation.

Notwithstanding this, where does construction innovation come from and what forms can it take? Innovation, like all of building, takes place within a system of inter-related actors and processes. As such, the source of an innovation may come from a variety of stakeholders including research and development organisations such as universities, manufacturers and product suppliers, designers, contractors (builders) and sub-contractors, as well as owners and occupants [15,16]. Reflecting this interlinked system, innovations may be described by the affect they have on the system as a whole. Incremental innovations are those that improve upon and existing product, practice or process but do not involve any substantial change, this type of innovation is common and ongoing and often originates from within construction companies. Modular innovations are also likely to develop within technically competent organisations such as manufacturers and suppliers, and involve a significant improvement to a particular component, but have a limited impact on the linkages between different parts of the overall system. Architectural innovations on the other hand, may involve only a slight change to a particular component but set in motion considerable modifications to the linkages between different actors in the system. Accordingly, these are likely to originate from parties that have a higher degree of control over relationships within the system, such as contractors and owners. Systems innovations are targeted specifically at modification of the linkages between the various actors, and so to be implemented require an expertise in managing both modular and architectural innovations, likely coming from companies with design and implementation responsibilities and strong ties to project owners [15]. Housing consumers remain largely outside of the system of linkages that form the industry, and so have little knowledge of the potential effect on other actors of requested changes, which are difficult enough to predict even by those inside the system, as the next section discusses. This severely restricts their ability to effectively advocate for change.

4. Uncertainty in the Residential Construction Industry

Historically within the building industry, the dominant relationship that promoted innovation was between manufacturers and product suppliers, and contractors. This relationship tended to try to drive innovation both from the supplier to the contractor (known as technological push), and from the contractor to the product supplier (known as market pull). That is, suppliers encouraged the uptake of new building products, and contractors attempt to influence suppliers to provide new products that are cost effective, quicker and safer to install. As noted above, at the mass produced, made-to-forecast end of the housing market, the influence of both consumers and designers has been much less. One of the reasons for this bias lies in the uncertainty inherent in housing innovation.

A high uncertainty innovation differs from low uncertainty ones in the amount of information that potential adopters are missing when they first hear about the innovation [17]. Incremental innovations have a low uncertainty as they are developed largely in house and by definition do not interrupt existing linkages within the industry. Architectural or systems based innovations do interrupt and change linkages, and as such may have a series of unintended consequences that are very hard to predict and quantify for innovators and so are likely to be considered highly uncertain. For adoption of an innovation to occur, a firm must be convinced that a relative advantage exists, that is, some tangible benefit from adoption will occur. In a typical firm, relative advantage has two primary components; the innovations ability to improve the performance of a particular work task, and/or the ability of the innovation to increase the survivability of the firm in the market ([17], p. 324). Judging the relative advantage of an innovation is difficult. On just the first issue of improving a particular task, the firm must consider several housing related variables including the considerable variation in housing types, the long time frame and wide range of conditions involved in house building, the fact that many parts of a house consist of interacting parts or dynamic systems, the tacit knowledge and skills required to complete the task, and finally that each task requires interaction with a large number of diverse entities (suppliers, sub-contractors, inspectors, clients). In addition, hostility and competition from other firms, the unpredictable and dynamic nature of the housing industry, and the level of complexity of any particular housing developer (who might also be involved in land speculation, financing, sales *etc.*), add considerably to levels of uncertainty of outcome when considering new innovations. Any innovation must be able to satisfactorily negotiate all of these factors. In these circumstances, firms seek advice from trusted sources of information. Research from the US suggests that these sources are primarily other builders, in-house testing facilities, and experienced sub-contractor firms. Only in cases of low uncertainty innovations were designers or homeowners actively consulted ([17], p. 328). Innovations necessary to move an established house building firm into an area with a further set of multiple variations and potential unknowns, such as accessible housing for people with disabilities, will be seen as highly uncertain to bring about the required market advantage to justify the risk. At present, there is no market leader to evaluate or emulate.

5. The NDIS and Innovation: Prospects for a Greater Engagement with Housing for Disability

In setting out to separate housing from disability service provision, the NDIS may create a space for the private housing industry to engage with the disability sector that it has not had to date. The intimate, and institutionalised, connection between care and dwelling effectively excluded mass market producers who need a broad customer base for their products, not just for the initial sale, but for multiple resales afterwards. Loosening this connection may provide opportunity. Nevertheless, significant market-based barriers exist to encouraging innovation in residential housing due to the complexity and uncertainty of the relationships of the many actors involved in housing design, production, financing and sales. Being able to transition from a make-to-forecast to a make-to-order model that would be able to accommodate modifications suitable for people with a disability has the potential to open up a substantial new market for private housing producers. From the current make-to-forecast model with only a single level of (low) accessibility, to a make-to-order situation where a choice of accessibility levels were available that might include mobility, hearing, vision, or calmness and clarity (for cognitive illness) packages. If designed well, these packages could have a much wider customer appeal than just the housing for disability market, particularly among consumers looking to accommodate aging in place concerns. Despite the appearance of a positive business opportunity for the development industry however, research from the UK shows that the experience of people with disabilities looking to purchase their own house from builders is often unsatisfactory, due to a lack of understanding and training of sales staff, and lack of provision of accessible entrances to display homes [18]. This mirrors the experience of the tourism industry in Australia, where again frontline staff were unaware or unprepared for questions about the disability related appropriateness of hotel rooms, notwithstanding current legislation requirements [19]. In both these cases, there had been little development of strategies that treated people with disabilities as a distinct, and valuable, market segment, despite studies that highlighted their likely economic value. Where there was interaction, it was focused primarily on access issues, and was reactive rather than proactive [19]. Moving to a mass customisation strategy would allow for an earlier, and more cost effective, voice of the consumer in final housing outcomes, without necessarily weakening the existing strong innovation axis between manufacturers and contractors. However the market for truly flexible housing designs will need an opportunity to mature and develop before anything resembling a system where 'innovation occurs due to the opportunities created by competitive forces in the marketplace' exists. The challenge for the administrators of the NDIS is to create an incentive system that will underpin the person-centred approach, giving their participants the freedom, choice and control advocated for in the housing market, while providing an acceptable level of certainty to producers willing to innovate with their supply chain in an unfamiliar, and as yet not-well-understood, market.

Acknowledgments: This research has been funded by the Melbourne Sustainable Society Institute (MSSI) and the Melbourne Social Equity Institute (MSEI) of the University of Melbourne. Parts of this paper were presented at the MSEI Conference 'Disability, Human Rights, and Equity' held at the University of Melbourne on the 3rd to 5th of February, 2016.

Conflicts of Interest: The author declares no conflict of interest.

References

1. Kirkman, Maggie. "Person-Centred approaches to disability service provision." 2010. Available online: www.melbournecitymission.org.au/docs/default-source/research-documents/kirkman-literature-review-november-2010.pdf (accessed on 10 November 2015).
2. Howard, Marilyn. *Enabling Government: Joined Up Policies for a National Disability Strategy*. London: Fabian Society, 1999.
3. United Nations. "Convention on the rights of persons with disabilities and optional protocol." 2006. Available online: www.un.org/disabilities/documents/convention/convoptprot-e.pdf (accessed on 21 October 2015).
4. Morris, Jenny. *Independent Lives: Community Care and Disabled People*. Basingstoke: Macmillan, 1993.
5. Rummary, Kirstein. "A comparative discussion of the gendered implications of cash-for-care schemes: Markets, independence and social citizenship in crisis." *Social Policy and Administration* 43 (2009): 634–48. [CrossRef]
6. Bourke, Eddy. "The housing needs of NDIS participants." *Parity* 27 (2014): 10. Available online: https://www.carersnsw.org.au/Assets/Files/Parity_Vol27-05.pdf (accessed on 13 June 2016).
7. Qu, Lixia, Ben Edwards, and Matthew Gray. "Ageing parents of people with a disability." *Australia Institute of Family Studies*, 2012. Available online: https://aifs.gov.au/sites/default/files/publication-documents/carers.pdf (accessed on 25 November 2015).
8. National Disability Insurance Agency. "Optimising the 'User Cost of Capital' for housing as part of delivering the NDIS sustainably and efficiently." 2014. Available online: https://www.dss.gov.au/sites/default/files/documents/07_2015/foi_request_no._14.15-166_-_document_for_release.pdf (accessed on 10 November 2015).
9. Burke, Terry, and Kath Hulse. "The institutional structure of housing and the sub-prime crisis: An Australian case study." *Housing Studies* 25 (2010): 821–38. [CrossRef]
10. Wiesel, Ilan, and Christine Bigby. "Movement on shifting sands: Deinstitutionalisation and people with intellectual disability in Australia, 1974–2014." *Urban Policy and Research* 33 (2015): 178–94. [CrossRef]
11. Australian Institute of Health and Welfare. "Disability support services appendix 2012–13." 2014. Available online: http://www.aihw.gov.au/publication-detail/?id=60129547855 (accessed on 25 November 2015).
12. Australian Bureau of Statistics. "Disability, aging and carers, Australia, 2012: Summary of findings." 2013. Available online: http://www.abs.gov.au/ausstats/abs@.nsf/mf/4430.0 (accessed on 18 July 2014).
13. Winch, Graham. "Models of manufacturing and the construction process: The genesis of re-engineering construction." *Building Research and Information* 31 (2003): 107–18. [CrossRef]
14. Ball, Michael. *Housing Policy and Economic Power: The Political Economy of Owner Occupation*. London: Methuen, 1993.
15. Slaughter, E. Sarah. "Models of construction innovation." *Journal of Construction Engineering and Management* 124 (1998): 226–31. [CrossRef]
16. Seaden, George, and André Manseau. "Public policy and construction innovation." *Building Research and Information* 29 (2001): 182–96. [CrossRef]
17. Toole, T. Michael. "Uncertainty and home builders' adoption of technological innovations." *Journal of Construction Engineering and Management* 124 (1998): 323–32. [CrossRef]
18. Thomas, Pam. "The experience of disabled people as customers in the owner occupation market." *Housing Studies* 19 (2004): 781–94. [CrossRef]
19. Darcy, Simon, and Shane Pegg. "Towards strategic intent: Perceptions of disability service provision amongst hotel accommodation managers." *International Journal of Hospitality Management* 30 (2011): 468–76. [CrossRef]

laws

MDPI

Article

Can International Human Rights Law Help Restore Access to Justice for Disabled Workers?

Rupert Harwood

Department of Human Resources & Organisational Behaviour, University of Greenwich, Old Royal Naval College, 30 Park Row, London SE10 9LS, UK; r.b.harwood@greenwich.ac.uk

Academic Editor: Anna Arstein-Kerslake
Received: 31 December 2015; Accepted: 30 March 2016; Published: 6 April 2016

Abstract: The research literature indicates that legislative changes in recent years, including the introduction of tribunal fees, have made it harder for workers in general to enforce their rights under UK employment laws. Drawing on the author's qualitative study, conducted in 2015 and with information from 265 participants, this paper finds that these legislative changes could be having disproportionate adverse impacts on disabled workers. Of particular note, fees had deterred substantial numbers from submitting discrimination claims; and it appeared that this reluctance to take legal action had in turn emboldened some employers to commit what might have been found to constitute unlawful acts if taken to tribunal. The paper goes onto consider whether these adverse impacts on disabled workers could render fees unlawful under UK and European equality and human rights law and/or could entail violations of rights under the United Nations Convention on the Rights of Persons with Disabilities. The paper concludes that the intent behind UK laws might (in relation to the lawfulness of fees) have been frustrated in the domestic courts and that the impact of any future successes in the domestic courts, or under international law, might be dependent upon public opinion and political expediency. The paper also briefly compares developments in Britain with developments in neighbouring and other comparable jurisdictions.

Keywords: UN Convention on the Rights of Persons with Disabilities; Equality Act; discrimination; disability; tribunal fees; justice; employment

1. Introduction

Disabled individuals in the UK have long experienced work-related disadvantage [1], including higher levels of unemployment and lower wages ([2], p. viii) and being more likely to be subject to ill-treatment in the work-place [3]. Disability employment protections in the Equality Act (EqA) 2010, and in the predecessor Disability Discrimination Act (DDA) 1995, have played an important role in reducing this disadvantage for many disabled workers. In particular, adjustments (to working arrangements and the working environment) have facilitated recruitment, progression, and retention (e.g., [4], pp. 81–83); and the DDA/EqA Reasonable Adjustments Duty has encouraged adjustments (e.g., [5], Figure 4.2). There are, however, indications that disability employment laws are quite often breached, with, for example, adjustments not being made when there could have been a legal duty to make them (e.g., [6]). A wide range of factors have contributed to failures to comply with disability employment law requirements. These might usefully be divided into individual factors, such as the attitude of particular line managers (e.g., [7], p. 412); organisational factors, including the size of an organisation ([8], p. 66); and external factors, including problems with enforcement, which are the focus of this paper.

As Elias LJ put it in *Unison v The Lord Chancellor* ([9], para. 26), "A right is rendered illusory if there is no practical mechanism for enforcing it." The research literature indicates that legislative and policy changes in recent years have made it harder for workers in general to enforce their rights at the employment tribunals [10], with relevant changes having included a narrowing in the scope of legal aid ([11], para. 3.1), as well as cuts in grants to voluntary sector advice providers ([12], p. 7); changes to tribunal procedures ([13], pp. 416–17); and the introduction of fees to take a case to tribunal [12]. Of particular note, with fees introduced in July 2013, total claims to employment tribunals went down by 81% between the first quarter of the 2013/14 financial year and the first quarter of the 2014/15 financial year ([14], Table 1.2), as shown in Table 1 below. There are also grounds to suspect that fees could have had disproportionate adverse impacts on disabled workers. Except for a small number of passing references (e.g., [11], p. 79; [15], p. 8), however, the research literature does not address this matter. If it turns out that there have been disproportionate adverse impacts, these might render the fees scheme unlawful under UK, EU, and/or international law.

Table 1. Changes in tribunal claims following the introduction of fees.

Adapted from data from the Office for National Statistics, Table 1.2 [14], licensed under the Open Government License v.3.0.	Change Q1 of 2013/14 to Q1 of 2014/15
Change in total employment tribunal claims accepted	−81%
Change in disability discrimination claims accepted	−63%

Whilst challenges to the lawfulness of the fees scheme have so far failed in the High Court (*Unison v The Lord Chancellor* [2014] EWHC 218 (Admin) (henceforth referred to as *Unison 1*) [16], and *Unison v The Lord Chancellor* [2014] EWHC 4198 (Admin) (*Unison 2*) [9], and in the Court of Appeal (*Unison v Lord Chancellor* [2015] EWCA Civ 935 (*Unison 3*) [17], the door has in effect been left open for parties to return to court with additional evidence and argument. First, in relation to whether the EU "principle of effectiveness" had been breached, the High Court in *Unison 2* indicated that more evidence was needed to show that the fees scheme makes it virtually impossible or excessively difficult for individuals to take a case to an employment tribunal ([9], para. 60), with the Court of Appeal in general concurring ([17], para. 68). Second, as regards the indirect discrimination claim, the claimants—and, in their stead, the courts—focussed on the disproportionate impact of the fees scheme on women as a group and did not other than nominally address the impact on disabled people as a group ([9], para. 65). In the light of this, there *might* be thought to be some value in presenting the High Court with evidence of indirect disability discrimination. However, the court's findings in relation to justification ([9], paras. 82–91) might be argued to have closed off the possibility of a successful disability claim. Third, the Public Sector Equality Duty (PSED), which the High Court in *Unison 1* [16] found had been complied with in relation to the introduction of the fees scheme, may subsequently have been breached in relation to requirements to monitor the impact of the scheme. There also appear to be possibilities under the United Nations Convention on the Rights of Persons with Disabilities and the European Convention on Human Rights. There are, however, problems with all of the above legal routes. Not least of these is that (even with legal decisions hostile to the fees scheme) any decision to remove tribunal fees in England and Wales appears likely to depend in large part upon changes in public opinion convincing the government that it would be politically expedient to do so.

Against this background, this paper draws upon the author's qualitative study (hereafter referred to as the *Disabled Workers Study*), and an analysis of the literature and some of the principal relevant case law, to address the following questions:

- What has been the impact of tribunal fees, and other potential barriers to justice, on whether and how disabled workers have enforced their rights under equality and employment laws?
- How if at all have restrictions on access to employment justice influenced employer behaviour towards disabled workers?
- Have restrictions on access to justice for disabled workers entailed breaches of UK, EU, and/or international law?
- How can legal and campaign action together help improve access to justice?

The author's Disabled Workers Study was conducted between April and September 2015; and involved collecting information from 265 disabled workers, using two qualitative online surveys, follow-up questions emailed to the third of respondents who agreed to be sent these, and 11 semi-structured in-depth telephone interviews. The paper approaches the above questions from the social sciences side of socio-legal studies.

The study methodology is outlined in the next section; then the findings are presented—in the context of the existing literature and in the context of the legal environment; and the paper finishes with conclusions and discussion.

2. Methods

2.1. A Pragmatic, and Exploratory, Qualitative Study

The study was pragmatic in that it aimed to produce, within a reasonable space of time, robust evidence to feed into ongoing policy and legal debates, and, in particular, in relation to the House of Commons Justice Committee's *Court and Tribunals Fees and Charges Inquiry* [18] and expected future legal challenges to the fees regime. In addition, the study aimed to help fill gaps in the research literature referred to above. The reason for taking a qualitative approach was that qualitative approaches appear better suited, than quantitative ones, to the study's purpose of identifying causal processes [19], concerning, for example, why and how disabled workers achieve or do not achieve access to employment justice. It is accepted here that limited and provisional generalisations, including what Williams calls *moderatum* generalisations [20], can be drawn from qualitative research ([20], p. 216). Ideally, however, qualitative research based generalisations require more detailed data (such as from a greater number of in-depth interviews), as well as a wider range of perspectives (including from managers and HR officers), than was available in this study. In addition, to go beyond moderatum generalisations, it might be argued to be necessary to use quantitative methods [21]. Therefore, while the study indicated the presence of relevant processes in particular cases and indicated where some of these processes were common across cases, the study is best regarded as exploratory and the findings cannot be assumed to be generalizable to wider populations. The findings do, however, suggest questions which could be used in a quantitative survey of a representative sample of disabled workers.

2.2. Data Collection and Analysis

Data collection and analysis ran in parallel. In particular, drawing on Strauss and Corbin [22], concepts developed from collected data suggested additional data that needed to be collected to further develop and test these concepts. For example, answers to the qualitative survey suggested that fees might have a particularly strong deterrent effect on casual workers, and, therefore, some of the follow-up semi-structured telephone interviews discussed what it was about being a casual worker which militated against taking legal action. The Framework Method [23] was used as a tool to help organise and analyse the data. The principal sources of study data were the following:

- *The literature review.* This included government documents and the research literature. The findings from the review are reported alongside the study findings in Sections 3 and 4 below.
- *Two online qualitative surveys.* These surveys asked disabled individuals principally open-ended questions about their work-related experiences, including, for example, "What has been your experience of taking...legal action?" The first survey was conducted between April and June 2015; and the second between June and September 2015, with the findings from the first survey having suggested topics to explore in the second. The surveys were publicised with help from the UK campaign Disabled People against Cuts and links to the surveys were posted on organisational websites and extensively tweeted (see Appendix 1). 154 individuals responded to the first survey and 158 to the second. Where respondents gave email addresses, it was clear that some had responded to both surveys; and it was estimated that a total of around 265 individuals responded

to the first and/or the second survey. A short extract from the second survey is shown at Appendix 2.

- *Follow-up email information and in-depth telephone interviews.* The surveys asked respondents to indicate if it would be OK to email them follow-up questions and around a third indicated that it would be. This provided an opportunity to seek clarification of answers and further details about experiences referred to. All those who emailed the author additional information, and referred to tribunals, were asked whether they would be prepared to be interviewed on the phone. Twenty five agreed to be interviewed and 11 in-depth semi-structured telephone interviews had been conducted at the time of writing.

The data analysis drew upon the grounded theory "constant comparative method" [22], including, for example, when comparing cases where legal action was taken with cases where it was not taken. With a self-selecting on-line sample of respondents, threats to validity were manifold. In addition, it seems likely that the places where the surveys were publicised (see Appendix 1)—including, for example, in tweets from trade unions—would have significantly increased the likelihood of attracting respondents opposed to tribunal fees and whose answers would include comments critical of fees and their impact. That the surveys indicated the involvement of Disabled People against Cuts could well have increased the possibility of such bias. It is also worth noting that the composition of the sample did not appear to reflect the composition of the workforce along a number of important dimensions. There was, for example, a disproportionate number of public sector workers. Along with making clear the study limitations (including in relation to bias and generalisability), attempts to address threats to validity included, in particular, "member checking" (e.g., [24], p. 322) searching for "discrepant data" (e.g., [19], p. 258); and individual triangulation. As regards member checking, the 15 survey respondents, sent the draft interpretations of their responses, in general agreed with the thrust of the interpretations; while, in a significant number of cases, suggesting some changes in detail. HR officers and managers sent some of the study conclusions in general expressed the opinion that the recorded problematic organisational practices might happen but far less frequently than appeared to be indicated in the draft study conclusions. The findings and conclusions were amended in the light of this feedback. As regards discrepant data, this led, in some cases, to a concept being abandoned; and, in others, to it being amended. For example, the initial conclusion that serious health problems and no representation would in most cases prevent legal action was amended as a result of finding that a number of individuals with serious health problems took action without representation (albeit without success) where a family member was able to provide considerable support. Individual triangulation included exploring, during the in-depth interviews, some of the assertions (such as about fees deterring action) that the interviewee had made in his/her survey responses. This was particularly aimed at addressing the possible biases arising from how the study sample was recruited.

In the findings sections below, the author's study presented in this paper is referred to as the "Disabled Workers Study".

3. Findings in the Context of the Existing Literature

3.1. The Impact of Law on Practice

Consistent with the literature (e.g., [5], Figure 4.2) discussed in the "Introduction", legal requirements appear to have encouraged improvements in disability employment practice in many of the organisations in the author's Disabled Workers Study. This was most apparent in the case of the Equality Act 2010 Reasonable Adjustments Duty. There were indications that adjustments (to working arrangements and the working environment) had facilitated the recruitment and retention of disabled workers; reduced sickness absence; and improved performance. An NHS worker, for instance, wrote—"I have a very low sickness rate because of my adjustments. It's lower than the able bodied in my building." It also appeared that the Reasonable Adjustments Duty could have encouraged the adjustments in a substantial number of cases. This was clearest in the nine cases where study respondents reported that an employer had initially refused an adjustment and then later agreed to it when the respondent was able to show that he/she was disabled under the Equality Act. It was hard or impossible from the limited information provided (and that from one source in each case) to assess the likelihood of the legal requirements having been breached in particular instances, except where the study respondent reported that he/she had won his/her case at tribunal. Nonetheless, again consistent with the existing literature (e.g., [6]), it appeared that practice may well have quite often fallen short of what was required in law. In some cases, it was said that no adjustments were made; and, in others, that adjustments were inadequate. For example, a central government worker, referring to additional adjustments that he had needed but did not get, wrote—"MS is progressive and what might have been an adequate adjustment 5 years ago would now not be adequate." This might have been inconsistent with the Reasonable Adjustment Duty being in law a continuing one.

There appear to have been a wide range of factors contributing to what could have been failures to comply with legal requirements. These included individual factors, such as the perceived importance of the disabled worker to the organisation, with casual workers being least well served; organisational factors, including organisational policies; and external factors, which might be taken to include, among others, social norms and (the focus of this paper) the enforcement of legal requirements. Arguably, the effectiveness of anti-discrimination law depends, in large part, upon a realistic prospect of workers being able (if poor practice continues) to enforce their rights at an employment tribunal. The findings of the Disabled Workers Study reported here suggest the possibility that the limited availability of free legal advice and representation, combined with the introduction of fees, and fear of victimisation, could have left the majority of study respondents with no realistic prospect of enforcing their employment rights. For example, referring to fees and lack of legal advice, a local council officer wrote —"The whole lot has a chilling effect on even contemplating a case, no matter how bad or personally hurtful the level of discrimination."

This section next looks at some of the impediments to enforcement encountered at different stages between what might be a discriminatory workplace incident and possibly fighting a case at tribunal.

3.2. Pre/No Legal Claim Actions

The coalition government justified the introduction of tribunal fees in part on the grounds that informal dispute resolution within the workplace is preferable to enforcement action and that fees will encourage the former ([25], para. 1). However, in addition to it appearing, from the existing literature, that tribunal fees could in fact have discouraged informal dispute resolution ([12], pp. 6–7), the mechanisms for such resolution appear in general to be ineffective. For example, Kirk *et al.* ([10], p. 3) found that "[p]articipants who attempted to resolve disputes within workplace procedures frequently found their grievances were ignored, hearings were pointless or managers simply covered one another." Being in a trade union can assist workers in obtaining their rights through informal means [26], with, for example, unions helping disabled workers to negotiate adjustments [27]). However, the general weakening of unions—with laws curtailing union activities ([28], p. 221), and the decline in membership ([29], p. 5) and in collective industrial relations (e.g., ([30], p. 359)—has reduced the power of unions to influence decisions in favour of individual workers (e.g., [31], p. 1521). Informal dispute resolution action does not, of course, take place in isolation from the legal environment. In some cases, for example, employees referring to legal requirements (without explicitly or at all threatening legal action) led to previously denied adjustments being made (e.g., [31], p. 1517).

The author's Disabled Workers Study, in general, reflected these findings about informal resolution in the existing literature. Of particular note, the study provides little or no evidence to support the government's claim that fees would encourage internal resolution of disputes. Indeed, consistent with Rose *et al.* [12], there were indications that tribunal fees have reduced the incentive for employers to resolve disputes through internal procedures, as employers, according to some respondents, know that non-resolution of disputes is now unlikely to lead to an employment tribunal case (on account of their employees not being able to afford tribunal fees). In addition, 35 of the 43 respondents who referred to grievance procedures either indicated that they had little faith in them, and so had not used them; or that they had used them and were disappointed with the results. A central government worker, for example, wrote—"took out a grievance, which is managed by the two managers against whom the grievance was." Union representatives did appear to have helped some study respondents to use internal procedures to secure their rights, with union support being referred to in 5 of the 8 cases in which the respondent appeared satisfied with the outcome of the grievance procedure. In one case, for example, a union rep assisted in making a successful complaint about reasonable adjustments not having been made, with the study respondent, a government agency control room operator, reporting—"Assessments, new chairs, less screens. When I and my union complained." A number of respondents, however, indicated that their union had provided insufficient help. Even where legal action was not initiated, threats of initiating it appear to have brought about improvements in practice. However, fear of an adverse reaction left some disabled workers reluctant to threaten legal action. This seemed to be particularly the case with casual workers, on account of regarding their positions as vulnerable. A retail worker, for example, referring to being bullied after requesting adjustments, wrote—"I didn't do anything about it because I was on a temporary zero hours contract, and they could have reduced my hours to zero at any time. After they found out I was disabled, they halved my hours."

3.3. Submitting a Claim

The Coalition government Business Secretary, Vince Cable, justified plans to "radically reform the tribunals system" in part on the grounds that "there is a widespread feeling it is too easy to make unmerited claims" [32]. Government representations of the tribunal system did not, however, strongly reflect the statistics or the realities that potential claimants appear (from the existing literature) to face. First, that the majority of claims are permitted to go onto a full hearing (*i.e.*, are not dismissed at a preliminary hearing) (e.g., [33], Table E.2) supports a conclusion that a majority of claims have merit. Second, the discrepancy between indications that potentially unlawful treatment could be relatively common place (e.g., [2]) among the millions ([34], p. 10) of UK disabled workers, and there only having been 7492 disability discrimination claims in the year before fees came in ([14], Table 1.2), suggests that it might in fact be too difficult to make merited claims, rather than too easy to make unmerited ones. Third, claims which are made appear in general to be made reluctantly and sometimes after years of ill-treatment ([10], p. 2). Reasons why most disabled workers do not attempt to enforce their rights at an employment tribunal include workers not knowing that their legal rights could have been breached. Edwards and Boxall ([35], p. 448), for example, report that the Disability Discrimination Act "featured little in the experiences of the participants with CF (cystic fibrosis). Few were aware of the [A]ct and others questioned whether they would be covered by it". For those who feel that their employment rights might have been breached, there are a number of principal deterrents to taking legal action.

These deterrents might include a not unrealistic perception that the odds will be stacked against them. Ewing and Hendy ([36], p. 120), for instance, referring to claims that have been submitted to the employment tribunal, report that "only 8% of unfair dismissal claims ultimately succeed at full hearing..." Difficulties getting initial legal advice can further discourage claims, with Holgate *et al.* ([37], p. 772), for example, finding "a paucity of individual employment advice...". It also seems that lack of advice at this stage has the potential to impact upon the likelihood of winning at tribunal later on, and, in particular, as a result of how well the case is made out in the ET1 tribunal claim form. Busby and McDermont ([38], p. 175), for example, found, in their interviews with Citizens Advice Bureau clients, that "[t]hose who completed the ET1 themselves found this a daunting experience". As with representation throughout the process, employees will in general be at a disadvantage compared to employers at the submission stage. For example, Harding *et al.* ([39], p. 6) found that "Three in ten claimants (31 percent) nominated a representative on the ET1 tribunal claim form, compared to five in ten (49 percent) of employers on the ET3 tribunal response form". Problems arise in part from the restriction of employment legal aid to discrimination cases; and legal aid in discrimination cases having become more limited in application and scope, and more difficult to access ([40], para. 27). There can also be fears that initiating a claim will lead to victimisation. Suggesting possible substance to these fears, O'Sullivan *et al.*, in their study of union officials' views in Ireland, found ([41], p. 236) that "half of survey respondents" indicated "that claimants are victimised by their employer".

Again reflecting the existing literature (e.g., [10], p. 2), as well as contradicting the Business Secretary's claim quoted above, the author's Disabled Workers Study suggested that workers do not easily or readily submit tribunal claims. In 17 of the 55 cases in which a reason for not submitting a claim was given, it was indicated that the employer's behaviour, or the dispute that this led to, had contributed to the disabled worker being too ill to go onto submit and see through a legal claim. This appears to have been the case with a speech therapist who wrote,—"If I had not felt so ill and upset by the time I left I would have explored my legal options for constructive dismissal". However, a more commonly cited reason for not submitting a claim was fear of victimisation and/or aggravating an already difficult situation (this being cited in 26 of the 55 cases in which a reason was given). One voluntary sector worker, for example, stated—"I've not taken legal action...because I fear my employer making me redundant as a result". There were also fears that taking action could make it harder to find work in future; and, for one local authority officer, it was not only being without a job that he feared, it was the changed and punitive conditions for those not working. He stated—"I know, and my family know, there is no longer any financial safety net if I lose the job I have now".

3.4. The New Requirement to Pay Tribunal Fees

The most powerful obstacle to submitting a disability discrimination claim could now be the requirement, introduced in July 2013, to pay a fee of £1200 to have a discrimination or other class B claim heard at an employment tribunal. This is the first time that fees have been charged to take a claim to tribunal since the UK tribunals were established in 1964 ([42], p. 136). There is, however, a remission scheme, with individuals qualifying to pay a reduced fee or no fee if their disposable capital and monthly income are below the specified thresholds. The government's fees consultation document suggested the possibility ([43], p. 19) that "Tribunal users required to pay a fee would not be especially price sensitive...". What, in fact, happened was a striking fall of 81% in claims accepted by the employment tribunals between the first quarter of the financial year 2013/14 and the first quarter of the financial year 2014/15 ([14], Table 1.2), as shown in Table 1 above. In addition, the government took a sanguine view of potential equality impacts. It's equality impact assessment of its proposed fee structure concluded that the structure would have few if any adverse impacts on equality [44]; and that "the measures" they "have put in place would mitigate any equality impacts" ([44], p. 9). Subsequent evidence, however, indicates that fees could be having disproportionate adverse impacts on disabled workers.

A principal impact has been reduced access to legal redress for disability discrimination. Following the introduction of tribunal fees, there was a fall in accepted disability discrimination tribunal claims of 63% between the first quarter of the financial year 2013/14 and the first quarter of 2014/15 ([14], Table 1.2), as also shown in Table 1 above. As well as the sequence and timing of this fall being suggestive of fees having contributed to it, research indicates that fees have deterred large numbers from submitting employment claims ([12], pp. 4–5). In addition, the evidence does not support the government's assertion that fees would be about "filtering out weaker and non-meritorious" employment claims ([45], p. 18). Of particular note, Anthony and Crilly ([11], p. 78) report that "success rates for employment tribunals remained broadly the same in the year before and after the introduction of fees." The reduced access to legal redress for disability discrimination would appear to entail a number of disproportionate adverse impacts on disabled workers. It is self-evident that disabled workers are more likely than non-disabled workers to experience unlawful disability discrimination, as only those who meet the Equality Act 2010 definition of disabled can be the subject of such discrimination. Therefore, a measure (in this case tribunal fees) which makes it harder for all groups to take a disability discrimination case to an employment tribunal will have a disproportionate adverse impact on those groups with the greatest likelihood of needing to take such a case, *i.e.*, disabled workers. The government's principal defence (in its equality impact assessment) to the argument that fees could have disproportionate adverse impacts on disabled people was that "disabled people are more likely to fall into the lower income brackets", than non-disabled people, and so "would be more likely to qualify for partial or full fee remissions" ([44], p. 7). This, however, gives insufficient weight to the fact that individuals can be on low incomes and ineligible for a substantial or any fees remission. The impact question in relation to low income groups should arguably have been whether the greater likelihood of those in such groups being eligible for a fee remission compensates (in terms of numbers affected and individual impacts) for the greater likelihood that individuals on low incomes will find it harder to pay whatever fee is not remitted. In addition, as disabled workers may be prevented by fees from bringing claims involving breaches of employment provisions other than those dealing with disability discrimination, the potential impact of fees on disabled workers is greater than the drop in disability discrimination claims reveals. Reduced access to redress for disability discrimination, and for other employment law breaches, could in turn embolden some employers to discriminate against disabled employees or to subject them to other detriment. Rose *et al.* ([12], pp. 6–7) lend indirect support to this possibility, in so far as their study indicates that fees have left workers in general in a weaker position vis-à-vis employers in relation to workplace disputes.

As the existing literature does not address the impact of fees on disabled workers, other than in passing (e.g., [15]) or to record the drop in disability claims [14], there is a limited basis for making comparisons with the author's Disabled Workers Study. The author's study findings do, however, add substance to concerns that the Equality and Human Rights Commission ([46], para. 19) and others have expressed about the possible negative impact of fees on disabled workers. Only a minority (73 out of 265) of respondents, in the Disabled Workers Study, addressed the issue of whether fees deterred claims. One of these respondents stated that "the fee would not prevent" him if he "needed to go to tribunal"; and five indicated uncertainty as to the impact of fees. All the others indicated a deterrent effect. First, this included respondents indicating that the fee would have deterred them if it had been in place when they took their case. Second, some respondents suggested that fees would deter them from taking another case in future. For instance, a third sector worker, with a visual impairment, referring to fees, wrote—"I wouldn't do it again. The financial implications are too high...and the service for those on legal aid is not fit for purpose". Third, there were those who had not taken a case before and stated that fees would stop them from doing so in future. In some cases, the additional costs of being disabled were indicated to have helped push the fee out of reach. For example, the just quoted third sector worker wrote—"It's a lot of money to lose—money that many of us simply don't have access to. Being disabled is incredibly expensive". In another case, the suggestion was that the money was there but that it was needed for difficult times ahead as the respondent's condition deteriorated. A data analyst wrote—"With a fee of £1200 to pay, and not being eligible for any relief (my wife received a relatively small sum...we have kept it against when times get even worse than they already are). I don't think that I could possibly file a claim against a large, well-funded organisation that already employs its own legal staff". Fee remissions could, of course, allow some not to pay all or part of the fee. However, just one respondent indicated being found eligible for a remission (though many more might well have so indicated if there had been a specific question about remissions). She wrote—"I was very wary of making a claim. Luckily I had the fee waived due to my disability (or paid by legal aid, I'm not sure...it's all so very confusing)".

Not feeling able to make a claim seems to have contributed to some individuals feeling compelled to put up with what they considered to be discrimination. For example, one respondent wrote—"I'm unlikely to make a claim. Things have on occasion been disgustingly discriminatory (getting trapped during a fire evacuation, anyone?) but I'm not likely to risk justice now. I will simply lump it until the stress of it simply drives me from my job". In addition, a significant number of respondents (19 of the 73 who discussed tribunal fees) seemed to suggest that employers realised that employees could not afford tribunal fees, and that this realisation had or would embolden some employers to behave in ways which before fees were introduced might have landed them at an employment tribunal. For instance, a voluntary sector worker wrote, with reference to fees,—"I think employers care much less about following rules because they know there is little or no comeback for their behavior". Another respondent suggested an impact on dismissal, writing that employers were now "willing to let people go due to lack of action. Tribunal fees stop people taking their case further".

3.5. Fighting the Case

For claimants who get as far as the employment tribunal, the chances of losing are higher than those of winning (e.g., [33], Table E.2 on unfair dismissal). A case might be lost in large part as a result of the statute and how the courts have interpreted it. Of particular note, despite having experienced substantial disadvantage, there would have been no unlawful disability discrimination if the affected individual did not meet the quite restrictive definition of disabled in the Equality Act 2010. Even if the definition is met, it can be difficult or impossible to prove this to the satisfaction of the tribunal. For instance, Bell ([47], p. 202) notes that "there are examples in the law reports of first instance tribunals and courts doubting, for example, whether even a condition as well-recognised as schizophrenia satisfies the test". A case might also be lost as result of a lack of representation. Employers are more likely than claimants to be represented at the tribunal hearing ([39], p. 6); and the tribunal process is heavily weighted against the unrepresented party ([48], p. iv). In addition to legal aid reforms ([11], para. 3.1), a number of other recent government policies further tilted the balance against the unrepresented claimant. For example, changes to tribunal procedures made it easier to reject claims without a full hearing ([13], p. 417); and the discrimination questionnaire procedure was abolished ([49], p. 207). This procedure had provided a statutory incentive for the employer to give non-evasive answers to questions about its actions, with the answers providing a potentially useful resource at any subsequent tribunal hearing.

Among respondents in the author's Disabled Workers Study, the biggest problem in fighting a case seemed, consistent with the literature (e.g., [48], p. iv), to be lack of representation. While it was far from clear, it appeared that all those who indicated that they had won at tribunal had some kind of representation. That one successful claimant had representation was implied, for example, in her comment that the case was "awarded to" her "without" her "having to appear". Without formal representation or access to professional advice, steering a case through the tribunal process would tend to prove difficult or impossible. For instance, a carer's support worker wrote—"Fighting that case was the hardest thing I have ever done and probably the most stressful. There is virtually no advice if you don't have legal representation and no legal aid. You have to work out how the system operates for yourself at every stage". In some cases, inadequate advice or representation, rather than none at all, appears to have been the problem. For instance, referring to advice provided through legal aid, a voluntary sector worker wrote—"the service I got was outsourced to another part of the country and I had no representation and minimal support". Once at tribunal, it appeared that there could be problems with accessibility. Of particular note, the carer's support worker, quoted above, wrote—"trying to get the Tribunal to make the same reasonable adjustments I was at the Tribunal about was a complete nightmare at every hearing." However, only two other respondents referred to problems getting reasonable adjustments to the tribunal process, with this suggesting the possibility that tribunal adjustments related practice could have improved since earlier studies (e.g., [50], para. 5.6.3). Whilst none of the respondents in the author's Disabled Workers Study referred to the recent government policies (additional to fees), which seem (as referred to in the previous paragraph) to tilt the balance further against the unrepresented claimant, there were indications that these policies could have been having an impact. For example, as regards the tightening up of tribunal procedures, all three of the telephone interviewees who referred to their cases being dismissed at a preliminary hearing appear to have been unrepresented, and their cases appear to have been dismissed for procedural reasons.

4. Findings in the Context of the Legal Environment

The existing literature (e.g., [15]), and the Disabled Workers Study reported here, suggest that the fees scheme, and some of the other barriers to justice discussed above (at Sections 3.1–3.5), could be at odds with domestic, European, and/or international law. However, there appear to be major obstacles to establishing this in relevant courts. In addition, it is far from certain that any judgements finding the fees scheme unlawful would lead to its abandonment or even to its substantial modification.

4.1. The Equality Act 2010 Public Sector Equality Duty (PSED)

The PSED requires that a "public authority" must, in the exercise of its functions, have due regard to a number of specified needs, including, for instance, "the need to" "eliminate discrimination...". The High Court in *Unison 1* dismissed Unison's argument that fees had been introduced in breach of the PSED ([16], para. 69), and the Court of Appeal in *Unison 3* dismissed Unison's appeal ([17], para. 125). The High Court's grounds for dismissing Unison's PSED challenge included, it seems, that (1) whilst the duty requires the public authority to collect and consider all relevant information, "it is for the public authority to decide what is relevant..., subject only to challenge on conventional public law grounds" ([16], para. 59), *i.e.*, on the grounds that the decision is outwith the range of reasonable decisions; and (2) in any event, the Lord Chancellor did collect and adequately consider an impressive amount of information ([16], para. 60). However, as Fredman argues ([51], p. 357), Moses LJ, in *Unison 1*, adopted "a very light touch standard of review of the duty to have due regard under the PSED"; and, as Fredman seems to imply, Moses LJ did not take adequate account of the extent to which requirements under the PSED go beyond what would be required in public law without the PSED ([51], p. 358). Amongst specific requirements under the PSED, the judgment in *R (Brown) v Secretary of State for Work and Pensions* [2008] EWHC 3158 (Admin) (para. 92) seems of particular relevance, stating that the due regard "duty must be exercised...with rigour and with an open mind". Moses LJ does ([16], para. 58) cite the reference to "rigour" in *Brown* but not the reference to "an open mind"; and it is the absence of an open mind, and a consequent lack of rigour, which might be argued to have entailed a breach of the PSED. Both the consultations and the equality impact assessments (EIAs) appear to have been directed at supporting an already reached policy decision to introduce fees. The second EIA, for instance, seems to dismiss the consultation evidence wherever it goes against this policy decision (e.g., [44], pp. 23–24).

The pre-fees introduction EIAs, despite their apparent inadequacies, are now effectively clear of possible domestic legal trouble. The PSED, however, is a continuing duty. That the author's research reported here (at Section 3.4), and other research (e.g., [15], p. 6), indicate that the now implemented fees regime could be having disproportionate adverse impacts on "equality groups" seems to provide a compelling reason as to why the government needs (if it is to remain compliant with the PSED) to conduct a fresh impact assessment (albeit not necessarily a formal EIA). However, despite evidence [52] that PSED judicial reviews can hinder unwelcome policies, it is not clear that a great deal would be gained in this case. Even if the High Court were to instruct the Ministry of Justice to conduct a new assessment, and this assessment was to prove damming, there would seem to be no consequent requirement under the PSED to abandon or even adjust the fees scheme. As Dyson LJ said in comments about the Race Equality Duty which also apply to the PSED, it "is not a duty to achieve a result..." (*R (Baker and others) v Secretary of State for Communities and Local Government [2008]* EWCA Civ 141, para. 31).

4.2. The European Union Principle of Effectiveness

In Unison's second case (*Unison 2*) [9], there were two principal challenges to fees carried over from *Unison 1*. The first was that the fees scheme breaches the "principle of effectiveness". As Elias LJ explains ([9], para. 23)—"That principle has been defined by the CJEU (Court of Justice of the European Union) in the following terms: 'The procedural requirements for domestic actions must not make it virtually impossible or excessively difficult to exercise rights conferred by [EU] law'." This principle is of relevance to fees in that their payment is a procedural requirement which has the potential to prevent individuals from enforcing employment rights conferred under EU directives. Whilst Elias LJ could "see the force of" Unison's "submission" on effectiveness ([9], para. 60), he rejected it, arguing that "the court has no evidence at all that any individual has even asserted that he or she has been unable to bring a claim because of costs" ([9], para. 60). The Court of Appeal agreed that additional evidence was needed, but was more amenable than the High Court to the idea that the individuals, whose circumstances constituted this evidence, could be "notional" ([17], para. 69) *i.e.*, hypothetical case studies could be relied upon. The principle of effectiveness ground would, therefore, appear to remain open, with Unison needing examples of individuals for whom fees made it "virtually impossible or excessively difficult" to take their case to tribunal. There again, the High Court had raised the possibility ([9], para. 63), which the Court of Appeal ran with ([17], para. 72), that the Lord Chancellor's existing discretion to waive fees in "exceptional circumstances" meant that such additional evidence might not be sufficient to show a breach of the effectiveness principle. In essence, the suggestion appears to be that this discretion could be used to accommodate the rights of those whose access to justice is rendered illusory by the fees scheme as currently administered, so long as the number of individuals involved is "very small" ([9], para. 63). Whilst the focus in this section is on the lawfulness of the tribunal fees scheme, other policies which restricted access to justice (such as changes to legal aid) also need to be born in mind, in the sense that (combined with fees) these other policies might have reduced access to such a degree as to render fees unlawful. The following comment from Elias LJ in *Unison 2* ([9], para. 51) suggests some authority for this approach—"As the CJEU observed in the *Duarte Heros (sic)* case (*Soledad Duarte Hueros v Autociba SA* [2014] 1 CMLR 53, para. 34), the effect of any restrictions must be considered in the context of the procedures as a whole...".

The author's Disabled Workers Study produced findings of potential relevance to the effectiveness claim. The study—consistent with the literature (e.g., [39], p. 5)—indicated that fees could be having a substantial deterrent effect on tribunal claims (as discussed at Section 3.4). Further, it appeared that, in some cases, fees might have made it "virtually impossible or excessively difficult" to take a claim to tribunal (suggesting the possibility that the principle of effectiveness had been breached). For instance, five of the study respondents, whose survey responses had indicated that fees had a strong deterrent effect, agreed to take part in telephone interviews, and four of these credibly maintained during the interviews that they simply could not afford the fee. In general, survey responses cited the fee as a barrier which deterred a claim when combined with other barriers. Of particular note, there was indicated to have been concern that paying a fee would (in the absence of legal aid) have necessitated forgoing legal representation and that without representation it would have been difficult or impossible to successfully pursue a case. In addition, it did appear, also consistent with the literature [38], that legal representation could make a substantial difference to outcomes. The author's Disabled Worker Study findings might be thought to lend support to the argument that, in determining the lawfulness of fees, the courts should give more weight, than the High Court did [9], to the deterrent effect arising from the interaction between tribunal fees and the cost of legal representation, as well as from the interaction between these factors and other impediments to action indicated in this study. These other impediments included, for example, the impact of health problems on the ability of some disabled workers to take a case without legal assistance. However, as referred to above, the Lord Chancellor's discretion to waive the fee could prove a stumbling block to any attempt to show that the effectiveness principle has been breached. The Disabled Workers Study casts some possible light on this issue. While the sample was not representative, the significant numbers who, it appears, might have been prevented from making a disability claim (as a result of the fee) suggests the possibility that the total numbers across Britain prevented from making any kind of employment tribunal claim could well be greater than the "very small" numbers that the High Court ([9], para. 63) appears to imply could be accommodated through the Lord Chancellor's existing discretion to waive the fee in "exceptional circumstances". It is also possible that there are individuals among the study respondents who would be willing to provide evidence to the Court of having been prevented by fees from pursuing legitimate employment claims. However, this would present potential ethical difficulties; and, instead, a separate study (with this legal purpose flagged up from the start) might need to be conducted. In addition, as Busby writes ([53], p. 257), referring to individuals who were refused a fees remission,—"to require such individuals to participate in litigation which is not directly concerned with resolving their personal dispute is a lot to ask."

4.3. Indirect Discrimination

The second principal challenge to fees carried over from *Unison 1* to *Unison 2* was that the fees scheme constitutes indirect discrimination under EU law and under the UK Equality Act (EqA) 2010. Under EqA section 19 (indirect discrimination), which Elias LJ focussed on in *Unison 2* ([9], para. 67), a provision, criterion or practice (PCP) is discriminatory where (to take the case of disability) it is applied or would be applied to non-disabled persons; it puts or would put disabled persons at a particular disadvantage compared to non-disabled persons; it puts or would put the disabled person in question at that disadvantage; and the person who applies or would apply the PCP cannot show it to be a proportionate means of achieving a legitimate aim. Elias LJ ([9], para. 65) states that Unison's case "focussed almost exclusively on discrimination against women", and that "The court does not have the material to determine whether there has been any other form of discrimination", such as against disabled people. The first two arguments that Unison put forward, as to why there was indirect discrimination, were rejected on the grounds that the comparisons (which Unison argued established disproportionate impact) were not legitimate (e.g., [9], para. 71) and the third argument was rejected on the grounds that (with the most recent statistics) the comparison did not support its claim that women were discriminated against ([9], paras. 77–78), as well as on the grounds of justification ([9], para. 90). The Court of Appeal upheld the High Court's rejection of Unison's indirect discrimination challenge [17]. However, in addition to it not being clear that the High Court had good reasons in law to reject the first two arguments, the third argument, which failed on the statistical facts in relation to women as a group, might (if a court were to consider the matter) be thought to have some hope of succeeding on the statistical facts in relation to disabled people as a group. For this reason, Elias LJ might not have been correct in asserting—"if the sex discrimination claim does not succeed, it is unlikely that any claim based on any other protected characteristic would do so" ([9], para. 65). The third argument alleged that the fees scheme "as applied to all class B cases discriminates against women" ([9], para. 76), with class B fees being higher than class A fees. While the latest statistics may or not support this argument ([9], paras. 77–81), they appear fairly likely to support the argument that the fees scheme as applied to all class B claims discriminates against disabled persons. In essence, this is because it is likely that the ratio of disabled to non-disabled persons caught by the class B fees (which apply to discrimination and, for instance, unfair dismissal claims) is greater than the ratio of disabled to non-disabled persons in the labour force as a whole. It is notable, for instance, that 52% of all discrimination claimants (not just those making disability claims) in 2013 had a long-term disability ([54], p. 84 cited in [11], p. 79). However, even if the courts were to accept that the higher class B fees put disabled persons at a particular disadvantage, the tenor of the High Court and Court of Appeal judgments (in *Unison 2* and *3*), including comments on how "legitimate" policies justified disproportionate adverse impacts on women (e.g., [9], para. 69), suggest that the courts may well be minded to regard any discriminatory impact on disabled persons as justified in law. Indeed, as the Court of Appeal notes ([17], para. 88), the High Court judgment includes a section "which appears to be intended to address the question of justification rather more generally in respect of any disparate impact which the Fees Order might have been shown to have on members of protected classes"; and this section in the High Court judgement ([9], p. 90) concludes that "the scheme taken overall...is justified and proportionate to any discriminatory effect". In short, the indirect disability discrimination claim could well be a legal cul de sac. There again, additional evidence (including that from the author's Disabled Workers Study discussed next) may contribute to showing that the discriminatory effect of the fees scheme on disabled workers is greater than the "very small" "extent of any adverse impact" ([9], p. 81) that the High Court refers to in relation to women as a group, thus potentially making the impact harder to justify. Additional evidence may also contribute to showing that some of the aims (that fees are taken to be a proportionate means of achieving) might not be as legitimate as the High Court assumed.

The findings of the author's Disabled Workers Study provide some support for the argument that fees have had disproportionate adverse impacts on disabled workers (see Section 3.4). This includes in relation to barriers to legal redress for discrimination and in relation to the consequences of weakened enforcement. In relation to barriers to legal redress, there were, for example, indications that the fees remission scheme itself entailed indirect disability discrimination. First, disposable capital—which individuals are in effect expected to expend on fees to below a specified threshold before being granted a remission—can be of greater importance to disabled individuals. For example, an individual might need to finance medical treatment not available from the UK National Health Service. Second, it can be harder for work-limited disabled individuals to replenish disposable capital expended on fees during a case. In relation to the consequences of weakened enforcement, the study findings were consistent with Rose *et al.'s* ([12], pp. 6–7) more general finding that fees tilted the power balance in the workplace further against the employee. However, the Disabled Workers Study reported here more specifically indicated that fees could have contributed to disabled workers being subject to increased workplace ill-treatment, including possible discrimination (as discussed at Section 3.4). As regards the suggestion above that the courts may be minded to regard fees as a proportionate means of achieving a legitimate aim, the Disabled Workers Study, along with earlier studies (e.g., [11], p. 79), arguably chip away at the legitimacy of these stated aims. For example, the information from study respondents did not seem to suggest that fees were helping to achieve the government's indicated aim of principally reducing unmeritorious claims and claims which could be settled informally ([45], p. 50). Indeed, it was telling that all the individuals who indicated that they had won a case in the past (suggesting, of course, that their case had merit), and who discussed fees, stated that they would not have taken the case if fees had been in place at the time. However, for the reasons discussed in the previous paragraph, it remains questionable as to whether a future indirect disability discrimination claim would have a realistic prospect of success.

4.4. United Nations Convention on the Rights of Persons with Disabilities (UN CRPD)

The UNCRPD was ratified by the UK on 8 June 2009 ([55], p. 428). A central motivation behind the Convention was to help ensure that disabled individuals can enjoy on an equal basis, with non-disabled individuals, rights provided for in international human rights treaties ([56], pp. 752–53); and the Convention aims to achieve this in part through requirements to make reasonable accommodations ([57], p. 5). CRPD Article 13 (Access to Justice) (1), for instance, requires—"procedural...accommodations, in order to facilitate" disabled persons' "effective role...in all legal proceedings..."; with it being notable that the UK Employment Appeal Tribunal recently drew on this Article in considering the reasonable adjustments that courts are required to make for disabled litigants (*Rackman v NHS Professionals Ltd* [2015] UKEAT/0110/15/LA, para. 59). Reiss ([58], pp. 113–14) argues that to "properly comply", with the CRPD, "governments may have to review nearly the entire corpus of existing law for lacunae, ignoring the needs of the disabled...". The CRPD also imposes monitoring obligations on States Parties [59]. These include the requirement to submit periodic reports to the Committee on the Rights of Persons with Disabilities (the Committee) on the steps that the state has taken to implement the Convention, and to respond in these reports to concerns raised by the Committee in its concluding observations to previous reports. In addition, as Bartlett ([56], pp. 754–55) points out—"for those countries such as the UK that have signed the optional protocol to the CRPD, individuals or groups of individuals may complain to the Committee regarding alleged breaches of the CRPD, and the Committee adjudicates the matter in quasi-judicial fashion"; with the Committee also having "authority to undertake inquiries into systematic violations of the CRPD" ([55], p. 429).

A number of the barriers to justice discussed above (Sections 3.1–5) appear at possible variance with the CRPD. These include what was referred to above (at Section 3.5) as the "quite restrictive definition of disabled in the Equality Act". In 2007, as Lane and Munkholm report ([60], p. 6), the European Union (EU) ratified the CRPD, "making it an integral part of the EU legal order, thus placing an obligation on the ECJ (European Court of Justice) to interpret the (EU Equal Treatment Framework) Directive in a manner consistent with the Convention" (wording in brackets added). Lane and Munkholm go onto note that, in the joined cases of *Jette Ring* and *Skoube Werge*, the Court of Justice of the European Union (CJEU) concept of disability was, in the light of the CRPD, brought "much more into line with the social model" ([60], p. 6). In essence, the social model focuses on external factors—such as inaccessible work environments—as a principal cause of a disabled person's disadvantage ([61], pp. 29–36). With this CJEU change in how disability is understood, and reasonable adjustments required under the Framework Directive, it could be argued that the right to reasonable adjustments should not be restricted to those who meet the definition of disabled in the UK Equality Act 2010 (which focuses on the nature of the individual's impairment and so is based on a predominantly medical model of disability) but instead should be extended (at least in relation to matters covered in the Framework Directive) to those who would meet the broader definition of disabled in the CRPD.

Where the arguments against fees have failed so far under domestic and EU legislation, similar arguments could potentially succeed under the CRPD. For example, as noted earlier (at Section 4.1), the Equality Act 2010 Public Sector Equality Duty (PSED) requires public authorities to have "due regard" to the "need to—(a) eliminate" unlawful discrimination, and Moses LJ appeared in *Unison 1* [16] to consider that the government's impact assessments met this requirement, regardless of whether these assessments had led to any action to eliminate discrimination. In contrast, CRPD Article 4 (1) (e) requires States Parties "to take all appropriate measures to eliminate discrimination on the basis of disability...". If fees for disability discrimination claims are emboldening a significant number of employers to discriminate against disabled workers—as the author's Disabled Workers Study suggests could be happening (Section 3.4)—then abolishing fees (outright or for disability discrimination claims) might be taken to be an "appropriate" measure "to eliminate" this additional discrimination.

Some of the other CRPD Articles which, in combination with others, tribunal fees might be argued to have the potential to be at variance with include Articles 5 and 27. Under Article 5 (Equality and non-discrimination) (2), "States Parties shall...guarantee to persons with disabilities equal and effective legal protection against discrimination...". The UK might be argued to be violating this article if, as the author's study suggests could be the case (Section 3.4), the fees scheme has resulted in many disabled workers no longer being able to afford to enforce their rights at tribunal and so, for them, there is no "effective legal protection...". Under Article 27 (Work and employment) (1), "...States Parties shall safeguard and promote the realization of the right to work,...by taking appropriate steps, including through legislation, to, inter alia:...(b) Protect the rights of persons with disabilities, on an equal basis with others, to just and favourable conditions of work..., including protection from harassment, and the redress of grievances". Tribunal fees could go against all of these specified obligations. This is most clearly indicated in relation to the Equality Act 2010 Reasonable Adjustments Duty, as this duty is in essence about safeguarding and promoting the realisation of the right to work (e.g., [31], p. 1511). However, if workers cannot afford, as a result of tribunal fees, to enforce their rights under the Reasonable Adjustments Duty, then the duty and its impact could be greatly diminished.

The impact of fees, in relation to these CRPD Articles, might provide the basis for an inquiry, by the UN Committee on the Rights of Persons with Disabilities, into whether the fees scheme entails systematic violations of the CRPD. There could also be grounds for individuals to bring complaints of violations of their rights under the Convention. Indeed, it is not impossible that such violations occurred in the case of some of the study respondents (though it was not possible to hear employer accounts of alleged incidents). One study respondent, for example, indicated that his workplace disability discrimination grievance was not taken seriously; and that the tribunal fee prevented him from going onto to take legal action. The problem, he explained, was that his disposable capital was just above the eligibility limit for a fee remission but he could not use this capital to pay the fee, since it was needed to fund care as his progressive condition deteriorated. It might be argued that, in these circumstances, he was denied his right under CRPD Article 5 (2) to "effective legal protection against discrimination" and under CRPRD Article 27 (1) (b) to "redress of grievances". While the Committee on the Rights of Persons with Disabilities will examine the impact of a national law on a particular individual (e.g., CRPD/C/12/D/5/2011, para. 10.2) [62], the Committee's recommendations in these cases can have wider effect; and, in particular, in so far as the State Party can be placed under an obligation to take measures to prevent similar violations in future (e.g., CRPD/C/14/D/21/2014, para. 9. (b))[63]. In addition, the CRPD periodic reporting requirements (referred to above) could provide opportunities to raise concerns about fees and for the UN Committee to recommend changes. Indeed, the Equality and Human Rights Commission writes that, as part of the UK Independent Mechanism on the CRPD, it contributed to a report which "called on the UN CRPD Committee to ask the UK government to provide evidence of the effect on disabled people of the introduction of fees for ET cases..." ([46], para. 19). There are also possibilities arising from the CRPD's role in strengthening, from a disability rights perspective, international human rights agreements. For example, in so far as the CRPD is used as "a reference point for interpreting...ECHR (European Convention on Human Rights) law relating to discrimination on the grounds of disability..." ([64], p. 38), the CRPD could add weight to what might already be a good case under the ECHR against fees in the case of particular disabled individuals. Of particular note, in a number of non-UK cases (e.g., *Podbielski and PPU Popure v Poland* [2005] ECHR 543, para. 64), the application of court fees has been found to have compromised a claimant's rights under Article 6 (covering the right to a fair trial); and, assuming that the UK fees regime has a particular impact on disabled people (which the study reported here suggests could be the case), Article 6 read with Article 14 (which guarantees non-discrimination in the enjoyment of the other Convention rights) might be engaged.

There are, however, major limitations on the potential usefulness of the CRPD. These include the slow pace at which UN procedures progress. For example, referring to the periodic reporting requirements, Lawson and Priestly ([59], p. 742) "estimate the likely time from submission of state parties' reports to their scrutiny by the UN Committee on the Rights of Persons with Disabilities may now be approaching seven years". In addition, domestic political priorities could render pyrrhic any victories in international law. In recent years, UK governments do not appear to have taken allegations from international bodies very seriously. For example, the 22 page letter to the UK government in 2014 from the Office of the United Nations High Commissioner for Human Rights [65] sets out, in considerable detail and with 116 citations, why austerity policies could amount to retrogressive measures prohibited under the International Covenant on Economic, Social and Cultural Rights. The heart of the UK government's 2 page response [66], however, is—"We were disappointed that your letter cites generalised rather than specific allegations with few sources cited". It seems possible that the government might give similarly short shrift to any recommendations regarding the CRPD and tribunal fees. Further, bearing in mind that the government is committed to abolishing the Human Rights Act 1998 ([67], p. 58), and the Prime Minister would not rule out quitting the European Convention on Human Rights [68], it would not be surprising if a series of adverse decisions from the Committee on the Rights of Persons with Disabilities prompted the government to talk about opting out of the inquiry procedure under the CRPD optional protocol. In such circumstance, in which national governments can ignore judgments or rescind international obligations, the impact of decisions under international law could depend to a considerable degree upon the state of domestic public opinion. It also seems that influencing public opinion in contradiction to dominant media and government narratives presents a major challenge. For example, government plans to abolish the Human Rights Act (HRA) might be expected to have provoked outcry from the public whose freedoms the Act is designed to protect; and yet the UK government has succeeded in portraying the HRA as akin to a terrorist's charter [69]. A similarly hostile reception could well await any adverse CPRD decision on tribunal fees. Indeed, the media reaction to the ongoing UN CRPD inquiry might give a taste of what to expect, with the Daily Mail headline [70] announcing—"Now UN sparks fury after launching human rights investigation into Britain's disability benefit reforms".

5. Conclusions and Discussion

Currie and Tegue ([71], p. 2) refer to a "huge expansion in individual employment rights that has occurred almost simultaneously across Anglo-American (sic) countries", and which "can be traced back to the 1970s" ([71], p. 7). However, the authors go onto argue ([71], p. 11) that "active efforts are occurring to design institutional arrangements to dull the impact of" this expansion. These efforts might be argued to have accelerated under the UK coalition government (2010–2015) and to have focussed on weakening enforcement, including through curtailing the enforcement powers and resources of the Equality and Human Rights Commission 2011 ([72], p. 319); cuts to legal aid and to legal advice services ([40], para. 27), and (the focus of this paper) the introduction in 2013 of fees to have a case heard at a British employment tribunal. UK governments have also begun reversing the expansion of the individual employment rights themselves, with, for instance, a doubling in the qualification period for protection from unfair dismissal ([49], p. 206). A number of Currie and Tegue's other so-called "Anglo-American" countries seem set to introduce or increase fees and/or make them non-refundable (see, for example, recommendation 17.1 of the Productivity Commission to the Australian government ([73], p. 56)). The picture with regards to fees, however, is different in jurisdictions neighbouring Britain. In the case of the devolved Northern Ireland administration, the Minister for Employment and Learning "ruled out the introduction of fees..." ([74], p. 2); and, in the Republic of Ireland, a fee is only payable where a party who failed to appear at the Workplace Relations Commission without good cause wishes to appeal the decision to the Labour Court [75]. In addition, within Britain, the ruling Scottish National Party has indicated that it would abolish tribunal fees if and when further devolution gives the Scottish government the power to do so ([76], p. 3).

With a majority UK government committed to fees, and the possibility of it continuing in power after the 2020 General Election, it seems that fees might be there to stay in England and Wales. That is unless fees are found unlawful. Fees have been successfully challenged in a number of jurisdictions. Of particular note, the Canadian Supreme Court (*Trial Lawyers Association of British Columbia v British Columbia (Attorney-General)* [2014] SCC 59) ([77], para. 46) found—"A fee that is so high that it requires litigants who are not impoverished to sacrifice reasonable expenses in order to bring a claim may, absent adequate exemptions, be unconstitutional because it subjects litigants to undue hardship, thereby effectively preventing access to the courts". In addition, criticisms on constitutional grounds (e.g., [78], paras. 40–72) of the Productivity Commission's recommendations on fees (referred to above) suggest the possibility of legal action if the Australian government implements these recommendations. Challenges to the lawfulness of the fees scheme have so far, however, failed in the UK High Court (*Unison v The Lord Chancellor* [2014] EWHC 218 (Admin) ("Unison 1") [16] and *Unison v The Lord Chancellor* [2014] EWHC 4198 (Admin) ("Unison 2") [9], and in the Court of Appeal (*Unison v Lord Chancellor* [2015] EWCA Civ 935 ("Unison 3") [17]. This seems to have been in part on account of the courts requiring that fees cause more hardship (to be taken to be unlawful) than in the test that the Canadian Supreme Court indicated. There again, the door has in effect been left open for parties to return to the UK courts with additional evidence and argument. First, in relation to whether the EU "principle of effectiveness" had been breached (Section 4.2), the High Court indicated that more evidence was needed to show that fees make it virtually impossible or excessively difficult for individuals to take a case to an employment tribunal (e.g., [9], para. 60), with the Court of Appeal in general concurring ([17], para. 68). Second, as regards the indirect discrimination claim, the claimants—and, in their stead, the courts—focussed on the alleged disproportionate impact of the fees scheme on women as a group, with the court ruling that the latest tribunal statistics did not indicate such an impact, as well concluding that "the scheme taken overall...is justified" ([9], para. 90). There might, therefore, be thought to be some value in the High Court being presented with evidence of indirect *disability* discrimination (though, as returned to below, an indirect disability discrimination claim may now have little prospect of success). Third, while the High Court dismissed Unison's argument that fees had been introduced in breach of the Public Sector Equality Duty (PSED) [16], the PSED is an ongoing duty, which might be argued to require the Ministry of Justice to re-assess the equality impact of the fees scheme now that it has been in place for several years (Section 4.1).

As discussed in this paper (Sections 4.1–4), the author's Disabled Workers Study produced findings of potential relevance to the effectiveness and indirect discrimination claims and to whether the PSED has been breached. A total of 265 disabled workers took part in the study; with the study including two qualitative surveys, emailed follow-up questions, and 11 in-depth semi-structured telephone interviews. As regards the principle of effectiveness (Section 4.2), the study suggested, for example, that fees, combined with the limited availability of legal aid, could have made it "virtually impossible or excessively difficult" for dozens of the study respondents to take their claims to tribunal. As regards indirect discrimination (Section 4.3), the study provided support for the argument that fees have had a disproportionate adverse impact on disabled workers. This includes in relation to barriers to legal redress for discrimination and in relation to the consequences of weakened enforcement. Of particular note, 19 of the 73 study respondents, who discussed tribunal fees, seemed to suggest that employers realised that employees could not afford tribunal fees, and that this realisation had or would embolden some employers to commit what might have been found to constitute unlawful acts if taken to tribunal. Study evidence of disproportionate adverse impacts on disabled individuals also adds weight to the argument that the Ministry of Justice should, so as to remain compliant with the PSED, reassess the equality impact of the fees scheme. There are, however, major obstacles to bringing about change through these domestic law approaches. The principle of effectiveness challenge, presented with the kind of evidence that the courts have called for, appears to have the greatest prospect of meaningful success. However, from the Court of Appeal judgement, it seems that the most that might be hoped for is that "the level of fees and/or the remission criteria will need to be revisited" ([17], para. 75), and presumably adjusted. A possible problem with an indirect disability discrimination claim is that, even if the courts were to accept that the fees scheme put disabled persons at a particular disadvantage, the tenor of the High Court judgement (in *Unison 2* and *3*) suggests that the courts may well decide that the particular disadvantage (that disabled people are put at) is justified in law. A PSED judicial review application might succeed. However, a finding against the Ministry of Justice would, at best, require a new assessment, subsequent to which there would appear to be no requirement under the PSED to make changes to the fees scheme.

In these circumstances, there could be value in additionally seeking remedy in international law and with European or international bodies. There are indications from the author's study (Section 4.4) that the fees scheme could be at variance with a number of Articles of the UN Convention on the Rights of Persons with Disabilities (CRPD), and that this could provide the grounds for an inquiry by the UN Committee on the Rights of Persons with Disabilities into possible systematic violations of the CRPD, as well as providing grounds for an individual to bring a complaint that their individual rights under the CRPD have been violated. Indeed, it seems possible that violations had occurred in the case of some of the study respondents. There are, of course, major obstacles to using international law to successfully oppose fees. Problems include the slow speed at which UN quasi-judicial wheels turn. However, the more substantial problem is that the UK government appears inclined to reject or ignore adverse decisions from the UN; with the foreign secretary, for example, describing as "ridiculous" the recent UN panel finding that Julian Assange [79] had been subject to "arbitrary detention". In addition, the media appears in general prepared to present government dismissal of UN decisions as defending British sovereignty (e.g., [70]) rather than as flouting international law that the UK has signed up to. Indeed, bearing in mind that the UK government has talked about leaving the ECHR [68], it seems unlikely to baulk at the prospect of opting out of the CRPD optional protocol inquiry mechanism. In these circumstances, an important challenge will be how to use the CRPD to help see off fees without the CRPD itself being seen off.

Indeed, none of the (domestic and international) legal options discussed above may be enough on their own or together to see off fees or the current fees scheme in England and Wales, even if the applicants are successful in court. In contrast, fees could well be abolished in Scotland without the need for any further legal action ([76], p. 3). The future of fees will ultimately be a political decision. With the UK government ideologically committed to charging fees ([45], pp. 49–50), any decision to end them in England and Wales is likely to depend upon it being made politically expedient to do so. Efforts to make it politically expedient might in turn benefit from combining legal actions and wider campaigning so as to generate coverage for the most egregious cases, provide a platform from which to address the more general arguments, and help persuade public opinion that tribunal fees are an unacceptable denial of access to employment justice. That the Lord Chief Justice has recently stated that "our justice system has become unaffordable to most" [80] can only bolster the effectiveness of these efforts. In addition, at the time of writing, Unison is waiting to find out if it has been granted permission to appeal its tribunal fees claim to the Supreme Court [81].

Acknowledgments: There were no sources of funding. The author would like to thank the study participants; the anonymous reviewers; and Jenny Dimond, Carole Stuart-McIvor, Bob Ellard, Debbie Jolly, Linda Burnip, and Anita Bellows.

Conflicts of Interest: The author declares no conflict of interest.

Abbreviations

The following abbreviations are used in this manuscript:

DDA	Disability Discrimination Act 1995
EqA	Equality Act 2010
PSED	Public Sector Equality Duty
UNCRPD	United Nations Convention on the Rights of Persons with Disabilities

Appendix 1

The following table lists every third website, facebook page and tweet which (during an internet search) was found to have publicised one or both of the qualitative surveys. Non-organisational tweets were not included for ethical reasons. The table provides links to the organisational home page or the page which publicises the survey.

Table A1. Sample of places publicising the study.

Name of Organisation	Link to Website, Facebook Page, or Tweet
Bakers Food and Allied Workers Union	http://www.bfawu.org/dpac_launches_survey_into_reasonable_adjustments_for_disabled_workers
Black Triangle Campaign	http://blacktrianglecampaign.org
Breakthrough UK	http://www.breakthrough-uk.co.uk
British Association for Supported Employment	http://base-uk.org/
Disabled Living Foundation	https://twitter.com/DLFUK
Disabled People Against Cuts	http://dpac.uk.net/
Ehlers-Danlos Support UK	https://www.facebook.com/EhlersDanlosUK/posts/10155456255180414
Legal Action Group	https://twitter.com/LegalActionGrp?cn=cmV0d2Vld F9tZW50aW9uZWRfdXNlcg%3D%3D&refsrc=em
Sense	https://twitter.com/sensetweets/status/644083632370487296
SEN RT	https://twitter.com/rt_sen
Trade Union Congress	https://www.tuc.org.uk/equality-issues/disability-issues/campaigning-disability-equality/impact-uk-coalition-government

Appendix 2

The following is a short extract from the second qualitative survey. The complete surveys will be emailed on request. There were a total of 60 questions asked across the two surveys.

Why Were Reasonable Adjustments Made for You?

1. What reasonable adjustments have been made for you by an employer (you worked for or applied for a job with) and when were these adjustments made?
2. What factors do you think contributed to the adjustment(s) being made? For example,

   (a) Who suggested an adjustment? Was it you or someone else?
   (b) Who supported the request for an adjustment; who, if any one, opposed the request; and what form did any support or opposition take?
   (c) Was an adjustment considered inexpensive and/or was it considered essential to you doing your job?
   (d) Did you have to fight for an adjustment; and, if so, what did this involve?
   (e) Did your organisation have a central fund to pay for reasonable adjustments?

3. Did the fact that there is a legal duty to make reasonable adjustments seem to contribute to you getting an adjustment, and, if so, how?"

References and Notes

1. John Hills, Mike Brewer, Stephen Jenkins, Ruth Lister, Ruth Lupton, Stephen Machin, Colin Mills, Tariq Modood, Teresa Rees, and Sheila Riddell. "An Anatomy of Economic Inequality in the UK: Report of the National Equality Panel." *Government Equalities Office*, 2010. Available online: http://eprints.lse.ac.uk/28344/1/CASEreport60.pdf (accessed on 10 June 2015).
2. Nick Coleman, Wendy Sykes, and Carola Groom. "Barriers to Employment and Unfair Treatment at Work: A Quantitative Analysis of Disabled People's Experiences." *Equality and Human Rights Commission*, 2013. Available online: http://www.equalityhumanrights.com/sites/default/files/documents/barriers_and_unfair_treatment_final.pdf (accessed on 5 April 2014).
3. Ralph Fevre, Amanda Robinson, Duncan Lewis, and Trevor Jones. "The Ill-treatment of Employees with Disabilities in British Workplaces." *Work, Employment and Society* 27 (2013): 288–307. [CrossRef]
4. John Horton, and Faith Tucker. "Disabilities in Academic Workplaces: Experiences of Human and Physical Geographers." *Transactions of the Institute of British Geographers* 39 (2014): 76–89. [CrossRef]
5. Sara Dewson, Ceri Williams, Jane Aston, Emanuela Carta, Rebecca Willison, and Rose Martin. "Organisations' Responses to the Disability Discrimination Act: 2009 Study." 2010. Available online: https://www.gov.uk/government/uploads/system/uploads/attachment_data/file/214456/rrep685.pdf (accessed on 20 March 2015).
6. Deborah Foster, and Victoria Wass. "Disability in the Labour Market: An Exploration of Concepts of the Ideal Worker and Organisational Fit that Disadvantage Employees with Impairments." *Sociology* 47 (2012): 705–21. [CrossRef]
7. Kelly Williams-Whitt. "Impediments to Disability Accommodation." *Relations Industrielles, Industrial Relations* 62 (2007): 405–32. [CrossRef]
8. Claire Simm, Jane Aston, Ceri Williams, Darcy Hill, Anne Bellis, and Nigel Meager. "Organisations' Responses to the Disability Discrimination Act." 2007. Available online: http://webarchive.nationalarchives.gov.uk/20130128102031/http://research.dwp.gov.uk/asd/asd5/rports2007-2008/rrep410.pdf (accessed on 20 March 2015).
9. *R (on the application of Unison (No.2)) v The Lord Chancellor and the Equality and Human Rights Commission (intervening)* [2014] EWHC 4198 (Admin) ("Unison 2").

10. Eleanor Kirk, Morag McDermont, and Nicole Busby. "Employment Tribunal Claims: Debunking the Myths." 2015. Available online: http://www.bris.ac.uk/media-library/sites/policybristol/documents/employment_tribunal_claims.pdf (accessed on 10 December 2015).

11. Helen Anthony, and Charlotte Crilly. "Equality, Human Rights and Access to Civil Law Justice: A Literature Review." 2015. Available online: http://www.equalityhumanrights.com/sites/default/files/publication_pdf/Equality%20human%20rights%20and%20access%20to%20civil%20law%20justice_0.pdf (accessed on 2 December 2015).

12. Emily Rose, Lauren Wood, and Eleanor Kirk. "The Impact of Employment Tribunal Fees: A Perspective from Citizens Advice Advisers in Scotland." 2015. Available online: http://www.cas.org.uk/system/files/publications/The%20Price%20of%20Justice%20final%20with%20cover%20and%20back.pdf (accessed on 3 December 2015).

13. David Mangan. "Employment Tribunal Reforms to Boost the Economy." *Industrial Law Journal* 42 (2013): 409–21. [CrossRef]

14. MOJ (Ministry of Justice). "Tribunal Statistics Tables—April to June 2014." *MOJ*, 2014. Available online: https://www.gov.uk/government/statistics/tribunal-statistics-quarterly-april-to-june-2014 (accessed on 15 November 2015).

15. TUC (Trade Union Congress). "At What Price Justice? The Impact of Employment Tribunal Fees." *TUC*, 2014. Available online: https://www.tuc.org.uk/sites/default/files/TUC_Report_At_what_price_justice.pdf (accessed on 20 March 2015).

16. *R (on the application of Unison) v the Lord Chancellor and the Equality and Human Rights Commission (intervening)* [2014] EWHC 218 (Admin) ("Unison 1").

17. *R (on the application of Unison) v The Lord Chancellor and the Equality and Human Rights Commission (intervening)* [2015] EWCA Civ 935.

18. UK House of Commons Justice Committee. "Court and Tribunal Fees and Charges Inquiry." 2015. Available online: http://www.parliament.uk/business/committees/committees-a-z/commons-select/justice-committee/news-parliament-20151/courts-tribunals-fees-charges-inquiry/ (accessed on 5 January 2016).

19. Joseph Maxwell. "Using Qualitative Methods for Causal Explanation." *Field Methods* 16 (2004): 243–64. [CrossRef]

20. Malcolm Williams. "Interpretivism and Generalisation." *Sociology* 34 (2000): 209–24. [CrossRef]

21. John Fairweather, and Tiffany Rinne. "Clarifying a Basis for Qualitative Generalization Using Approaches That Identify Shared Culture." *Qualitative Research* 12 (2012): 473–85. [CrossRef]

22. Anselm Strauss, and Juliet Corbin. *Basics of Qualitative Research—Grounded Theory Procedures and Techniques.* London: Sage, 1990.

23. Nicola K. Gale, Gemma Heath, Elaine Cameron, Sabina Rashid, and Sabi Redwood. "Using the Framework Method for the Analysis of Qualitative Data in Multi-disciplinary Health Research." *BMC Medical Research Methodology* 13 (2013): 1–8. [CrossRef] [PubMed]

24. Jeasik Cho, and Allen Trent. "Validity in Qualitative Research Revisited." *Qualitative Research* 6 (2006): 319–40. [CrossRef]

25. MOJ (Ministry of Justice). "Review of the Introduction of Employment Tribunal Fees: Terms of Reference." *MOJ*, 2015. Available online: https://www.gov.uk/government/uploads/system/uploads/attachment_data/file/434207/tor-employment-tribunal-fees.pdf (accessed on 2 December 2015).

26. Anna Pollert, and Andy Charlwood. "The Vulnerable Worker in Britain and Problems at Work." *Work, Employment and Society* 23 (2009): 343–62. [CrossRef]

27. Deborah Foster, and Patricia Fosh. "Negotiating 'Difference': Representing Disabled Employees in the British Workplace." *British Journal of Industrial Relations* 48 (2010): 560–82. [CrossRef]

28. Alan Bogg, and Keith D. Ewing. "The Implications of the *RMT* Case." *Industrial Law Journal* 43 (2014): 221–52. [CrossRef]

29. BIS (Department for Business, Innovation and Skills). "Trade Union Membership 2014: Statistical Bulletin." *BIS*, 2015. Available online: https://www.gov.uk/government/uploads/system/uploads/attachment_data/file/431564/Trade_Union_Membership_Statistics_2014.pdf (accessed on 14 December 2015).

30. Andy Charlwood, and Anna Pollert. "Informal Employment Dispute Resolution among Low-Wage Non-Union Workers: Does Managerially Initiated Workplace Voice Enhance Equity and Efficiency?" *British Journal of Industrial Relations* 52 (2014): 359–86. [CrossRef]

31. Rupert Harwood. "'The Dying of the Light': The Impact of the Spending Cuts, and Cuts to Employment Law Protections, on Disability Adjustments in British Local Authorities." *Disability and Society* 29 (2014): 1511–23. [CrossRef]

32. Vincent Cable. "Reforming Employment Relations." Speech to the Engineering Employers' Federation, London, UK, 23 November 2011. Available online: https://www.gov.uk/government/speeches/reforming-employment-relations (accessed on 14 December 2015).

33. MOJ (Ministry of Justice). "Tribunal Statistics Quarterly Tables—April to June 2013." *MOJ*, 2013. Available online: https://www.gov.uk/government/statistics/tribunal-statistics-quarterly-april-to-june-2013 (accessed on 20 March 2015).

34. DWP (Department for Work and Pensions). "Fulfilling Potential—Outcomes and Indicators Framework Progress Report." *DWP*, 2014. Available online: https://www.gov.uk/government/uploads/system/uploads/attachment_data/file/348867/Fulfilling_Potential_Outcomes_and_Indicators_Framework_Progress_Report_2014.pdf (accessed on 14 December 2015).

35. Jill Edwards, and Kathy Boxall. "Adults with Cystic Fibrosis and Barriers to Employment." *Disability and Society* 25 (2010): 441–53. [CrossRef]

36. Keith D. Ewing, and John Hendy. "Unfair Dismissal Law Changes—Unfair? " *Industrial Law Journal* 41 (2012): 115–21. [CrossRef]

37. Jane Holgate, Anna Pollert, Janroj Keles, and Leena Kumarappan. "De-Collectivisation and Employment Problems: The Experiences of Minority Ethnic Workers Seeking Help through Citizens Advice." *Work, Employment and Society* 26 (2012): 772–88. [CrossRef]

38. Nicole Busby, and Morag McDermont. "Workers, Marginalised Voices and the Employment Tribunal System: Some Preliminary Findings." *Industrial Law Journal* 41 (2012): 166–83. [CrossRef]

39. Carrie Harding, Shadi Ghezelayagh, Amy Busby, and Nick Coleman. "Findings from the Survey of Employment Tribunal Applications 2013." 2014. Available online: https://www.gov.uk/government/uploads/system/uploads/attachment_data/file/316704/bis-14-708-survey-of-employment-tribunal-applications-2013.pdf (accessed on 20 November 2015).

40. Law Centres Network. "Law Centres Network—Written Evidence (EQD0135) (to the House of Lords Equality Act 2010 and Disability Committee)." 2015. Available online: http://data.parliament.uk/writtenevidence/committeeevidence.svc/evidencedocument/equality-act-2010-and-disability-committee/equality-act-2010-and-disability/written/20891.pdf (accessed on 20 December 2015).

41. Michelle O'Sullivan, Thomas Turner, Mahon Kennedy, and Joseph Wallace. "Is Individual Employment Law Displacing the Role of Trade Unions? " *Industrial Law Journal* 44 (2015): 222–45. [CrossRef]

42. David Mangan. "No longer. Not Yet. The Promise of Labour Law." *King's Law Journal* 26 (2015): 129–50.

43. MOJ (Ministry of Justice). "Charging Fees in Employment Tribunals and the Employment Appeal Tribunal (Consultation Paper CP22/2011)." 2011. Available online: https://consult.justice.gov.uk/digital-communications/et-fee-charging-regime-cp22-2011/supporting_documents/chargingfeesinetandeat1.pdf (accessed on 20 November 2015).

44. MOJ (Ministry of Justice). "Charging Fees in Employment Tribunals and the Employment Appeal Tribunal: Government Response—Equality Impact Assessment." *MOJ*, 2012. Available online: https://consult.justice.gov.uk/digital-communications/et-fee-charging-regime-cp22–2011/results/et-fees-response-eia.pdf (accessed on 20 March 2015).

45. BIS (Department for Business, Innovation and Skills), and Tribunals Service. "Resolving Workplace Disputes: A Consultation." *BIS*, 2011. Available online: https://www.gov.uk/government/uploads/system/uploads/attachment_data/file/31435/11-511-resolving-workplace-disputes-consultation.pdf (accessed on 20 March 2015).

46. Equality and Human Rights Commission. "Equality and Human Rights Commission—Written Evidence (to the House of Commons Justice Committee)." *House of Commons*, 2015. Available online: http://data.parliament.uk/writtenevidence/committeeevidence.svc/evidencedocument/justice-committee/courts-and-tribunals-fees-and-charges/written/22872.pdf (accessed on 4 January 2016).

47. Mark Bell. "Mental Health at Work and the Duty to Make Reasonable Adjustments." *Industrial Law Journal* 44 (2015): 194–221. [CrossRef]

48. Sarah Leverton. *Monitoring the Disability Discrimination Act 1995 (Phase 2)*. London: Equality Commission for Northern Ireland/Disability Rights Commission, 2002.

49. Bob Hepple. "Back to the Future: Employment Law under the Coalition Government." *Industrial Law Journal* 42 (2013): 203–23. [CrossRef]
50. J. Hurstfield, Nigel Meager, J. Aston, J. Davies, K. Mann, H. Mitchell, Siobhan O'Regan, and A. Sinclair. "Monitoring the Disability Discrimination Act (DDA) 1995." 2004. Available online: http://disability-studies.leeds.ac.uk/files/library/hurstfield-Final-pdf.pdf (accessed on 24 December 2015).
51. Sandra Fredman. "Addressing Disparate Impact: Indirect Discrimination and the Public Sector Equality Duty." *Industrial Law Journal* 43 (2014): 349–63. [CrossRef]
52. Aileen McColgan. "Litigating the Public Sector Equality Duty: The Story So Far." *Oxford Journal of Legal Studies*, 2015, 1–33. [CrossRef]
53. Nicole Busby. "Challenging Employment Tribunal Fees: R (Unison) v Lord Chancellor and Another (No 2)." *The Edinburgh Law Review* 19 (2015): 254–59. [CrossRef]
54. BIS (Department for Business Innovation and Skills). "Findings from the Survey of Employment Tribunal Applications 2013." *BIS*, 2014. Available online: https://www.gov.uk/government/uploads/system/uploads/attachment_data/file/316704/bis-14-708-survey-of-employment-tribunal-applications-2013.pdf (accessed on 20 November 2015).
55. Sarah Fraser Butlin. "The UN Convention on the Rights of Persons with Disabilities: Does the Equality Act 2010 Measure up to UK International Commitments? " *Industrial Law Journal* 40 (2011): 428–38. [CrossRef]
56. Peter Bartlett. "The United Nations Convention on the Rights of Persons with Disabilities and Mental Health Law." *The Modern Law Review* 75 (2012): 752–78. [CrossRef]
57. Paul Harpur. "Embracing the New Disability Rights Paradigm: The Importance of the Convention on the Rights of Persons with Disabilities." *Disability and Society* 27 (2012): 1–14. [CrossRef]
58. Jennifer W. Reiss. "Innovative Governance in a Federal Europe: Implementing the Convention on the Rights of Persons with Disabilities." *European Law Journal* 20 (2014): 107–25. [CrossRef]
59. Anna Lawson, and Mark Priestley. "Potential, Principle and Pragmatism in Concurrent Multinational Monitoring: Disability Rights in the European Union." *International Journal of Human Rights* 17 (2013): 739–57. [CrossRef]
60. Jackie Lane, and Natalie Videbaek Munkholm. "Danish and British Protection from Disability Discrimination at Work—Past, Present and Future." *International Journal of Comparative Labour Law and Industrial Relations* 31 (2015): 91–112.
61. Colin Barnes, and Geof Mercer. *Exploring Disability*. Cambridge: Polity Press, 2010.
62. Committee on the Rights of Persons with Disabilities. "Communication No. 5/2011: Views Adopted by the Committee at its Twelfth Session. CRPD/C/12/D/5/2011." 2011. Available online: http://www.ohchr.org/EN/HRBodies/CRPD/Pages/Jurisprudence.aspx (accessed on 4 November 2015).
63. Committee on the Rights of Persons with Disabilities. "Communication No 21/2014: Views Adopted by the Committee at its Fourteenth Session. CRPD/C/14/D/21/2014." 2014. Available online: http://www.ohchr.org/EN/HRBodies/CRPD/Pages/Jurisprudence.aspx (accessed on 4 November 2015).
64. Gregor Maucec. "Tackling Disability-based Discrimination in International and European Law." *International Journal of Discrimination and the Law* 13 (2013): 34–49. [CrossRef]
65. Maria M. S. Carmona, Olivier De Schutter, and Raquel Rolnik. Letter from the Office of the United Nations High Commissioner for Human Rights to Karen Pierce, UK Ambassador and Permanent Representative to the UN, 20 May 2014.
66. Karen Pierce. Letter from Karen Pierce, UK Ambassador and Permanent Representative to the UN, to the Office of the United Nations High Commissioner for Human Rights, 10 July 2014.
67. The Conservative Party. "The Conservative Party Manifesto 2015." 2015. Available online: https://s3-eu-west-1.amazonaws.com/manifesto2015/ConservativeManifesto2015.pdf (accessed on 20 November 2015).
68. Matt Dathan. "David Cameron Refuses to Rule out Quitting the European Convention on Human Rights." *Independent*, 3 June 2015. Available online: http://www.independent.co.uk/news/uk/politics/david-cameron-refuses-to-rule-out-quitting-the-european-convention-on-human-rights-10294385.html (accessed on 15 January 2016).
69. Robert Mendick. "Human Rights Act Has Helped 28 Terrorists to Stay in UK." *Telegraph*, 31 January 2015. Available online: http://www.telegraph.co.uk/news/uknews/terrorism-in-the-uk/11381944/Human-Rights-Act-has-helped-28-terrorists-to-stay-in-UK.html (accessed on 15 January 2016).

70. Jack Doyle. "Now UN Sparks Fury after Launching Human Rights Investigation into Britain's Disability Benefit Reforms." *Dailymail.co.uk*, 27 August 2014. Available online: http://www.dailymail.co.uk/news/article-2735958/UN-sparks-fury-launching-human-rights-investigation-Britain-s-treatment-disabled.html (accessed on 5 January 2015).
71. Denise Currie, and Paul Teague. "Economic Citizenship and Workplace Conflict in Anglo-American Industrial Relations Systems." *British Journal of Industrial Relations*, 2015. [CrossRef]
72. Bob Hepple. "Enforcing Equality Law: Two Steps Forward and Two Steps Backwards for Reflexive Regulation." *Industrial Law Journal* 40 (2011): 315–35. [CrossRef]
73. Productivity Commission. "Workplace Relations Framework: Productivity Commission Inquiry Report, Volume 1." 2015. Available online: http://www.pc.gov.au/inquiries/completed/workplace-relations/report/workplace-relations-volume1.pdf (accessed on 23 December 2015).
74. DEL (Department for Employment and Learning). "Developing Modern, Efficient, and Effective Employment Tribunals." *DEL*, 2015. Available online: https://www.delni.gov.uk/sites/default/files/consultations/del/employment-tribunals-consultation-june-2015.pdf (accessed on 10 December 2015).
75. Workplace Relations. "Labour Court." 2015. Available online: https://www.workplacerelations.ie/en/WR_Bodies/Labour_Court/ (accessed on 10 December 2015).
76. The Scottish Government. "A Stronger Scotland: The Government's Programme for Scotland 2015–16." 2015. Available online: http://www.gov.scot/Resource/0048/00484439.pdf (accessed on 29 January 2016).
77. *Trial Lawyers Association of British Columbia v British Columbia (Attorney-General)* [2014] SCC 59.
78. Steven Rares. "Is Access to Justice a Right or a Service?" 2015. Available online: http://www.civiljustice.info/cgi/viewcontent.cgi?article=1038&context=access (accessed on 20 December 2015).
79. Esther Addley, Owen Boycott, David Crouch, and Jessica Elgot. "Julian Assange: 'Sweet' Victory Soured by British and Swedish Rejection." 5 February 2016. Available online: http://www.theguardian.com/media/2016/feb/05/julian-assange-sweet-victory-soured-by-british-and-swedish-rejection (accessed on 28 January 2016).
80. Charles Falconer, and Willy Bach. "The Lack of Access to Justice is a National Disgrace." 16 January 2016. Available online: http://www.theguardian.com/commentisfree/2016/jan/16/legal-aid-review-lack-of-access-to-justice (accessed on 28 January 2016).
81. Anonymous (Unison, London). Personal communication, 2016.

laws

MDPI

Opinion

A Word of Caution: Human Rights, Disability, and Implementation of the Post-2015 Sustainable Development Goals

Claire E. Brolan

School of Public Health, University of Queensland, Public Health Building, Herston Road, Herston, Brisbane St Lucia 4006, Australia; c.brolan@uq.edu.au; Tel.: +61-733-655-345

Academic Editor: Anna Arstein-Kerslake
Received: 30 March 2016; Accepted: 6 May 2016; Published: 14 May 2016

Abstract: On 25 September 2015, the United Nations (UN) General Assembly unanimously voted for the post-2015 UN resolution on the post-2015 Sustainable Development Goal (SDG) agenda. This article argues that although the post-2015 SDG agenda is an advance on its precursor the Millennium Development Goals (MDGs)—especially for progressing the human rights of persons with disabilities in development settings, everywhere—it should nonetheless be approached with caution. This article will identify "three steps forward" for persons with disabilities within the broad content of the post-2015 SDGs, while also highlighting four potential "steps back". It concludes persons with disabilities, disability rights advocates and their supporters must remain vigilant as the post-SDG UN resolution is now operationalised and implemented by UN Member States and their many partners. This is particularly so if the content of the Convention on the Rights of Persons with Disabilities is to be effectively integrated into the post-2015 development policy and planning landscape.

Keywords: human rights; disability; sustainable development goals; SDGs; UN resolution; Convention on the Rights of Persons with Disabilities; CRPD

1. Introduction

The United Nations (UN) General Assembly's 25 September 2015 resolution, "Transforming our world: the 2030 Agenda for Sustainable Development", is a "plan of action for people, planet and prosperity" ([1], p. 1, preamble). Consisting of a 35-page, 91-paragraph document, this formative resolution sets out the global community's post-2015 Sustainable Development Goal (SDG) action plan for the next 15 years, until the year 2030. Although it contains much of the "unfinished business" of its precursor blueprint for development, the eight Millennium Development Goals (MDGs), which were introduced to the world in UN Secretary-General Kofi Annan's *Road map towards the implementation of the UN Millennium Declaration* (Road Map report) of September 2001 (Figure 1) [2], the 17 SDGs outlined in the September 2015 resolution undoubtedly advance the MDG agenda (Figure 2). This is primarily because the UN resolution on the post-2015 SDGs shifts the world's development focus from poverty eradication (as emphasised by the MDGs) to poverty eradication *and* sustainable development, while also reinforcing the inclusive nature of the new goals through its central principle—"that no one will be left behind" ([1], p. 1, preamble).

Figure 1. The eight MDGs contained in the UN Secretary-General's Road Map report of September 2001 [2].

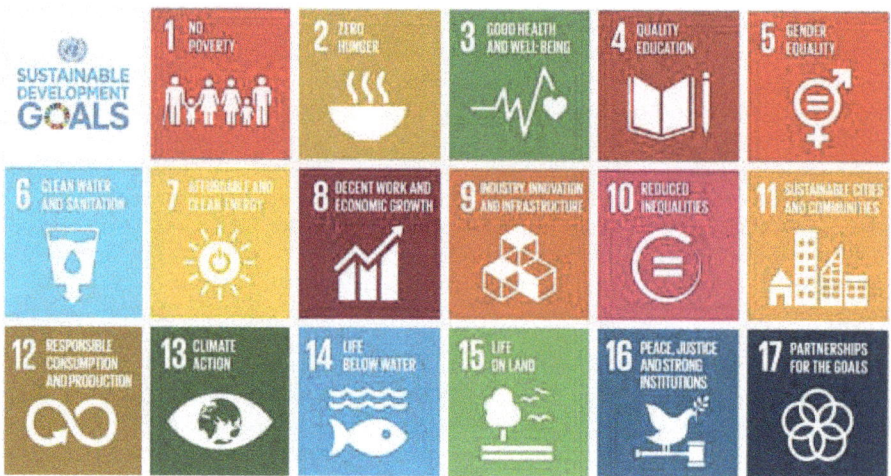

Figure 2. The 17 SDGs outlined in pages 14–27 of the UN resolution on the post-2015 SDG agenda [1].

The question I will seek to address in this article for Laws' Special Issue on *Disability and Human Rights*, however, is whether the 17 SDGs are as "bold and transformative" ([1], p. 1, preamble), if not adequately sufficient, to provide seminal instruction for the *de facto* advance of the human rights of persons with disabilities in the unfolding twenty-first century. My views in response to this question are based on having worked as part of a right to health research collaborative for the last three years, tasked with empirically monitoring and providing advice to the European Commission on health's location in the unfolding post-2015 SDGs [3–5]. These views are further grounded in my recent, parallel experience in both disability research and rights advocacy [6–10].

This article will begin by setting the scene through establishing the relationship of the Convention on the Rights of Persons with Disabilities (CRPD) with sustainable development, followed by examining the formulation of the post-2015 SDG agenda. Once this contextual landscape has been outlined, the three key ways in which the SDG framework is an advance on the MDG agenda for persons with disabilities will be highlighted. I will then proceed with trepidation; detailing four reasons why I fear that the cogency of the SDG moment is not all that it seems for advancing not only human rights generally, but more specifically, the human rights of persons with disabilities. I wil conclude by briefly recommending potential advocacy strategies for ensuring the rights of persons with disabilities in the next 15 years are in the post-2015 SDG spotlight. However, this will not be "a doddle".

2. Background

2.1. The CRPD and Sustainable Development

Since the eight MDGs were introduced to the world in 2001 in the wake of the Millennium Declaration of September 2000 [2,11], the international human rights legal landscape for persons with disabilities has significantly progressed. This is due to the international community's development and adoption of the CRPD [12], which builds upon the social model of disability and "introduces a new disability rights paradigm" [13]. The CRPD, along with its Optional Protocol, was adopted by the UN General Assembly on 13 December 2006 and entered into force on 3 May 2008 [12]. Within its preamble, the CRPD reiterates the "integral" rights-based relationship between persons with disabilities and the achievement of sustainable development; a relationship that must be mainstreamed ([12], preamble g). The CRPD's preamble further highlights how pursuit of the human rights of persons with disabilities will ultimately assist in overcoming poverty and the varied yet interconnected development challenges facing many millions of persons with disabilities, their families and communities ([12], preamble m).

Although it took until the new millennium and some 60 years since the birth of the UN Charter for a UN Convention to be devised to ensure affirmative steps are taken to respect, promote and fulfil the human rights of the "biggest definable disadvantaged group on the planet" ([14], p. 548), one positive burgeoning effect of the CRPD is no less evident—and most welcome—in the international development field. Article 32 of the CRPD (International Cooperation), for example, has been an instructive legal catalyst for high-income countries to devise and advance (and importantly allocate resources toward) disability-inclusive development programs in their foreign affairs and international development portfolios [15]. Therefore, what has traditionally been a neglected area in development policy and planning efforts—disability-inclusive development [16,17]—is now increasingly at the fore and must be lauded.

The growing global focus and promotion of disability-inclusive development, particularly since 2010, is without doubt intimately connected to the CRPD's parallel arrival on the world stage. Indeed, Article 32(1)(a) directs States Parties to ensure, among other measures, "that international cooperation, *including international development programmes,* is inclusive of and accessible to persons with disabilities" [emphasis added] [12]. Although Article 32 sets out *all* nation's extra-territorial obligations to support "the importance of international cooperation and its promotion, in support of national efforts for the realization of the purpose and objectives of the present Convention" [13], the primary onus is on State Parties to take the necessary measures to realise the CRPD's provisions in both *de jure* law and *de facto* reality inside their sovereign borders. Again, Article 32(2) makes this clear: "The provisions of this article are without prejudice to the obligations of each State Party to fulfil its obligations under the present Convention" [12].

It is estimated approximately 80% of the world's more than one billion persons with disabilities reside in a developing country context, frequently in poverty [1,18]. Accordingly, "Disability is a development issue, because of its bidirectional link to poverty: disability may increase the risk of poverty, and poverty may increase the risk of disability" ([19], p. 10). Subsequently, today there is great onus on low- and middle-income countries to step up and work hard to overcome the extraordinary legal, policy, social, structural, environmental, socio-cultural and other entrenched barriers (including those related to the human right to health and health's underlying social determinants) for persons with disabilities [18,19]. In turn, and pursuant to Article 32, high-income nations and their partners must also rise to support countries with lessor resources, technical capacity, and knowledge to implement the Convention's terms. It is of little wonder, therefore, that disability advocates are now asking whether or how the SDGs of September 2015 and Article 32 intersect.

2.2. A Closer Look at the Formulation of the Post-2015 SDG Agenda

Similar to the CRPD, the post-2015 SDG agenda emanates from a UN resolution that enjoys unanimous government support [1]. The September 2015 resolution is the output of a formidable global consultation process involving Member States, the UN, civil society, non-government organisations (NGOs), academic agencies, and a host of other actors and advocates. From the UN Conference on Sustainable Development (Rio+20 Conference) in Brazil in June 2012 to UN Director-General Ban Ki-moon's July 2012 appointment of a High-Level Panel of Eminent Persons on the Post-2015 Development Agenda (High-Level Panel), vigorous dialogue continued over the framing of the MDG's successors. The UN Development Group (UNDG) also took steps to realise the UN's aim to incorporate as many voices into a global post-2015 dialogue, including voices that may otherwise not be heard [20]. An ambitious post-2015 consultative strategy was thus embarked on. This involved the UNDG supporting at least 100 national-level dialogues, convening 11 global thematic consultations (in conjunction with its governmental partners), and creating an interactive web portal to stimulate citizen and stakeholder engagement [20].

The global thematic consultation process occurred between May 2012 and June 2013, and divided post-2015 discussion priorities into 11 thematic branches (Table 1) [21]. While disability was not a thematic topic in and of its own right, persons with disabilities and international disability advocacy agencies, and their supporters, certainly contributed to the dialogue within each thematic branch, as well as ensuing discussion in UN, country, and other forums. Within these forums, there was strong promotion by disability advocates, such as the International Disability Alliance and International Disability and Development Consortium, for the new SDG framework to be expressly underpinned by human rights [22]. The importance given to including the rights of persons with disabilities in the formulation of the post-2015 goals culminated in a High-Level Meeting on Disability and Development on 23 September 2013 at the UN headquarters in New York [23]. The overarching theme of this meeting, "The way forward: a disability inclusive development agenda towards 2015 and beyond", was attended by heads of state and government and resulted in an action-oriented outcome document in support of the aims of the CRPD and the realisation of the MDGs [23,24].

Table 1. Focus of the 11 global thematic consultations.

Thematic Consultation Number	Issue Focus
1	Conflict, Violence and Disaster
2	Water
3	Education
4	Energy
5	Environmental Sustainability
6	Food Security and Nutrition
7	Governance
8	Growth and Employment
9	Health
10	Addressing Inequalities
11	Population Dynamics

When the SDG document was adopted by UN Member States on 25 September 2015, the profile of—and need to prioritise—persons with disabilities within the new post-2015 development agenda was arguably high. This sharply contrasted with the wholesale lack of participation and focus on the development needs of the world's persons with disabilities in the MDG formulation process 14 years earlier [25]. In contrast, the MDGs were devised in a cloistered "top down" manner by a select cluster of high-level UN technocrats (and their associates) in the spring and summer of 2001 [26–29]. Although the content of the eight MDGs was allegedly based on the broadly worded goals of the Millennium Declaration that UN Member States had already collectively agreed to and signed in September 2000 [27,30], the MDGs release in the annexure of UN Secretary-General Kofi Annan's Road Map report a year later raised concern. The new United States government, led by President George W. Bush, especially queried the MDGs' legitimacy in light of the eight goals not being officially developed nor formally endorsed by the Member States at the UN General Assembly [31].

Human rights were a victim of this closed, high-level negotiation and decision-making process [28]. When reflecting on the MDGs' construction, co-chair of the UN inter-agency expert group responsible for the MDGs, Jan Vandemoortele, is unequivocal in terms of human rights' marginalisation from MDG decision-making:

> "[The MDGs] express targets that are feasible at the global level. They should not been seen as a normative statement of what is desirable in an ideal world, which is already embedded in the various human rights treaties that have been ratified by member state to varying degrees. There is no need to repeat or overlap with these instruments . . . " ([32], p. 14).

David Hulme, a second-hand informant who has written extensively on the MDGs formulation, reinforces the eight MDGs and their associated targets were configured in 2001 to avoid "potentially difficult-to-measure goals like human rights and participation" [33]. Hulme explains MDG architects were amenable to placing such concepts in the introductions and conclusions of the key documents "but not in the lists that were to guide plans of action" [33].

Although human rights were not expressly incorporated in the MDG list, they were repeatedly referred to in the UN Secretary-General's Road Map report, to which the MDGs were annexed. Moreover, the Millennium Declaration, which facilitated the release of UN Secretary-General Kofi Annan's Road Map report, was explicitly grounded in a vision for development that advanced human rights [34]. However this vision for development did not affirmatively identify persons with disabilities and constructive advancement of *their* rights [25].

As established, the CRPD was negotiated after the MDG's release. The positive participation of persons with disabilities in the CRPD's development between 2002 and 2006 reflected the international disability movement's long-standing mantra, "Nothing About Us Without Us" [35]. The successful, speedy formulation of this UN Convention clearly demonstrated to the UN and its Member States how the formulation of future human rights treaties, and future formulation of high-level policy and planning frameworks such as the post-2015 development goals, must be done. That is, inclusively; with the people at the heart of the document participating in formal UN deliberations. Of course, while it is unknown how much the voices (*and whose voices*) elicited through the vast post-2015 consultation process actually influenced the final SDG text in September 2015, the effort and resource invested in attempting to engage voices from the global community in the SDG's formulation is progress on the nature of the MDG's birth.

3. The Post-2015 SDGs Are an Advance on the MDG Agenda for Persons with Disabilities

Following the secretive manner in which the MDGs were born, the MDG framework became interpreted and applied by the UN, its Member States and development partners as a development agenda applicable to "the Other" residing in poor countries [36]. While the enormous positive, life-changing benefits that have flowed for millions of highly marginalised people and disadvantaged communities as a result of the eight MDGs should not be decried [37], there were two obvious deficits with the MDG framework that the post-2015 SDG agenda seeks to remedy (among others). These two factors are connected to, and pertinent for, advancing the human rights of persons with disabilities around the world. Firstly, the SDGs are a universal agenda and apply to everyone, everywhere; and secondly, the SDGs expressly include persons with disabilities.

3.1. The SDGs Are a Universal Agenda

In light of the basic principle of the post-2015 SDGs "that no one will be left behind", the SDGs contain a "new universal Agenda": they are applicable to all, everywhere, in low-, middle- and high-income countries alike ([1], p. 1, preamble). Paragraphs 4 and 5 of the UN Resolution of September 2015 are most eloquent in establishing the SDG's universal character:

"As we embark on this great collective journey, we pledge that no one will be left behind. Recognising that the dignity of the human person is fundamental, we wish to see the Goals and targets met for all nations and peoples and for all segments of society. And we will endeavour to reach the furthest behind first" ([1], para. 4).

"This is an Agenda of unprecedented scope and significance. It is accepted by all countries and is applicable to all, taking into account different national realities, capacities and levels of development and respecting national policies and priorities. These are universal goals and targets which involve the entire world, developed and developing countries alike. They are integrated and indivisible and balance the three dimensions of sustainable development" ([1], para. 5).

Iteration within the resolution that its contents are applicable to all, everywhere, ensures the SDGs clearly depart from the MDGs: the SDGs are to be applied to all rather than occidentally applied to "the other" in "those" lower income nations. While the world must not divert its attention from the plight of persons living in utterly desperate circumstances in low-income nations and fragile and conflict-affected states in pursuing the post-2015 SDG agenda [38,39], today the bulk of people living in poverty reside in middle-income countries [40]. Furthermore, in ensuring "that no one will be left behind" ([1], p. 1, preamble), the SDGs recognise the importance of redressing inequities experienced by vulnerable and marginalised groups and communities (including persons with disabilities) in high-income nations. Even though such persons do reside in high-income countries, their experience of relative poverty, disenfranchisement and disadvantage remains unjust, and their governments need to be held accountable and accordingly improve domestic policy and law in line with their SDG commitments [41].

3.2. The SDGs Explicitly Embrace a Human Rights Agenda

The UN General Assembly's September 2015 resolution reiterates the association between human rights and the post-2015 SDG agenda:

"[The 17 SDGs and 169 targets are a] ... new universal Agenda. They seek to build on the MDGs and complete what they did not achieve. *They seek to realise the human rights of all ...* " ([emphasis added] ([1], p. 1, preamble)).

The Declaration envisages a world "of universal respect for human rights and human dignity, the rule of law, justice, equality and non-discrimination" ([1], para. 8), noting the new SDG agenda is:

"*Guided by the purposes and principles of the Charter of the UN, including full respect for international law. It is grounded in the Universal Declaration of Human Rights, international human rights treaties,* the Millennium Declaration and the 2005 World Summit Outcome. *It is informed by other instruments such as the Declaration of the Right to Development*" ([emphasis added] ([1], para. 10)).

Within paragraph 19, the Declaration again reinforces human rights' centrality to the SDG's achievement, which expressly includes the "human rights and fundamental freedoms" of persons with disabilities:

"We reaffirm the importance of the Universal Declaration of Human Rights, as well as other international instruments relating to human rights and international law. *We emphasize the responsibilities of all States, in conformity with the Charter of the UNs, to respect, protect and promote human rights and fundamental freedoms for all, without distinction of any kind as to* race, colour, sex, language, religion, political or other opinion, national or social origin, property, birth, *disability* or other status" ([emphasis added] ([1], para. 19)).

Through the content of the resolution's preamble, and paragraphs 8, 10, 19 and 20, the following observations about human rights' intersection in the post-2015 SDG agenda can be made. First, not only are human rights prominent in the SDG agenda, they are integral to its realisation: the post-2015 agenda *is* a human rights agenda explicitly grounded in international law, and more specifically, the laws espoused in international human rights treaties. According to the resolution, sustainable development cannot and will not occur if human rights for all as established in international law, and especially the human rights of women and girls ("half of humanity") are not respected, protected and promoted ([1], para. 20). Therefore, human rights permeate, and are fundamental to, the post-2015 outcome document; international human rights law underpins the post-2015 policy agreed to by UN Member States.

It is also important to illuminate that unlike the Millennium Declaration of 2000, the UN resolution on the post-2015 SDG agenda *contains* the 17 SDGs. Inclusion of the goals, associated targets and means of implementation within the SDG text juxtapose the eight MDGs release a year after the Millennium Declaration in the annexure of a UN Secretary-General's report. Hence there can be no quibble among UN Member States as to the authority of the 17 SDGs, nor the human rights agenda that underpins them. Together, the latter is visible in the one UN document that the UN General Assembly cumulatively voted on after several years of post-2015 discussion and negotiation.

The UN resolution on the post-2015 SDG agenda also incrementally builds on the CRPD's reconciliation of the rights contained within the International Covenant on Political and Civil Rights and the International Covenant on Economic, Social and Cultural Rights of 1966 ([35], p. 10). The UN resolution of September 2015 repeatedly uses the phrase "integrated and indivisible" to describe *both* the interlinkage of all 17 SDGs and 169 associated targets, *and* the 17 SDG's subsequent interconnection with the remaining content of the UN resolution on the post-2015 agenda ([1], p. 1, preamble 5, 18, 55, 71). For example, the UN General Assembly states: "*We* [the UN General Assembly] *reiterate that this Agenda and SDGs and targets, including the means of implementation, are universal, indivisible and interlinked*" [emphasis added] ([1], para. 71). Use of the words "universal" and "indivisible" echo the Vienna Declaration and Programme of Action of 1993's historic affirmation "all human rights are universal, indivisible and interdependent and interrelated" ([42], para. 5), which the CRPD (the first international convention to be drafted following the Vienna Declaration of 1993) embraced ([35], p. 10).

Use of these terms by the UN General Assembly in September 2015 is not accidental: it is a nod to the Vienna Declaration of 1993 and the holistic nature of human rights (as interlinked and indivisible). Yet, and perhaps most significantly, paragraph 71 implicitly attaches human rights to the SDG metrics framework ([1], pp. 14–27). This significantly differs to the MDG list, wherein the UN technocratic decision-makers purposively sidelined human rights from the Millennium Declaration's plan of action: the eight MDGs released one year *after* the Millennium Declaration. Now, the post-2015 metrics framework is embedded in, and an expression of, political, civil, economic, social and cultural rights and their realisation. In other words, the 17 SDGs have metamorphosed into the new human rights and development post-2015 road map, which is not annexed to a UN Secretary-General report, but incorporated in *the* UN resolution adopted by the UN General Assembly in September 2015.

3.3. The SDGs Expressly Include Persons with Disabilities

Not only are persons with disabilities *implicitly* included in the SDGs through its universal agenda, they are *explicitly* identified:

"People who are vulnerable must be empowered. Those whose needs are reflected in the Agenda include all children, youth, *persons with disabilities (of whom more than 80 per cent live in poverty)*, people living with HIV/AIDS, older persons, indigenous peoples, refugees and internally displaced persons and migrants" ([emphasis added] ([1], para. 23)).

It follows that persons with disabilities are expressly referred to in four locations in the 17 goals and their 169 associated targets and means of implementation. Persons with disabilities are identified with respect to the achievement of three SDGs: Goal 4 (Quality education), Goal 8 (Decent work and economic growth) and Goal 11 (Sustainable cities and communities) (Table 2). In light of persons with disabilities omission from the eight MDGs and their associated targets annexed to the UN-Secretary General's Road Map report in 2001 [2], the specific inclusion of persons with disabilities in both the terms of the UN Declaration *and* the content of its 17 SDGs could be interpreted as a major win. Certainly, and as Mercer and MacDonald point out, it is "astonishing" that the MDGs excluded persons with disabilities, especially when many of the MDGs (if not all) "cannot be met without addressing disability issues in the developing world" ([14], p. 549).

Table 2. Inclusion of Persons with disabilities in the SDG metrics framework ([1], pp. 14–27).

SDG	Metric	Target Aim
Goal 4: Quality Education	Goal 4, Target 5	4.5 By 2030, eliminate gender disparities in education and ensure equal access to all levels of education and vocational training for the vulnerable, including persons with disabilities, indigenous peoples and children in vulnerable situations
Goal 8: Decent work and economic growth	Goal 8, Target 5	8.5 By 2030, achieve full and productive employment and decent work for all women and men, including for young people and persons with disabilities, and equal pay for work of equal value
Goal 11: Sustainable Cities and Communities	Goal 11, Target 2	11.2 By 2030, provide access to safe, affordable, accessible and sustainable transport systems for all, improving road safety, notably by expanding public transport, with special attention to the needs of those in vulnerable situations, women, children, persons with disabilities and older persons
Goal 11: Sustainable Cities and Communities	Goal 11, Target 7	By 2030, provide universal access to safe, inclusive and accessible, green and public spaces, in particular for women and children, older persons and persons with disabilities

4. Three Steps Forward, But Four Steps Back

The UN resolution on the post-2015 SDG agenda is a remarkable achievement—its contents definitively highlight and advance the rights of persons with disabilities in development contexts worldwide. This is especially so when compared to the vacuous hole in the MDG list regarding human rights *and* persons with disabilities, as well as in the MDG's antecedent the Millennium Declaration, which excluded persons with disabilities. Nonetheless, this article identifies four reasons why the post-2015 SDG agenda, as a human rights agenda *and* a human rights agenda for persons with disabilities, is to be cautiously approached. These four reasons include: the lack of binding status in international law for the UN resolution on the post-2015 SDG agenda; its weak governance and accountability mechanisms; the SDG metrics framework's (that is, the 17 SDGs and their 169 associated targets and means of implementation) sidelining of human rights; and finally, the SDG metrics framework's insufficient identification and inclusion of persons with disabilities.

4.1. The UN Resolution on the Post-2015 SDGs Is a High-Level Policy Document Only, It Is Not Binding Instrument of International Law

This article has established that the UN resolution on the post-2015 SDGs references, and is grounded in, the body that is international human rights law ([1], p. 1, preamble, para. 3, 8, 10, 19–20, 29, 35). And, this body of international human rights law (in its various iterations) has been widely adopted by the international community of UN Member States. However, the UN resolution on the post-2015 SDG agenda is not a UN treaty document or binding international human rights law instrument *per se*, which means it is not governed by international law. Rather, it is a piece of soft law: it is an expression of agreed-upon international goals and aspirations, despite espousing some norms of customary international law.

The lack of "hard law" status for the UN resolution on the post-2015 SDG agenda is problematic for several reasons. Even though there was widespread government endorsement (and vote) for the SDGs in September 2015, countries are not legally obliged to implement or realise within their domestic jurisdictions the terms of this human rights document, *or* the content *or* human rights framing of its 17 SDGs. As a piece of soft law, the provisions of the Vienna Convention on the Law of Treaties 1969 do not apply [43]. This includes the *Pacta Sunt Servanda* rule encapsulated in Article 26: Every treaty in force is binding upon the parties to it and must be performed by them in good faith ([43], Article 26).

Alternatively, others might argue that if the UN resolution on the post-2015 SDG agenda cannot be interpreted as a matter of international statutory law, then it should be construed as customary international law per Article 38(1)(b) of the Statute of International Court of Justice (ICJ) [44]. Supporters of this argument might point to the UN resolution on the post-2015 SDG agenda's international human rights law underpinning, and its ensuing containment of a cluster of customary international law rules. Yet successfully characterising the UN resolution on the post-2015 SDGs as a piece of customary international law pursuant Article 38(1)(b) is unlikely. This is because the ICJ is cautious in ascertaining the existence of customary international laws [45], and in its reticence has settled on two components necessary for the constitution of custom per Article 381(1)(b); the state practice (or the material fact) and the *opinio juris*; a subjective or psychological element that is related to the consent (or belief) of the State that such behaviour is "law" ([46], para. 10; [47], p. 58). The argument that either of these two components exists for this UN resolution to constitute customary international law is wanting.

Firstly, the state practice component is weak. Turning to *the historical*, it was UN Member State practice to treat the MDGs, the SDG's predecessor, as a non-binding policy commitment only. Also, the *opinio juris* component is equally feeble. This is because analysis of the high-level *contemporary discourse* on the formulation of the SDGs reveals it was never the collective intention of the UN General Assembly's Member States to create a piece of binding international law (especially *human rights* law) when engaging in the formulation of the text of the UN resolution on the post-2015 SDGs or in the formulation of its list of 17 goals therein [48]. Had this been otherwise, decision-making consensus between UN Member States would have been extremely difficult to reach at the UN in New York in September 2015 [48].

4.2. As a High-Level Policy Document without Legal Standing, Its Accountability Mechanisms Are Flimsy

The next reason the UN resolution on the post-2015 SDG's lack of standing in international law is problematic for the SDG's *de facto* achievement is because without such legal standing, the resolution cannot establish an authoritative international implementing body or accountability mechanism akin, for example, to the overseeing committees of the UN treaty documents. While the power and influence of these overseeing bodies has been criticised, at least there is an overarching implementation mechanism for the monitoring of UN treaty implementation, grounded in international law (however imperfect), in existence. The fact this is not the case for the ambitious post-2015 SDG action plan—a "plan of action for people, planet and prosperity" ([1], p. 1, preamble)—is a major deficit.[1]

Following on, "SDG 17: Strengthen the means of implementation and revitalize the Global Partnership for Sustainable Development" and its 19 targets ([1], pp. 26–27) appear to be an expanded yet recycled version of "MDG 8: Global Partnership for Development" and its six targets (Tables 3 and 4) [50]. As has been well-documented, government support for MDG 8 waned as the MDG agenda progressed in the mid-to-late 2000s, particularly in the wake of the Global Financial Crisis of 2008 [37,50], and

---

[1] I note that subsequent to writing this article, and such is the dynamic nature of the entire SDG process, a High-Level Political Forum on Sustainable Development (the "HLPF") has been advertised by the UN as the planned "central platform for the follow-up and review of the 2030 Agenda for Sustainable Development and the SDGs" [49]. As to whether the HLPF will be duly respected by the UN Member States (and their development partners), and duly funded, so as to become an effective overarching accountability mechanism remains to be seen.

government's viewed MDG 8 as a "weak goal" [51]. Compounding matters, MDG 8's targets and indicators were reported as being "indifferent to human rights principles", and perversely creating "dynamics and incentives for policy-making that were ultimately detrimental to the implementation of norms on international cooperation for the achievement of human rights" ([52], p. 276; [53]). Consequently, Member States *treatment* of MDG 8 combined with MDG 8's distilled content (*i.e.*, its emphasis on sweeping general statements as opposed to quantitative, time bound benchmarks: [53]), is a worrying precedent that the content of SDG 17 appears not to have adequately responded to.

Table 3. SDG 17: Strengthen the means of implementation and revitalize the Global Partnership for Sustainable Development.

Finance	SDG-Target Detail
17.1	Strengthen domestic resource mobilization, including through international support to developing countries, to improve domestic capacity for tax and other revenue collection
17.2	Developed countries to implement fully their official development assistance commitments, including the commitment by many developed countries to achieve the target of 0.7 per cent of gross national income for official development assistance (ODA/GNI) to developing countries and 0.15 to 0.20 per cent of ODA/GNI to least developed countries; ODA providers are encouraged to consider setting a target to provide at least 0.20 per cent of ODA/GNI to least developed countries
17.3	Mobilize additional financial resources for developing countries from multiple sources
17.4	Assist developing countries in attaining long-term debt sustainability through coordinated policies aimed at fostering debt financing, debt relief and debt restructuring, as appropriate, and address the external debt of highly indebted poor countries to reduce debt distress
17.5	Adopt and implement investment promotion regimes for least developed countries
Technology	
17.6	Enhance North-South, South-South and triangular regional and international cooperation on and access to science, technology and innovation and enhance knowledge sharing on mutually agreed terms, including through improved coordination among existing mechanisms, in particular at the United Nations level, and through a global technology facilitation mechanism
17.7	Promote the development, transfer, dissemination and diffusion of environmentally sound technologies to developing countries on favourable terms, including on concessional and preferential terms, as mutually agreed.
17.8	17.8 Fully operationalize the technology bank and science, technology and innovation capacity-building mechanism for least developed countries by 2017 and enhance the use of enabling technology, in particular information and communications technology
Capacity-Building	
17.9	Enhance international support for implementing effective and targeted capacity-building in developing countries to support national plans to implement all the Sustainable Development Goals, including through North-South, South-South and triangular cooperation
Trade	
17.10	Promote a universal, rules-based, open, non-discriminatory and equitable multilateral trading system under the World Trade Organization, including through the conclusion of negotiations under its Doha Development Agenda
17.11	Significantly increase the exports of developing countries, in particular with a view to doubling the least developed countries' share of global exports by 2020
17.12	Realize timely implementation of duty-free and quota-free market access on a lasting basis for all least developed countries, consistent with World Trade Organization decisions, including by ensuring that preferential rules of origin applicable to imports from least developed countries are transparent and simple, and contribute to facilitating market access
Systemic Issues	*Policy and institutional coherence*
17.13	Enhance global macroeconomic stability, including through policy coordination and policy coherence
17.14	Enhance policy coherence for sustainable development
17.15	Respect each country's policy space and leadership to establish and implement policies for poverty eradication and sustainable development
	Multi-stakeholder partnerships
17.16	Enhance the Global Partnership for Sustainable Development, complemented by multi-stakeholder partnerships that mobilize and share knowledge, expertise, technology and financial resources, to support the achievement of the Sustainable Development Goals in all countries, in particular developing countries
17.17	Encourage and promote effective public, public-private and civil society partnerships, building on the experience and resourcing strategies of partnerships
	Data, monitoring and accountability
17.18	By 2020, enhance capacity-building support to developing countries, including for least developed countries and small island developing States, to increase significantly the availability of high-quality, timely and reliable data disaggregated by income, gender, age, race, ethnicity, migratory status, disability, geographic location and other characteristics relevant in national contexts
17.19	By 2030, build on existing initiatives to develop measurements of progress on sustainable development that complement gross domestic product, and support statistical capacity-building in developing countries

Table 4. MDG 8: Develop a global partnership for development.

8.A	Develop further an open, rule-based, predictable, non-discriminatory trading and financial system Includes a commitment to good governance, development and poverty reduction—both nationally and internationally
8.B	Address the special needs of the least developed countries Includes tariff and quota free access for the least developed countries' exports; enhanced programme of debt relief for heavily indebted poor countries (HIPC) and cancellation of official bilateral debt; and more generous ODA for countries committed to poverty reduction
8.C	Address the special needs of landlocked developing countries and small island developing States (through the Programme of Action for the Sustainable Development of Small Island Developing States and the outcome of the twenty-second special session of the General Assembly)
8.D	Deal comprehensively with the debt problems of developing countries through national and international measures in order to make debt sustainable in the long term
8.E	In cooperation with pharmaceutical companies, provide access to affordable essential drugs in developing countries
8.F	In cooperation with the private sector, make available the benefits of new technologies, especially information and communications

In fact, whilst continuing to apply this dose of political realism, the likely obsequious treatment by UN Member States toward SDG 17 is only reinforced by way of the noncommittal (if not evasive) configuration of Target 17.15. This target advises UN Member States to (rather weakly) *"Respect each country's policy space* and leadership to establish and implement policies for poverty eradication and sustainable development" [emphasis added] ([1], p. 27). Thus, the governance and accountability mechanisms for the SDG's implementation are not only appearing increasingly weak—they are crumbling. Indeed, it is arguable the UN General Assembly's aspirational aim for MDG's 8 "resuscitated" Global Partnership for Development is undermined from the outset ([1], para. 60).

4.3. What Matters Is What Governments Will Prioritise for SDG Implementation: The 17 Goals, Their Targets and Means of Implementation, and Inter-Linked Country Indicators

What might a non-binding high-level policy document with questionable governance mechanisms practically offer persons with disabilities so as to substantively progress *their* human rights and sustainable development needs in the post-2015 context? In response, disability advocates might (rightly) cite the UN resolution on the post-2015 SDG agenda's gains over the MDG agenda. That is, the post-2015 SDG agenda embodies a (i) universal (ii) human rights agenda (grounded in international human rights law) that (iii) *expressly* includes persons with disabilities. Certainly on paper these gains are monumental. However, this "bold and transformative" ([1], p. 1, preamble) post-2015 vision for development might be a mirage not only for persons with disabilities, but for meeting the human rights and development needs of other potentially vulnerable groups identified in the post-2015 UN document (*i.e.*, children, youth, people living with HIV/AIDS, older persons, indigenous persons, refugees and internally displaced persons and migrants ([1], para. 23). Such cause for concern is again grounded in *the historical*, or on UN Member State's behaviour in interpreting their MDG commitments.

The MDG list of September 2001 did not explicitly contain a human rights agenda. Thus as the new millennium unfolded, a handful of scholars argued that a far greater overlap between human rights and development was needed [52–54]. As mentioned however, the multilateral interagency technocrats who constructed the MDGs in 2001 had no intention of expressly intersecting human rights law with the MDG action plan. Nor did governments, in turn, collectively interpret the eight MDGs through a human rights lens. If anything, the release of the MDG's by way of annexure to the UN Secretary General's Road Map report in 2001 ensured this schism existed between the eight MDGs and human rights located in the MDG's formative document, the Millennium Declaration. Unsurprisingly, in terms of MDG implementation, government at all levels (national, regional, international) focused on achieving the MDG metrics framework, or the eight goals and their associated targets and indicators, in a somewhat vertical or reductionist fashion. And, as the MDG decision-makers had ensured, there was a purposive human rights dearth in this framework.

If over ten years of MDG implementation is the litmus test, then it is unlikely the SDGs will be implemented by UN Member States and their partners with human rights foregrounding their SDG investment efforts. This is in spite of the fact the UN resolution on the post-2015 SDG agenda's preamble, the content of its declaration, *as well as its 17 SDGs* are clearly grounded in international human rights law. Conversely, following MDG experience, it is likely government focus on the SDGs will narrow to solely fixate on implementation of the SDG metrics framework; on achieving the 17 goals, their associated targets and means of implementation, and country-specific indicators. This aligns with the potent adage in international development circles—"what gets measured gets done".

If the SDG metrics will be the UN Member State's (and their partners) main focus, then this is concerning for human rights and disability rights advocates alike. This is because the treatment of human rights within this one UN document is not consistent. For instance on the one hand, human rights principles and international human rights law are privileged within the text of the preamble and larger declaration. Yet, on the other hand, the SDG metrics (found within the same document [1], pp. 14–27) scarcely mention human rights. In fact, "human rights" are referred to only once in the SDG metrics framework, while none of the 17 headline goals explicitly refer to "human rights".

Indeed, close examination of the 17 SDG's 169 targets and means of implementation serves to only reinforce human rights' marginal presence in the SDG metrics. Human rights' shortened version—"rights"—is explicitly found in six locations in the SDG metrics framework: in four targets and two means of implementation (Table 5). This ensures "rights" are expressed in only five of the 17 goals, or less than a third of the SDGs. Further, where "rights" are referred to as "human rights" in the one standalone—but inadequate—target, Target 4.7 (see Table 5), this phrase is inserted to affirm that *the learning* of human rights in educational settings is to be *promoted* in educational settings. Of course, the learning of human rights (and greater generation of human rights awareness) is important, but this insertion of human rights within the education goal does not go far enough. Instead, if the SDGs truly embodied a human rights agenda, then SDG 4 and its targets should be explicitly promoting the attainment of education *as a matter of human rights* for everyone, or express achievement of the human right to education as underscoring the post-2015 education goal [55].

Disparate meaning can also be attached to the framing of "rights" in the SDG metrics. For example, in Target 1.4 and Means of Implementation 5.a, rights are identified as *"equal rights to economic resources"* (*i.e.*, economic rights). On the other hand, Target 8.8 refers to rights in the context of *the protection of* "labour rights" (*i.e.*, employment rights). Whereas in Means of Implementation 3.b, rights are now being used to affirm country rights (*i.e.*, "the right of developing countries"). In each instance, the use of "rights" language lacks consistency, and is hardly contentious. Conversely, the lack of rights language to frame numerous targets, embedded in human rights, is particularly instructive. For example, the content of "Target 10.2: By 2030, empower and promote the social, economic and political inclusion of all, irrespective of age, sex, disability, race, ethnicity, origin, religion or economic or other status" and "Target 10.3: Ensure equal opportunity and reduce inequalities of outcome, including by eliminating discriminatory laws, policies and practices and promoting appropriate legislation, policies and action in this regard", are not presented as a matter of fundamental human rights *already entrenched* in international human rights law.

Table 5. Rights in the post-2015 SDG framework.

Post-2015 Goal	Target	Means of Implementation
Goal 1: End poverty in all its forms everywhere	1.4: By 2030, ensure that all men and women, in particular the poor and the vulnerable, have *equal rights* to economic resources, as well as access to basic services, ownership and control over land and other forms of property, inheritance, natural resources, appropriate new technology and financial services, including microfinance.	
Goal 3: Ensure healthy lives and promote well-being for all at all ages		3.b Support the research and development of vaccines and medicines for the communicable and non-communicable diseases that primarily affect developing countries, provide access to affordable essential medicines and vaccines, in accordance with the Doha Declaration on the TRIPS Agreement and Public Health, which affirms *the right of developing countries* to use to the full the provisions in the *Agreement on Trade-Related Aspects of Intellectual Property Rights* regarding flexibilities to protect public health, and, in particular, provide access to medicines.
Goal 4: Ensure inclusive and equitable quality education and promote lifelong learning opportunities for all	4.7: By 2030, ensure that all learners acquire the knowledge and skills needed to promote sustainable development and sustainable lifestyles, *human rights*, gender equality, promotion of a culture of peace and non-violence, global citizenship and appreciation of cultural diversity and of culture's contribution to sustainable development.	
Goal 5: Achieve gender equality and empower all women and girls	5.6: *Ensure universal access to sexual and reproductive health and reproductive rights* as agreed in accordance with the Programme of Action of the International Conference on Population and Development and the Beijing Platform for Action and the outcome documents of their review conferences.	5.a: Undertake reforms to give women *equal rights to economic resources*, as well as access to ownership and control over land and other forms of property, financial services, inheritance and natural resources, in accordance with national laws.
Goal 8: Promote sustained, inclusive and sustainable economic growth, full and productive employment and decent work for all	8.8: *Protect labour rights* and promote safe and secure working environments for all workers, including migrant workers in particular women migrants, and those in precarious employment.	

4.4. The SDG Metrics Framework Does Not Sufficiently Identify and Include Persons with Disabilities

If the UN resolution on the post-2015 SDG agenda amounts to a non-binding policy document with questionable governance mechanisms that do not adequately reference "human rights" (or even, "rights") in the SDG metrics framework (which will become, in light of MDG experience, the implementation action plan for "people, planet and prosperity" for the next 15 years), then concern the human rights of persons with disabilities will likely be sidelined from SDG implementation is well-founded. This concern is furthered by the SDG metrics' insufficient identification and inclusion of persons with disabilities (along with other vulnerable population's alluded to in paragraph 23 of the UN resolution on the post-2015 SDG agenda). While persons with disabilities are identified in the achievement of three post-2015 goals (see Table 2), if the rights of persons with disabilities are to be mainstreamed in development per the CRPD's preamble then persons with disabilities must be identified and named in the achievement of each and every SDG—not only three.

To summarise, if persons with disabilities are not affirmatively named in SDG metrics then, as with human rights omission from such metrics, it is unlikely governments will pro-actively identify and adequately include persons with disabilities in implementing their SDG targets and plans of action. Subsequently there is a real risk persons with disabilities will fall between the SDG cracks. Certainly, if MDG experience is anything to go by [56,57], if persons with disabilities are not named in the metrics of all 17 SDGs, it is highly unlikely affirmative action will be taken by UN Member States to specifically redress the development inequities, abuses and complex human rights breaches persons with disabilities unconscionably, and all too-often, silently suffer in low-, middle-, and high-income nations around the world.

5. Conclusions

Persons with disabilities and their advocates should not be deceived by the post-2015 SDG's appearance as a major accomplishment for advancing both human rights and the human rights of persons with disabilities, everywhere, in global development policy and planning efforts. Although the SDGs appear to be an advance for human rights and persons with disabilities, especially in contrast to parallel omission of both human rights and persons with disabilities from the MDG agenda, this "double coup" might transpire to be little more than subterfuge. This is because, as this article contends, a worrying disjunct exists between human rights' treatment in the one post-2015 SDG text agreed upon by the UN General Assembly. It follows the UN General Assembly's emphasis on human rights and the prioritisation of the development needs and issues of persons with disabilities in the preamble and content of the declaration of the UN resolution on the post-2015 SDG agenda is in keeping with the CRPD and enormously promising. Yet conversely, the marginalisation of human rights as well as persons with disabilities in the SDG metrics framework found within that same—unenforceable—UN policy document, creates intense unease. Based on over ten years of MDG experience this unease is well-founded: it is highly unlikely UN Member States will seek to extend their implementation of the UN resolution on the post-2015 SDG agenda beyond the parameters of its SDG metrics framework—from which human rights and persons with disabilities are sidelined.

Somewhat paradoxically, the UN resolution on the post-2015 SDG agenda reveals that as at September 2015, the UN General Assembly has not agreed on the location of, or overlap between, human rights and development in the post-MDG world. Thus it can be reasonably anticipated MDG antagonism and discord between rights and development will continue in UN Member State's implementation of the SDG program. Therefore, for persons with disabilities in particular, the UN resolution on the post-2015 SDG agenda might not be "the bold and transformative" development plan that it initially appears on paper. Rather, this article identifies a real risk exists that persons with disabilities, and other vulnerable populations, will be left behind in global post-2015 SDG planning and implementation efforts. Arguably, the post-2015 SDG action agenda might be inherently flawed.

Persons with disabilities and disability rights advocates must remain vigilant as the post-2015 SDG agenda moves into 2016 and beyond. Including, or better still mainstreaming, persons with disabilities in country-specific SDG targets and indicators is an excellent starting point. Ensuring that those same targets and indicators are integrated into *all* government SDG-related policy and planning efforts is the next step. Generating in-country, community awareness as to UN Member State's responsibilities under both the CRPD and the UN resolution on the post-2015 SDG agenda in progressing disability-inclusive development, and holding UN Member State's accountable, will be crucial. Disability advocates must also not forget to include vulnerable non-nationals with disabilities in post-2015 advocacy efforts, such as those individuals with disabilities fleeing persecution or caught in complex, irregular migration contexts. Tracing UN Member State's incorporation of persons with disabilities in their post-2015 SDG development policy and planning efforts outside State borders is of equal import, especially in relation to progressing Article 32 CRPD achievement.

Clearly, persons with disabilities and their advocates have much to monitor in the unfolding post-2015 SDG landscape. If such persons and advocates are dissatisfied that UN Member States (and their partner's) burgeoning implementation of the post-2015 SDGs lacks adequate focus on persons with disabilities, then further action must be taken. If this is the case (and I think it likely), then it is recommended that persons with disabilities, disability advocates and their supporters together press individual countries, SDG regional monitoring bodies, the recently devised High-Level Political Forum on Sustainable Development [49], as well as the UN General Assembly for a new goal and/or cluster of new disability-inclusive targets to be inserted into the SDG list. This new goal and/or cluster of targets (or indicators) must be explicitly linked to Article 32 of the CRPD, as well as the CRPD's broader content. It is also advisable that advocacy on this front begins *now* and not later. It is instructive that there is precedent for such action: sexual and reproductive health and rights advocates were successful in expanding MDG 5: Improve Maternal Health to include Target 5B (*Achieve, by 2015, universal access to reproductive health*) some years after the MDGs were devised [58], while Afghanistan and other nations introduced a country-relevant MDG 9 [59].

In addition to pressing for international, regional, and national accountability and monitoring mechanisms for the specific implementation of the SDG agenda for persons with disabilities, I further recommend that advocates call for a fourth and critical level of SDG monitoring [60]. Here, I recommend persons with disabilities and their advocates establish a specialist international disabilities and SDG commission (or peak body of similar nature), which could work with communities, countries, as well as other regional and international SDG monitoring agencies, to streamline and link Member States' SDG metrics reporting to their international reporting obligations under the CRPD [60]. In this way, the accountability concerns relating to the soft law nature of the post-2015 SDG outcome document might have greater chance of being remedied. This in turn leads to my final point: disability advocates must also press that implementation of the SDGs, and the parallel progression of the rights of persons with disabilities around the globe, is not "all about the metrics", or the numbers and the quantitative. Indeed, reducing disability-inclusive development to "the numbers" places the people at the heart of such development efforts—*the person* with disabilities—secondary to an all-consuming focus by government on quantitative measurement. This secondary positioning is arguably an insidious and repackaged form of the biomedical model approach toward disability creeping into the *human* development policy and planning efforts of the CRPD States Parties. This is not only morally unacceptable; it is unlawful pursuant the terms of the CRPD. Therefore, within efforts to measure SDG achievement for persons with disabilities, the qualitative must also be captured, or the voices and the experiences of SDG development on persons with disabilities and their supporters.

Acknowledgments: The funding for Go4Health, a research project of which this analysis was part, was provided by the European Union's Seventh Framework Programme (grant HEALTH-F1-2012-305240) and by the Australian Government's NH & MRC-European Union Collaborative Research Grants (grant 1055138). The views expressed in this article are the author's alone. The author thanks the two peer-reviewer's for their guidance and Peter Hill, School of Public Health, The University of Queensland, for feedback on the final manuscript.

Conflicts of Interest: The author declares no conflict of interest.

Abbreviations

The following abbreviations are used in this manuscript:

CRPD Convention on the Rights of Persons with Disabilities
MDG   Millennium Development Goal
NGOs Non-government organisations
SDG   Sustainable Development Goal
UN   United Nations
UNDG UN Development Group

References

1. UN General Assembly. "Transforming our World: The 2030 Agenda for Sustainable Development." 2015. Available online: http://www.un.org/ga/search/view_doc.asp?symbol=A/RES/70/1&Lang=E (accessed on 29 March 2016).
2. UN General Assembly. "Road Map towards the Implementation of the UN Millennium Declaration: Report of the Secretary-General." 6 September 2001. Available online: http://www.un.org/documents/ga/docs/56/a56326.pdf (accessed on 29 March 2016).
3. Ooms, Gorik, Claire Brolan, Natalie Eggermont, Asbjørn Eide, Walter Flores, Lisa Forman, Eric A. Friedman, Thomas Gebauer, Lawrence O. Gostin, and Peter S. Hill, *et al.* "Universal health coverage anchored in the right to health." *Bulletin of the World Health Organization* 91 (2013): 2. [CrossRef] [PubMed]
4. Hill, Peter S., Kent Buse, Claire E. Brolan, and Gorik Ooms. "How can health remain central post-2015 in a sustainable development paradigm? " *Globalization and Health* 10 (2014): 18. [CrossRef] [PubMed]

5. Brolan, Claire E., and Peter S. Hill. "Countdown for health to the post-2015 UN Sustainable Development Goals." *Medical Journal of Australia* 202 (2015): 289–90. [CrossRef] [PubMed]
6. Mulumba, Moses, Juliana Nantaba, Claire E. Brolan, Ana Lorena Ruano, Katie Brooker, and Rachel Hammonds. "Perceptions and experiences of access to public healthcare by people with disabilities and older people in Uganda." *International Journal for Equity in Health* 13 (2014): 76. [CrossRef] [PubMed]
7. Durham, Jo, Claire E. Brolan, and Bryan Mukandi. "The Convention on the Rights of Persons with Disabilities: A foundation for ethical disability and health research in developing countries." *American Journal of Public Health* 104 (2014): 2037–43. [CrossRef] [PubMed]
8. Ngo, Anh D., Claire Brolan, Lisa Fitzgerald, Van Pham, and Ha Phan. "Voices from Vietnam: Experiences of children and youth with disabilities, and their families, from an Agent Orange affected rural region." *Disability and Society* 28 (2012): 955–69. [CrossRef]
9. Brolan, Claire E., K. Van Dooren, M. Taylor Gomez, Robert S. Ware, and Nicholas G. Lennox. "Suranho healing: Filipino concepts of intellectual disability and treatment choices in Negros Occidental." *Disability and Society* 29 (2013): 71–85. [CrossRef]
10. Brolan, Claire E., M. Taylor Gomez, Nicholas G. Lennox, and Robert S. Ware. "Australians from a non-English speaking background with intellectual disability: The importance of research." *Journal of Intellectual and Developmental Disability* 38 (2013): 70–73. [CrossRef] [PubMed]
11. UN General Assembly. "Resolution adopted by the General Assembly. United Nations Millennium Declaration." 18 September 2000. Available online: http://www.un.org/millennium/declaration/ares552e.pdf (accessed on 29 March 2016).
12. United Nations. "Convention on the Rights of Persons with Disabilities. Adopted 13 December 2016, GA Res 61/106, UN Doc A/Res/61/106, Entered into Force 3 May 2008." Available online: http://www.un.org/disabilities/convention/conventionfull.shtml (accessed on 29 March 2016).
13. Harpur, Paul. "Embracing the new disability rights paradigm: The importance of the Convention on the Rights of Persons with Disabilities." *Disability and Society* 27 (2012): 1–14. [CrossRef]
14. Mercer, Stewart W., and Rhona MacDonald. "Disability and human rights." *The Lancet* 370 (2007): 548–49. [CrossRef]
15. Bhat, Neha. "Mainstreaming Disability in International Development: A Review of Article 32 on International Co-Operation on the Convention on the Rights of Persons with Disabilities." 6 May 2013. Available online: http://dx.doi.org/10.2139/ssrn.2262946 (accessed on 29 March 2016).
16. Officer, Alana, and Nora E. Groce. "Key concepts in disability." *The Lancet* 374 (2009): 1795–96. [CrossRef]
17. Kett, Maria, and Mark van Ommeren. "Disability, conflict, and emergencies." *The Lancet* 374 (2009): 1801–2. [CrossRef]
18. World Health Organization, and the World Bank. "World Report on Disability." 2011. Available online: http://www.who.int/disabilities/world_report/2011/en/ (accessed on 29 March 2016).
19. World Health Organization. "Disability and Health (Factsheet No. 352)." December 2015. Available online: http://www.who.int/mediacentre/factsheets/fs352/en/ (accessed on 29 March 2016).
20. UN Development Group (UNDG). "Developing the Post-2015 Development Agenda: Opportunities at the National and Local Levels." 2014. Available online: http://www.undp.org/content/dam/undp/library/MDG/Post2015-SDG/UNDP-MDG-Delivering-Post-2015-Report-2014.pdf (accessed on 29 March 2016).
21. Beyond2015. "UN Thematic Consultations." 2015. Available online: http://www.beyond2015.org/un-thematic-consultations (accessed on 29 March 2016).
22. International Disability Alliance, and the International Disability and Development Consortium. "Include Persons with Disabilities in the Sustainable Development Process." Available online: http://iddcconsortium.net/sites/default/files/pages/files/ida_and_iddc_owg_statement.pdf (accessed on 29 March 2016).
23. World Health Organization. "UN High-Level Meeting on Disability and Development." 2016. Available online: http://www.who.int/disabilities/hlm/en/ (accessed on 29 March 2016).
24. UN General Assembly. "Outcome Document of the High-Level Meeting of the General Assembly on the Realization of the Millennium Development Goals and Other Internationally Agreed Development Goals for Persons with Disabilities: The Way Forward, a Disability-Inclusive Development Agenda towards 2015 and Beyond." September 2013. Available online: http://www.un.org/ga/search/view_doc.asp?symbol=A/68/L.1 (accessed on 29 March 2016).

25. Groce, Nora E., and Jean-Francois Trani. "Millennium Development Goals and people with disabilities." *The Lancet* 374 (2009): 1800–1. [CrossRef]

26. Vandemoortele, Jan. "Making sense of the MDGs." *Development* 51 (2008): 220–27. [CrossRef]

27. Doyle, Michael W. "Dialectics of a global constitution: The struggle over the UN Charter." *European Journal of International Relations* 18 (2011): 601–24. [CrossRef]

28. Darrow, Mac. "The Millennium Development Goals: Milestones or Millstones? Human Rights Priorities for the Post-2015 Development Agenda." *Yale Human Rights and Development Law Journal* 15 (2012): 55–127.

29. Langford, Malcolm. "The Art of the Impossible: Measurement Choices and the Post-2015 Development Agenda (Background Paper Governance and Human Rights: Criteria and Measurement Proposals for a Post-2015 Development Agenda)." 2012. Available online: https://sustainabledevelopment.un.org/content/documents/776langford.pdf (accessed on 29 March 2016).

30. Vandemoortele, Jan. "The MDG Conundrum: Meeting the Targets without Missing the Point." *Development Policy Review* 27 (2009): 355–71. [CrossRef]

31. McArthur, John. "Own the Goals: What the Millennium Development Goals Have Accomplished." *Brookings.* 21 February 2013. Available online: http://www.brookings.edu/research/articles/2013/02/21-millennium-dev-goals-mcarthur (accessed on 29 March 2016).

32. Vandemoortele, Jan. "If not the Millennium Development Goals, then What? " *Third World Quarterly* 32 (2011): 9–25. [CrossRef]

33. Hulme, David. "Governing global Poverty? Global ambivalence and the Millennium Development Goals." In *Governance, Poverty and Inequality.* Edited by Jennifer Clapp and Rorden Wilkinson. London and New York: Routledge, 2010.

34. Fukuda-Parr, Sakiko. "Recapturing the narrative of international development." In *The Millennium Development Goals and Beyond.* Edited by Rorden Wilkinson and David Hulme. Milton Park: Routledge, 2012.

35. Brolan, Claire E., Robert S. Ware, Miriam Taylro Gomez, and Nicholas G. Lennox. "The right to health of Australians with intellectual disability." *Australian Journal of Human Rights* 17 (2011): 1–32.

36. Brolan, Claire E., Sameera Hussain, Eric A. Friedman, Ana Lorena Ruano, Moses Mulumba, Itai Rusike, Claudia Beiersmann, and Peter S. Hill. "Community participation in formulating the post-2015 health and development goal agenda: Reflections on a multi-country research collaboration." *International Journal for Equity in Health* 13 (2014): 66. [CrossRef] [PubMed]

37. United Nations. "The Millennium Development Goals Report 2015." Available online: http://www.un.org/millenniumgoals/2015_MDG_Report/pdf/MDG%202015%20rev%20%28July%201%29.pdf (accessed on 29 March 2016).

38. Chandran, Rahul, Hannah Cooper, and Alexandra Ivanovic. "Managing Major Risks to Sustainable Development: Conflict, Disaster, the SDGs and the United Nations: A Report Prepared for the United Nations Department of Economic and Social Affairs for the 2016 Quadrennial Comprehensive Policy Review." 17 December 2015. Available online: http://www.un.org/en/ecosoc/qcpr/pdf/sgr2016-deskreview-transition.pdf (accessed on 29 March 2016).

39. UNDP. "Helen Clark: Speech on 2030 Agenda and the SDGs in Fragile States." 3 March 2016. Available online: http://www.undp.org/content/undp/en/home/presscenter/speeches/2016/03/03/helen-clark-2030-agenda-and-the-sdgs-in-fragile-states-european-parliament.html (accessed on 29 March 2016).

40. Sumner, Andy. "The New Bottom Billion: What if Most of the World's Poor Live in Middle-Income Countries? Center for Global Development (CGD Brief)." March 2011. Available online: http://www.cgdev.org/files/1424922_file_Sumner_brief_MIC_poor_FINAL.pdf (accessed on 29 March 2016).

41. Lucas, Paul, Norichika Kanie, and Nina Weitz. "Translating the SDGs to High-Income Countries: Integration at Last? IISD Reporting Services." 17 March 2016. Available online: http://sd.iisd.org/guest-articles/translating-the-sdgs-to-high-income-countries-integration-at-last/ (accessed on 29 March 2016).

42. United Nations. "Vienna Declaration and Programme of Action: Adopted by the World Conference on Human Rights on 25 June 1993, UN Doc A/CONF.157/23." Available online: http://www.un-documents.net/ac157-23.htm (accessed on 29 March 2016).

43. United Nations. "Vienna Convention on the Law of Treaties Concluded at Vienna on 23 May 1969. Entered into Force on 27 January 1980." Available online: https://treaties.un.org/doc/Publication/UNTS/Volume%201155/volume-1155-I-18232-English.pdf (accessed on 29 March 2016).

44. International Court of Justice. "Statute of the International Court of Justice (Annexed to the Charter of the United Nations)." Available online: http://www.icj-cij.org/documents/?p1=4&p2=2#CHAPTER_II (accessed on 29 March 2016).
45. Da Rocha Ferreira, Andre, Cristieli Carvalho, Fernanda Graeff Machry, and Pedro Barreto Vianna Rigon. "Formation and Evidence of Customary International Law." *UFRGS Model United Nations Journal* 1 (2013): 182–201.
46. International Law Association. *London Statement of Principles Relating to the Formation of General Customary International Law.* London: International Law Association, 2000.
47. Shaw, Malcolm N. *International Law*, 4th ed. Cambridge: University of Cambridge Press, 1997.
48. Brolan, Claire E., Peter S. Hill, and Gorik Ooms. "'Everywhere but not specifically somewhere': A qualitative study on why the right to health is not explicit in the post-2015 negotiations." *BMC International Health and Human Rights* 15 (2015): 22. [CrossRef] [PubMed]
49. UN Sustainable Development Knowledge Platform. "High-Level Political Forum on Sustainable Development." Available online: https://sustainabledevelopment.un.org/hlpf (accessed on 11 May 2016).
50. United Nations. "Millennium Goal 8 the Global Partnership for Development: Making Rhetoric a Reality." Available online: http://www.who.int/medicines/mdg/mdg8report2012_en.pdf?ua=1 (accessed on 29 March 2016).
51. Kenny, Charles, and Sarah Dykstra. "The Global Partnership for Development: A Review of MDG 8 and Proposals for the Post-2015 Development Agenda (Background Research Paper)." Submitted to the High Level Panel on the Post-2015 Development Agenda. May 2013. Available online: http://www.post2015hlp.org/wp-content/uploads/2013/05/Kenny-Dykstra_The-Global-Partnership-for-Development-Proposals-for-the-Post-2015-Development-Agenda.pdf (accessed on 29 March 2016).
52. Caliari, Aldo. "Analysis of Millennium Development Goal 8: A Global Partnership for Development." *Journal of Human Development and Capabilities* 15 (2014): 275–87. [CrossRef]
53. Fukuda-Parr, Sakiko. "Millennium Development Goal 8: Indicators for International Human Rights Obligations? " *Human Rights Quarterly* 28 (2006): 966–97. [CrossRef]
54. Alston, Philip. "Ships Passing in the Night: The Current State of the Human Rights and Development Debate seen through the Lens of the Millennium Development Goals." *Human Rights Quarterly* 27 (2005): 755–829. [CrossRef]
55. Unterhalter, Elaine. "Measuring Education for the Millennium Development Goals: Reflections on Targets, Indicators, and a Post-2015 Framework." *Journal of Human Development and Capabilities* 15 (2014): 176–87. [CrossRef]
56. Brolan, Claire E., Peter S. Hill, and Ignacio Correa-Velez. "Refugees: The Millennium Development Goals' Overlooked Priority Group." *Journal of Immigrant and Refugee Studies* 10 (2012): 426–30. [CrossRef]
57. Brolan, Claire E., Stephanie Dagron, Lisa Forman, Rachel Hammonds, Lyla Latif Abdul, and Attiya Waris. "Health rights in the post-2015 development agenda: Including non-nations." *Bulletin of the World Health Organization* 91 (2013): 719. [CrossRef] [PubMed]
58. UNICEF. "Expanding Millennium Development Goal 5: Universal Access to Reproductive Health by 2015." Available online: http://www.unicef.org/sowc09/docs/SOWC09-Panel-1.4-EN.pdf (accessed on 29 March 2016).
59. Islamic Republic of Afghanistan (Ministry of Economy). "Afghanistan Millennium Development Goals Report 2012." Available online: http://www.af.undp.org/content/dam/afghanistan/docs/MDGs/Afghanistan%20MDGs%202012%20Report.pdf (accessed on 29 March 2016).
60. De la Mothe, Eve, Jessica Espey, and Guido Schmidt-Traub. "GSDR 2015 Brief. Measuring Progress on the SDGs: Multi-level Reporting." Available online: https://sustainabledevelopment.un.org/content/documents/6464102-Measuring%20Progress%20on%20the%20SDGs%20%20%20Multi-level%20Reporting.pdf (accessed on 30 April 2016).

laws

MDPI

Article

NGO-Ization and Human Rights Law: The CRPD's Civil Society Mandate

Stephen Meyers [1,2]

[1] Law, Societies & Justice Program, University of Washington, Box 353565, Seattle, WA 98195, USA;
     sjmeyers@uw.edu; Tel.: +1-206-616-8151
[2] The Jackson School of International Studies, University of Washington, Box 353565, Seattle, WA 98195, USA

Academic Editor: Anna Arstein-Kerslake
Received: 21 March 2016; Accepted: 6 May 2016; Published: 11 May 2016

Abstract: The Convention on the Rights of Persons with Disabilities (CRPD) is unique among international human rights instruments for including a "civil society mandate". Within the convention, disabled persons organizations (DPOs) are identified as having the responsibility to "be involved and participate fully in the monitoring process" of the CRPD. In response to this mandate, international funders, NGOs (non-governmental organizations), and networks committed to the CPRD have begun to implement capacity-building programs that target grassroots DPOs with the goal of ensuring they become advocates and monitors of the CRPD. While the goals of these capacity-building programs are admirable, they must be critically assessed. The NGO-ization theory within development studies offers a framework for analyzing the potential unintended consequences of donors providing new funding, NGOs providing training, and global networks integrating local partners. NGO-ization studies have identified how grassroots associations are co-opted by outside actors through formalization and professionalization processes that significantly alter local groups and alienate members, thus making those associations less representative and less responsive to local needs and interests. Human rights scholars and international organizations focused on the CRPD should incorporate an NGO-ization perspective into their research and project-implementation to ensure that grassroots voices are heard and local needs addressed.

Keywords: civil society; human rights law; non-governmental organizations; disabled persons organizations; capacity building; grassroots associations

1. Introduction

Law, obviously, is meant to change behavior. International treaties, including human rights conventions, are typically designed to change the behavior of the States Parties that have signed and ratified them. As such, socio-legal scholars researching human rights focus on the ways in which international rights instruments affect the actions of states in relation to their citizens. Indeed, Risse, Ropp, and Skikkink promoted this line of human rights research in their much-cited volume *The Power of Human Rights: International Norms and Domestic Change* (1999) by asking "Have the principles articulated in the Declaration (Universal Declaration of Human Rights) had any effect at all on the actual behavior of states towards their citizens?" ([1], p. 1). In turn, socio-legal researchers have alternately answered this question in the affirmative and in the negative, with human rights champions often pointing to the most successful cases and human rights critics pointing to the worst disasters. A more nuanced response to Risse, Ropp, and Sikkink's question, however, has emerged: Human rights success in altering states' behavior depends on an effective civil society.

International human rights laws do not succeed by themselves but only when there is an active global civil society promoting those rights abroad and a vibrant national civil society advocating for those rights on the ground. For example, the presence of non-governmental organizations (NGOs)

and transnational civil society networks is perhaps the most important correlation between state compliance and human rights treaty ratification [2,3]. Keck and Sikkink's *Activists Beyond Borders* (1998) provides the classic account as to why grassroots organizations in non-compliant countries are able to link with international groups that in turn can "name and shame" human rights violators and call upon other states and organizations to apply pressure and bring violating states into line [4]. Smith-Cannoy (2012) builds upon this line of argument by demonstrating that, while many states may adopt human rights instruments with no real intention of implementing them, the treaties themselves often empower and embolden local civic activists to begin filing complaints for violations and thus ultimately holding their states accountable [5]. This monitoring process has increasingly become institutionalized in international human rights instruments through optional provisions for treaty implementation that involve the right of citizens and civil society to report violations. These optional provisions, in fact, are a statistically significant factor in predicting the compliance of states with human rights standards [6]. What is overlooked, however, is that monitoring and complaint provisions within international treaties not only impact states, but also civil society, as well often reshaping local civil societies in profound ways.

The 2006 Convention on the Rights of Persons with Disabilities (CRPD) is not only the exemplar but the most advanced human rights treaty in terms of integrating a role for civil society and specifying the practices those civic associations should engage in. Not only does the CRPD's Optional Protocol allow the United Nations Committee on the Rights of Persons with Disabilities to "receive and consider communications from or on behalf of individuals or groups" (Article 1), but a monitoring role for persons with disabilities and their representative organizations is specified in the text of the Convention itself. As Maya Sabatello, international disability rights lawyer and permanent civil society representative to the UN on disability rights, writes:

> Although participation of NGOs and civil society organizations in human rights debates and enforcement has been on the rise, particularly in the past couple of decades, there is no doubt that the disability rights movement has taken it to a new level. For the first time in an international human rights treaty, the expertise of those to be protected under the Convention, including their representative organizations, is fully recognized. Importantly, the Convention established an explicit positive legal obligation on states to seek their input in all levels of development, monitoring, and implementation of disability rights ([7], p. 23).

In this "groundbreaking provision" ([7], p. 23) not only are States Parties required to "consult and actively involve persons with disabilities...through their representative organizations" in Article 4, "General Obligations", but Article 33, "National Implementation and Monitoring", specifically mandates that "Civil society, in particular persons with disabilities and their representative organizations, shall be involved and participate fully in the monitoring process" of their human rights. Additionally, Articles 29, 34, and 40 also refer to a role for disabled persons organizations (DPOs) in the interpretation, implementation, and monitoring of their rights. In short, a rights advocacy role for civil society organizations made up of or representing persons with disabilities is written into the Convention itself.

While this innovation in the CRPD is certainly a victory for the global disability rights movement—the dozens of international NGOs and networks that successfully advocated for the creation and adoption of a human rights convention specific to persons with disabilities—it raises important socio-legal questions regarding the ways in which the treaty is reshaping local civil societies and DPOs on the ground. The intended effect of the inclusion of "persons with disabilities and their representative organizations" in a monitoring role in the CRPD is to ensure that there is both bottom-up (as well as top-down) pressure upon states to not only ratify the CRPD but to actively implement it. But this inclusion of a role for civil society also carries the potential of fundamentally changing the mission and practice of grassroots associations.

Many local disability associations in developing countries have heretofore prioritized self-help and social service provision over and above human rights advocacy [8,9]. Furthermore, many persons with disabilities view human rights with suspicion, associating its ideology with the legacy of Western intervention in the Global South [10] or simply do not identify with the social model of disability or politically identify as persons with disabilities despite being individuals with impairments [11].

International funders, disability NGOs, and global DPO networks committed to the success of the CRPD have anticipated this disconnect and begun to implement capacity-building programs around the world focused on transforming local DPOs into human rights advocates. The immediate goal of these programs is often implicitly, if not explicitly, to change the very nature of what activities and aims grassroots DPOs work towards, thus creating a "new kind of disability NGO—or amalgam of NGOs—with a clear mandate to monitor human rights developments around the world" ([12], p. 179). While the specific objectives of these programs and the larger goal of integrating persons with disabilities into the monitoring and implementation of the CPRD are laudable, they raise important questions regarding the reshaping of grassroots civil society. What are the potential consequences of reorienting existing DPOs towards human rights advocacy? How does this change impact the persons with disabilities who are the members, volunteers, and beneficiaries of these local disability associations in their home communities? How can capacity-building programs be designed to ensure that local leaders continue to respond to members' priorities in context-specific ways rather than feel pressured to focus and utilize the objectives and global "best practices" introduced to them by international actors?

Because the civil society mandate within the CRPD is an unprecedented phenomenon, there has been very little research specific to the impact that human rights instruments have upon changing the behavior of grassroots civil society generally, much less DPOs. There is, however, existing literature in development studies on outside intervention in local civil societies. A large swathe of critical development studies theory falls under the rubric of "NGO-ization" [13], which is broadly concerned with the "institutionalization, professionalization, depoliticization and demobilization of movements for social and environmental change" ([14], p. 1). This research perspective raises significant questions regarding the legitimacy [15], autonomy [16], and accountability [17] of local associations that receive aid or benefit from capacity-building initiatives sponsored by states, businesses, multilateral organizations, and international NGOs. These latter two—multilateral organizations and international NGOs—have played an important role in promoting the CRPD by partnering with grassroots DPOs around the world and supporting their human rights advocacy activities. The purpose of the article is to advocate for critical self-reflection among international disability rights advocates in the design and implementation of outreach programs. If grassroots DPOs are to remain connected to their local constituencies and the rights-based approach to disability is to succeed worldwide, the international disability rights community must be aware of both the positive and *negative* potential of funding, training, and partnership hold in terms of DPOs achieving their goals.

In this article, I argue that disability human rights law scholars must go beyond simply researching and analyzing the CRPD's impact on states to also include the CRPD's impact on civil society. In doing so, critical development studies scholarship, namely NGO-ization theory, provides an important way forward. In this article, I will review NGO-ization theory, analyze public statements, documents, and reports of international foundations, NGOs, and networks implementing capacity-building projects for DPOs in developing countries, and discuss implications for human rights, civil society, and disability studies researchers.

2. NGO-Ization Theory

The potential power of the CRPD is often seen as hinging on civil society's role in advocating for disability rights. As such, "disability awareness-raising and coordinated actions among disabled peoples' organizations are prerequisites for transforming the CRPD's promises into reality" ([18], p. 27). This human rights perspective on civil society reflects both the long-established participatory development paradigm [19], which focuses on grassroots associations as the foundation of both economic and political development, and the newer human rights-based [20] and inclusive [21] development paradigms, which focus on the empowerment of marginalized groups by integrating political advocacy into development planning and practice. This turn towards civil society in development and human rights has resulted in the prioritization of capacity-building activities [22] and funding [23] meant to strengthen civil society throughout the Global South. The unintended consequences or negative implications of this rapid rise of transnational capacity-building projects and partnerships, however, are rarely questioned, much less examined [24]. Strengthening civil society initiatives, paradoxically, may actually weaken the voices of marginalized groups at the local level and, in the case of DPOs, rendering them silent or circumscribing their advocacy to pre-determined scripts focused exclusively on the rights inscribed in the CRPD [25]. It is also linked with shifting grassroots groups' (and the international NGOs that have typically funded and supported them) focus and resources from meeting the short-range, material needs of members in the community to national or international advocacy initiatives that may yield few or no practical benefits in the immediate future [26–28], thus making members of these groups more vulnerable in the interim. In short, political advocacy does not necessarily help marginalized people, such as disabled persons, address their daily needs for food, shelter, and health care in the "here and now". The effects of NGO-ization—the formalization and professionalization of local civil societies—can be profound, yet are rarely systematically addressed within human rights-based approaches to social marginalization.

Capacity-building projects benefiting civic associations can, in fact, decrease their ability to adequately represent the needs and wants of their members. Chahim and Prakash, for example, argue that foreign funding and corresponding professionalization initiatives "creates dualism among domestic civil society organizations" ([17], p. 487), increasing the influence of "modern" NGOs, which are essentially local incarnations of international NGOs, and decreasing the profiles of grassroots, membership-based organizations that reflect local culture and traditional (and particular) associational models. This "modernization" of NGOs through NGO-ization processes is often a one-size-fits-all pursuit, where the organizational attributes that international groups help local groups develop are chosen "without consideration for economic, social and political context within which these issues arise" ([16], p. 193) even if other organizational models have proven effective in the local environment [29].

Factors driving the transformation of the grassroots associations into modern NGOs are: local groups developing dependence on foreign funding, integrating into hierarchical networks, increasing professionalization where local community members are replaced by trained professionals, and/or the taking of cues from outside, agenda-setting entities, such as influential international NGOs. Grassroots groups that do not succumb to NGO-ization are often ignored, if not made invisible, by outsiders who see them as backwards, lacking the legal and financial infrastructure (*i.e.*, official certification or tax status) necessary for partnership, or simply do not recognize them as civic associations. "Formal NGOs", as opposed to the diversity of informal and formal associations based upon kinship, religious tradition, reciprocal relations, and self-help networks, however, are just one element of civil society, yet "often the part which external donors 'see' as civil society and find most bureaucratically amenable to engage with" ([30], p. 720). Thus, those groups most "in touch" with the people are sometimes the least likely to be listened to or included in larger discussions about the needs and interests of vulnerable groups.

In addition to the reordering of local civil societies, where certain types of grassroots associations are raised up over others, another principal concern within NGO-ization theory is that for those local groups that are targeted and chosen and whose "capacity" is built up by international organizations, there is a concomitant loss in autonomy and local accountability [13,16,17]. International organizations teach and "discipline" [31] grassroots groups through the provision of professional consultants and the communication of new ideas, both of which replace local leaders and existing beliefs about what needs to be done with alternatives that meet global, rather than local, expectations and interests. In essence, NGO-ization turns local organizations into satellites or franchises of international organizations, thus "de-localizing" them and pulling their leadership away from their members.

Or, outsider organizations will simply enter the local organizations and "manufacture civil society" [30], establishing in communities entirely new organizations that reflect international values, yet are meant to represent local concerns. This can result in a "dislocated new civil society" ([32], p. 50) that has little connection to the actual populus, yet claims to speak for "the people" at the grassroots level.

Traditionally, NGO-ization research has focused on the ways in which local groups are co-opted by the "state and capital" [14], thus making them a part of the "development hegemony" [13] by which states and markets dictate the direction of political and economic development. What is often overlooked by development studies (and human rights researchers), however, is that the co-optation of grassroots associations goes far beyond governments and businesses to also include other civil society actors, such as international NGOs, foreign donors, and global networks, all of whom have an interest in having local partners who support their global agendas. The shaping of local civil society for this purpose thus requires some exercise of power; whether that power be hard or soft, it still has consequences. As Eschle has argued, "oppression and conflict *within civil society* and *between social movement actors* cannot simply be wished away or ignored" ([33], my emphasis, p. 74).

The result, however, is that attempts to build up grassroots associations can actually pull the rug out from under local civil society by alienating the very citizens who supposedly belong to it. Human rights, which has been so instrumental in advancing the rights of citizens around the world, can play a role in denuding local groups of the power to represent their members. Within grassroots groups themselves, elites can form, made up of leaders capable of interacting with the staff of international NGOs, leaving regular participants out of the conversation ([34], pp. 298–99). As Clifford Bob has noted, funding initiatives, for example, reward groups led by leaders with "marketing" savvy and the willingness to adopt the priorities of international donors, which can in turn pull local leaders away from their base in their quest for resources. Unfortunately, there is often an inverse relationship between the types of things local groups need to say and do to get international support and those things the members and beneficiaries of their organizations are saying or want done themselves, as "what plays best overseas seldom corresponds to what matters most domestically" ([26], p. 193).

In regards to networks, which often consciously adopt horizontal forms of participation, power still concentrates in the hands of the full-time, media savvy, or well-positioned (*i.e.*, in Washington D.C. or Geneva) few who have the time or wherewithal to respond to calls or attend meetings with governments, multilateral organizations or other international NGOs. This can leave partners marginalized from the agenda-setting process ([35], p. 51; [36]) and lead to "oligarchy". Several critical studies of international NGOs [37] and transnational networks [36] have cited Michels' "iron law of oligarchy", first enunciated in his *Political Parties: A sociological study of the oligarchic tendencies of modern democracy*. In it, Michels argues that within ostensibly democratic parties representing their members, anti-democratic tendencies develop to deal with the "tactical and technical necessities" ([38], p. 365) of organizing and representation. An elite is formed, usually made up of an elected chair or council, in some cases "self-appointed" [36], who, for the sake of efficiency, begin to set agendas and make decisions without consulting their base.

A common response to these concerns above is for international NGOs, networks, and movements to commit to a greater "consciousness" regarding their activities. Consciousness, however, does little to address the underlying power differential between the Global North and Global South in terms of economic, cultural, and organizational resources. For example, studies on the international feminist movement have found that even when northern women's groups sought to "reverse the North-to-South flow of ideas and development strategies, the organization and its [southern] counterparts were circumscribed in locally-specific ways by the very power imbalances they were attempting to undo" ([39], p. 45). Not only do offers of grants and other forms of assistance "nudge" local groups into meeting outsiders' expectations, but capacity-training workshops provided by international NGOs are often activities with the explicit mission of bringing in new forms of social knowledge and identities (*i.e.*, women-as-citizens) that displace local knowledge or silence alternative (and often more complex and intersecting) identities [40]. These sorts of changes can take place independently of NGO and network activities by being communicated by the law itself. Masaki [41], for example, shows how the UN Declaration on the Rights of Indigenous Peoples defines indigenous persons on the basis of outsider oppression (*i.e.*, colonialization), a facet of their identity that may be far less important than gender, class, and even occupational group. As a result, rights protected in law and policies that pre-suppose a "shared will" on the basis of "shared oppression" silence intersecting and often marginalized identities within indigenous groups.

Transitioning from service-provision to political advocacy is one of the most important directions that international funders, NGOs, and networks, especially those centered on human rights, try to move grassroots associations. The service *vs.* advocacy divide is perhaps the most significant divide within civil societies, including global civil society. In a study of only formal NGOs that have contact with the UN system, Sikkink found that NGOs based in the North were far more likely to be in contact with the UN's human rights apparatus, such as the Human Rights Centre in Geneva, while southern NGOs were far more likely to be in contact with the UN's more service-oriented agencies, such as UNICEF and the UN Development Program ([42], p. 307). The split is even wider when informal NGOs are taken into account, including kinship networks, religious groups, and other forms of traditional association, many of which are based on norms of reciprocity and a focus on social support, self-help, charity, and/or mutual beneficence.

When grassroots groups are incentivized or pressured to adopt advocacy practices, their members are likely to resist. For example, in a study of "local survival initiatives" in Africa, Cheru warns that "the more the representatives of African social movements spend their time on worthy international [human rights] campaigns that are little understood by their own constituencies, and devote less time to critical local 'bread-and-butter and rights' issues, the more they risk losing legitimacy and fostering an ethic of isolationism" ([27], p. 125). However, perhaps the most significant effect is that these new professionalization activities focused on advocacy are replacing prior programming focused on training local individuals in providing substantive social and economic services (*i.e.*, teacher or health care worker training) to marginalized populations. Rugendycke has observed that "where once NGOs concentrated their work on establishing projects to do things like build water supplies or encourage income generation, the same NGOs have increasingly devoted resources to advocacy campaigns directed at global actors" ([28], p. 2).This shift in funding focus is evident in training programs implemented in the Global South where a new class of professionals has been created who are adept in "watchdogging" government activities, but are unable to meet the more immediate material needs of their followers.

3. Disabled Persons Organizations Capacity Building around the World

The passage of the CRPD in 2006, with its important civil society mandate, has acted as a clarion call for international disability NGOs and global disability networks to reach out to local DPOs around the world, especially the Global South, to build their capacity and integrate them into their networks. In recognition of the fact that the CRPD established an "explicit positive legal obligation on states to seek ('representative disability organizations') input in all levels of development, monitoring, and implementation of disability rights" ([7], p. 23) international disability organizations have implemented funding, training, and other forms of outreach to local DPOs. The stated purpose of these activities is for DPOs to adopt a new, rights-based perspective on disability and to incorporate advocacy into their organizational practice. This new role for DPOs, thus, "involves a change in identity of the organization and in its strategic direction" in which "they now actively aim to convey the rights-based approach to disability" ([43], p. 369).

Changes in "identity" and the adoption of a new "strategic directions" can have both a positive and negative impact on the ability of DPOs to remain relevant in the lives of their members. I argue that capacity-building activities that formalize grassroots associations and orient their activities towards human rights advocacy and away from service-provision and other non-advocacy-related practices may succeed in bringing them in line with international priorities, but, if designed in ways that are not sensitive to local needs and contexts, could fail in terms of ensuring that their activities remain germane to their members. While it is important that local DPOs fulfill their responsibilities as outlined in the CPRD, their foremost responsibility is to the persons with disabilities that belong to them. As such, international capacity-building initiatives must be aware of their potential to NGO-ize local groups and, in fact, distance them from their memberships or render them ineffective in their specific social and political contexts. These processes are carried out through the creation of new funding opportunities, organizational development trainings, and integration into global networks, all of which have a narrow vision of DPOs around the world as supporters of the CRPD and, therefore, advocates. DPO research, unfortunately, has often been complicit in this process, dismissing local organizational diversity and dissidence, thus demonstrating the need for a critical development studies perspective in this era of transnational outreach towards civil society.

3.1. Funding

A wide array of international actors based in the Global North, ranging from government agencies for international cooperation through to disability and mainstream foundations and funds have begun funding DPOs in the Global South. The grant-giving criteria institutionalizes specific organizational forms and activities through funding priorities and eligibility requirements.

The majority of official foreign aid for DPOs is specific towards activities, limiting the money to only include "organizational capacity, advocacy efforts, cross-disability coalition building, coordination, and leadership and training" [44]. This holds both an implicit and explicit expectation that DPOs should be focused on advocacy rather than service provision or social support. These funds are also limited to formal DPOs. For example, the Australian Agency for International Development (AusAID)-funded Pacific DPO Fund specifies that grantees must "be non-governmental, non-profit and a DPO" and, furthermore, that "the organisation should have a plan to meet its purpose and objectives, a transparent organisational structure, clear administrative and financial systems to manage funds" [45]. These sorts of requirements create a selection-bias against less formal, traditional, and grassroots associations of persons with disabilities and towards professionalized groups that are "bureaucratically amenable" ([30], p. 720) for AusAID to partner with, even if these formal groups are both geographically and socially distant (*i.e.*, in the capital and staffed by an educated elite) from the majority of persons with disabilities in the developing country they represent.

Both disability and mainstream international foundations prioritize disability rights advocacy over and above other forms of organizational practice. For example, the disability-specific Disability Rights Fund's grants program based in the United States explicitly states that its grants are to be used to "strengthen local stakeholders who can hold governments accountable for fulfilling the rights of persons with disabilities", and frames its grants program strategy in terms of the CRPD, stating "By supporting civil society efforts at country level to ratify, implement, and monitor the CRPD, DRF seeks to make a more direct impact on improving the conditions of (persons with disabilities)" [46]. The ABILIS Foundation of Finland similarly provides capacity-building grants to DPOs in developing countries, again framing their mission in terms of disability human rights advocacy: "ABILIS makes grants to carefully chosen DPOs in developing countries in order to strengthen the capacity of disabled peoples organizations (DPOs) in the global South so that they are better able to advocate for their Human Rights as articulated by the Convention on the Rights of Persons with Disabilities (CRPD)" [47]. Along with this advocacy priority, ABILIS also notes it only funds organizations with a formal "certificate of registration". In addition to these disability-specific foundations, mainstream funders such as the Open Society Foundation also emphasize human rights advocacy. Open Society explains its DPO grantmaking program as ensuring "persons with disabilities enjoy human rights on an equal basis with others" and outlining project activities as those that "tackle deeply entrenched discriminatory laws, practices, and attitudes that hinder full equality and inclusion of persons with disabilities" [48].

This prioritization of rights advocacy over service provision is, obviously, no accident, but, as shown above, explicitly linked to the CRPD, which provides a blueprint of what DPOs in developing countries should be doing. It may also display the historical experiences of the Northern (or Western) disability movements, where many of the needs for persons with disabilities were achieved through rights advocacy and legislative change, success that may not be as replicable in states where governments lack the institutional capacity to implement many of the rights they promise their citizens.

3.2. Training

A number of international disability NGOs, such as Action for Disability and Development, CBM International, and Handicap International have implemented global capacity-building projects aimed at increasing the rights advocacy and monitoring role of DPOs in developing countries. Virtually all programs directly reference human rights and the CRPD. The specific types of outreach ranging from organizing activities (*i.e.*, bringing persons with disabilities together) through to consciousness raising and advocacy skill training.

Action for Disability and Development, an international NGO based in the United Kingdom, explains its approach as "We work with Disabled People's Organizations throughout Africa and Asia because the fight for equality starts with disabled people themselves", going on to outline a civil society outreach program wherein they "fight alongside disabled people's organizations and the disability movement to eradicate the injustice and the discrimination disabled people face" through activities such as organizing workshops, giving advice, and so forth.

CBM (Christian Blind Mission) International's International Advocacy and Alliances program is a global partnership program to promote human rights advocacy "within the guiding frameworks of the UNCRPD" (CBM 2013) that guides their activities around the world, specifying that "DPOs are a priority for capacity development by CBM, particularly in management and PCM (project cycle management)." As such, the focus is not only on advocacy, but also on professionalization—transforming grassroots advocates into project managers, presumably to implement projects funded by CBM or other international donors. In addition to CBM's direct outreach to DPOs, it also encourages other NGOs to do the same. In its Disability Inclusive Development Toolkit, which was developed as a guide for other international actors, it advises that groups assess DPOs in terms of the question: "Are people with disabilities able to exercise their right to be part of debate, advocacy and responsibility within their communities" ([49], p. 112) and, if not, building their capacity to do so. The toolkit explicitly outlines a human rights basis to its work and the civil society mandate in the CRPD, pointing to the importance of DPO involvement, because "A shadow/alternative report gives civil society an opportunity to have its voice heard on how the State is implementing the CRPD" ([50], p. 96).

Handicap International has its own global capacity-building campaign called Making It Work, which provides technical assistance to local DPOs in developing countries around the world to "strengthen their advocacy to influence social change". The "It" in Making It Work refers to the Convention on the Rights of Persons with disabilities. A Handicap International policy paper on supporting DPOs states that the CRPD constitutes a "roadmap for DPOs" and encourages them to use it, arguing that "the CRPD represents a major step, it is a tool that can be effective and make a difference for persons with disabilities only if used and enacted. This calls for all stakeholders to play their role to make these rights a reality" ([51], p. 16). The report goes on to advocate that DPOs are assisted in developing the "relevant capacities and resources" to become effective human rights advocates and that "DPOs have a responsibility" to do such advocacy. The policy paper goes on to explain that "HI has observed that in most developing countries there is a discrepancy between the important role that DPOs have to play and the limited opportunities, resources and capacities they have had to fulfill their role" ([50], p. 23) and to then outline project components meant to address the DPOs' (1) organization and technical weaknesses; (2) lack of awareness and knowledge of the "new conceptual models of disability developed at the international level"; (3) experience as human rights monitors; and (4) lack of actions that empower individual members ([50], pp. 23–64). Again, the role that DPOs are to play and the deficits identified are based on the CPRD and not the expressed needs or interests of persons with disabilities themselves within the targeted DPOs.

All of these programs are based on the global prioritization of the CRPD, an international instrument, rather than the expressed needs or mission of the DPOs targeted by these campaigns. The specific capacities strengthened range from project management through to human rights reporting, but not social service or self-help provision, the original purpose of many of the DPOs found in the world today. In that way, the local groups are engaged on the international NGOs terms, which are focused on their mission to ensure that DPOs are advocates for the CRPD. This, obviously, risks being a top-down process where grassroots groups are NGO-ized according to a globally-defined template.

3.3. Network Integration

Lastly, there are a number of global DPO networks, the two most prominent of which are hierarchical, moving from national to regional to the global network, which then claim to speak on behalf of persons with disabilities worldwide. For example, the International Disability Alliance (IDA) describes itself as "the most authoritative representative voice of persons with disabilities" ([51], p. 7) globally and Disabled People International (DPI), another global network, uses "A Voice of Our Own" as its motto, presumably also representing the voice of persons with disabilities around the world. These networks also emphasize unity in message, which they instill through their own capacity-building programs and guidance, much of which teaches regional and national coalitions how to be "good" network members by using the CRPD in advocacy and developing human rights monitoring reports that contribute towards the goals of global unity in message. This, however, may come at the cost of covering up diversity and regional and national particularity.

Disabled People International is the older of the two international DPO networks. DPI was founded in 1981 as a "human rights organization committed to the protection of the rights of people with disability and equal participation in society" and was instrumental in advocating for the CRPD. It claims over 130 member cross-disability DPOs. It was founded in the Global North, but has since expanded globally to include national DPOs that are then aggregated into regional DPO networks for North America, South America, Africa, Arab Nations, the Asia-Pacific, and Europe that are then members of the World Council and report to the world headquarters in Canada. Acknowledgement of diversity was present from the beginning of DPI. Jim Derksen, who was a disability advocate in Canada who believed in unity, argued to DPOs "Let us reason together, let us deliberate on our problems and needs, let us consider our abilities, and when we have agreed on the problems and solutions let us articulate our opinions and ideas in a strong and united voice" ([52], p. 1).

The idea of collectively agreeing upon problems and solutions, however, has not been achieved in DPI. In an extraordinarily honest report from DPI's World Council Meeting in Dhaka in 2015, which resulted in "withdrawing of confidence" in DPI's Chair, the report lays out its grievances, stating that "Most decisions in the name of DPI have been taken unilaterally by the chair without any approval by the World Council and consultation with the executive officers", listing such instances as the headquarters making "The unilateral announcement of controversial DPI political decisions in the United Nations and other platforms that undermined the unity of the disability movement without any approval from the executive officers", the "unconstitutional intervention in countries where DPI is established by revoking elected leadership and replacing it by a new one", and other complaints demonstrating a flagrant disregard to democratic norms within the organization [53].

The other global disability network is the International Disability Alliance, which was created in 1999 by seven transnational DPO networks and several disability NGOs that were principal advocates for the creation of a UN disability convention. In 2007, IDA changed into a global alliance of global and regional DPO coalitions and was subsequently given full consultative status within the UN, giving it an official advisory role on international disability rights. The mission of IDA is "to promote the effective and full implementation of the United Nations Convention on the Rights of Persons with Disabilities worldwide, as well as compliance with the CRPD within the UN system, through the active and coordinated involvement of representative organisations of persons with disabilities at the national, regional and international levels" [54]. This global coordination is promoted in two ways: direct advocacy capacity building and CRPD-reporting guidelines. The reporting guidelines for parallel reports, which are outlined as a responsibility of civil society in the CRPD, contain recommendations that paradoxically "ensures that issues that are important to small organizations are given a voice", but also ensure that DPOs submitting to the report speak with a "unified voice" and only submit "one comprehensive report" ([51], p. 28), thus creating obstacles to DPOs focused on community or disability-specific issues [25]. The report is also based upon the CRPD, specifying specific rights to be addressed and how their implementation is to be measured. IDA also has its own capacity-building program that "includes long-term coaching of few national coalitions in the preparation of parallel reports, punctual trainings at national and regional for key DPO representatives and other stakeholders on the monitoring of CRPD" [55]. There are no public reports of dissent (or confidence) as there is for DPI, but a similar emphasis on unity of message is present in IDA as it is in DPI, but without acknowledgement of diversity.

Within global networks, there is cause for concern with "oligarchy", as Ghirmire [36] found with transnational networks, wherein a chair, as evidenced by DPI's Dhaka Statement, is empowered (or takes the power) to set agendas and make unilateral decisions without consultation of members. A critical development studies perspective is needed in the face of procedures and processes by which grassroots groups are integrated in international disability networks through hierarchical patterns (local-national-regional-global) that are meant to create a unity in message. Top-down capacity building and guidance, wherein network headquarters "coach" and "advise" and "guide" members groups have the potential to NGO-ize grassroots groups, thus shaping them according to global concerns rather than enabling them to be organic, bottom-up representations of their local memberships. The importance of network integration and the difficulty of including and consulting highly diverse groups of persons with disabilities around the globe potentially increases the risk of such networks misrepresenting their base, especially in the face of the bureaucratic complexity of representing those groups to the CRPD Council of Experts.

3.4. Research Deficit

Much of the current research on DPO capacity building fails to take a critical stance on funding, training, and network integration initiatives. Instead, much research specifically advises how international NGOs and other actors can better achieve their goal of turning local DPOs into advocates for the CRPD and becoming part of a worldwide movement.

For example, in a study on an organizational development initiative involving six disability-specific NGOs and DPOs in East Africa implemented by Light for the World, a Netherlands-based disability rights NGO, the authors describe how the "six organizations have translated the legal responsibilities enshrined in the CRPD into new activities" ([43], p. 362) for the purposes of lessons being applied to other DPOs making the transition around the world. While the authors note that, as the DPOs in the study began to focus increasingly on human rights activities, this "led to tensions with the beneficiaries" and the DPO's members were "afraid that their group would be forgotten", they then go on to uncritically and positively report that the changes were accomplished because "most employees of the organisations and their partners had found a collective drive, confidence and fostered the ambition to realise the new desired role" ([43], p. 371). From an NGO-ization perspective, however, the "collective drive and confidence" of the DPOs' staff and management to forge ahead despite resistance from their base supporters (*i.e.*, persons with disabilities themselves) should raise questions about the costs of professionalization in member participation in organizational decision-making. Further in the article, the authors note that the DPOs were able to make these changes because of their ability to "*market* their new approach" ([43], my emphasis, p. 379) to funders, without questioning their usage of the term "marketing", a strategy Clifford Bob [26] suggested, as reviewed above, that can lead to grassroots leaders adopting the priorities of foreign funders over and above domestic audiences and local movement participants in the quest for resources.

In a different context, but with a similar outcome concerning the adequacy of pre-existing NGOs in low-income countries to advance the disability rights agenda, Sarah Phillips, an anthropologist studying the Ukrainian disability movement, states that contemporary DPO coalitions in Eastern Europe are "plagued by socialist legacies" because "these groups have unwieldy, rather ossified structures and tend to have a narrow focus on shoring up social programs for certain groups of the disabled" ([56], p. 283). She sees this as antithetical to the human rights approach she supports for DPOs in the age of the CRPD. In her concluding remarks, Phillips suggests that Ukrainian NGOs need to pursue more international partnerships so that they have the "opportunities to travel to the United States, Canada, and other countries to participate in seminars, meet fellow activists, and become familiar with different approaches to rights issues" ([56], p. 291) and also "pursue international partnerships that can teach them a new model" ([56], p. 283). In short, she wants these groups to change and be brought in line with international, rather than local, priorities.

Research such as this is based on a northern priority of encouraging DPOs to take up their responsibilities under the CPRD as rights advocates, regardless of local priorities or purposes of organizing. It fails to integrate a critical development studies perspective that could open up important questions about international funder, NGO, and network interventions into local civil societies and the possible consequences that may have for those groups to remain connected to and answerable to their local members. An example of the latter is important.

One critical exception to the predominant DPO research is a consultancy report on capacity-building initiatives implemented by Northern DPOs and NGOs for grassroots DPOs in Mozambique. By taking an unbiased research position, the author demonstrates why an NGO-ization perspective is necessary to uncover real issues in the interactions between DPOs and international actors. The author reports that the initiatives of the international actors working in Africa often overlook the needs of local groups, noting that local DPOs saw "Northern NGO partners as concentrating their limited support on technical inputs, without paying attention to how organisations survive from day to day" and also "expressed anger at what they saw as unequal power with their Northern NGO partners" and that the local "DPOs reported feeling as if they are treated more like clients or objects than the primary constituency" [57], often noting that they were used by the North to fundraise for monies the Mozambique NGOs only benefitted from indirectly. In this case, rather than call for the local DPOs to fall in line, the consultant suggests that the international NGOs should question their practices. This is the sort of research where NGO-ization theory, which questions international funder, NGO, and network practices from the beginning is helpful in highlighting local voices rather than global agendas.

4. Implications and Conclusions

Human rights instruments can offer a blueprint of what civic associations should be doing by specifying "communication" (or complaint) processes and spelling out the specific issues (*i.e.*, rights and violations) and "identities" (*i.e.*, definitions of specific groups) that local organizations should pay attention to and represent. Equally, if not more importantly, global human rights campaigns led by international donors, professional NGOs, and transnational networks often implement civil society capacity-building programs meant to educate and empower local civil societies by teaching marginalized groups about their rights and building up grassroots associations operating on the ground by providing small grants, holding workshops and training, and integrating those groups into transnational networks. These activities, however, can fundamentally reshape local civil societies by prioritizing some groups over others and implicitly (or explicitly) setting organizations' agenda.

The civil society mandate in the CRPD has made grassroots DPOs targets for change. While human rights protecting persons with disabilities are vital, the consequences of DPOs being specified within the convention as monitors must be investigated. The transformation of local associations may not be an unmitigated good—it may also have negative consequences in terms of the ability of local members to continue to exercise ownership over the groups that they have joined and supported, often for decades before the CRPD was written and signed and ratified around the world. In many cases, DPOs are critical service providers and social support mechanisms that persons with disabilities in poor communities rely on. A shift towards advocacy is often a shift towards a long-term strategy where recognition of disability rights by states will eventually address needs and create opportunities for disabled persons. But it may have short-term, or in the case of states with limited capacity, long-term consequences when DPOs shift their time, resources, and attention towards advocacy over and above their founding purpose to provide material assistance to their members. As such, these groups can, in fact, work against the very people they claim to represent.

NGO-ization theory within critical development studies raises important questions regarding the way grassroots associations can be co-opted by other actors, including representatives of global civil society such as foreign donors, international NGOs, and transnational networks. Utilizing this perspective is important to ensure that the voices of all persons with disabilities are heard and not simply an international elite. It also holds the promise of better allocating resources, providing training, and organizing representation to and for local DPOs in a way that reflects their members' priorities, thus ultimately and organically strengthening grassroots civil society rather than transforming it in accordance with a pre-determined and global blueprint.

For the civil society mandate within the CRPD to truly be empowering for grassroots DPOs and for the unmet needs of persons with disabilities in the Global South to be met, the mandate's interpretation and implementation must be left to local groups. The international disability rights community can (and often does) play an important role in helping DPOs reach their full potential. It is, however, the responsibility of those involved in designing and implementing global capacity-building programs to engage in critical self-reflection so as to be aware of the power that funding, training, and other forms of assistance hold to both bring grassroots associations closer or to push grassroots associations *further away* from their memberships. Outside interventions should be assessed not only from the point of view of their ability to introduce and support a rights-based approach, but to allow local DPOs to interpret and integrate that approach in context-specific ways that remain focused on local priorities and can flexibly accommodate a range of interpretations and practices.

Conflicts of Interest: The author declares no conflict of interest.

References

1. Risse, Thomas, Stephen C. Ropp, and Kathryn Sikkink. *The Power of Human Rights: International Norms and Domestic Change.* Cambridge: Cambridge University Press, 1999.
2. Hafner-Burton, Emilie, and Kiyoteru Tsutsui. "Human Rights in a Globalizing World: The Paradox of Empty Promises." *American Journal of Sociology* 110 (2005): 1373–411. [CrossRef]
3. Simmons, Beth. *Mobilizing for Human Rights: International Law and Domestic Enforcement.* New York: Cambridge University Press, 2009.
4. Keck, Margaret, and Kathryn Sikkink. *Activists beyond Borders.* Ithaca: Cornell University Press, 1998.
5. Smith-Cannoy, Heather. *Insincere Commitments: Human Rights Treaties, Abusive States, and Citizen Activism.* Washington: Georgetown University Press, 2012.
6. Cole, Wade. "Human Rights as Myth and Ceremony? Reevaluating the effectiveness of human rights treaties, 1981–2007." *American Journal of Sociology* 117 (2012): 1131–71. [CrossRef]
7. Sabatello, Maya. "A Short History of the International Disability Rights Movement." In *Human Rights & Disability Advocacy.* Edited by Maya Sabatello and Marianne Schulze. Philadelphia: University of Pennsylvania Press, 2014, pp. 13–24.
8. Ingstad, Benedict, and Susan Whyte, eds. "Disability and culture: An overview." In *Disability and Culture.* Berkeley: University of California Press, 1995, pp. 1–37.
9. Turmasani, Majid. *Disabled People and Economic Needs in the Developing World: A Political Perspective from Jordan.* Hampshire: Ashgate Publishing, 2003.

10. Meekosha, Helen, and Karen Soldatic. "Human Rights & the Global South: The case of disability." *Third World Quarterly* 32 (2011): 1383–97.
11. Meyers, Stephen. "The Social Model of Disability Under the Shadow of the Revolution: Ex-Combatants Negotiating Disability Identity in Nicaragua." *Qualitative Sociology* 37 (2014): 403–24. [CrossRef]
12. Quinn, Gerard, and Theresia Degener. *Human Rights and Disability*. New York: United Nations, 2002.
13. Kamat, Sangeeta. *Development Hegemony*. New York: Oxford University Press, 2002.
14. Choudry, Aziz, and Dip Kapoor. *NGOization: Complicity, Contradictions and Prospects*. New York: Zed Books, 2013.
15. Howell, Jude, and Jenny Pearce. *Civil Society and Development*. Boulder: Lynne Rienner Publishers, 2001.
16. Nazneen, Sohela, and Maheen Sultan. "Struggling for Survival and Autonomy: The NGOisation of women's organizations in Bangladesh." *Development* 52 (2009): 193–99. [CrossRef]
17. Chahim, Dean, and Asseem Prakash. "NGOization, Foreign Funding, and the Nicaraguan Civil Society." *VOLUNTAS: International Journal of Voluntary and Nonprofit Organizations* 25 (2013): 487–513. [CrossRef]
18. Stein, Michael, and Janet Lord. "Forging Effective International Agreements: Lesson for the UN Convention on the Rights of Persons with Disabilities." In *Making Equal Rights Real: Taking Effective Action*. Edited by Jody Heymann and Adele Cassola. Cambridge: Cambridge University Press, 2009, pp. 27–50.
19. Mohan, Giles, and Kristian Stokke. "Participatory Development and Empowerment: The Dangers of Localism." *Third World Quarterly* 21 (2000): 247–68. [CrossRef]
20. Uvin, Peter. *Human Rights and Development*. Bloomfield: Kumarian Press, 2004.
21. Hickey, Sam, Kendall Sen, and Badru Bukenya. *The Politics of Inclusive Development*. Oxford: Oxford University Press, 2015.
22. Eade, Deborah. *Capacity-Building: An Approach to People-Centred Development*. Oxford: Oxfam, 1997.
23. Stiles, Kendall. "International support for NGOs in Bangladesh: Some unintended consequences." *World Development* 30 (2002): 835–46. [CrossRef]
24. Batliwala, Srilatha. "Grassroots movements as transnational actors: Implications for global civil society." *Voluntas: International Journal of Voluntary and Nonprofit Organizations* 13 (2002): 393–409. [CrossRef]
25. Meyers, Stephen. "Global Civil Society as Megaphone or Echo Chamber?: Formalizing voice in the international disability rights movement." *International Journal of Politics, Culture, and Society* 27 (2014): 459–76. [CrossRef]
26. Bob, Clifford. *The Marketing of Rebellion: Insurgents, Media, and International Activism*. New York: Cambridge University Press, 2005.
27. Cheru, Fantu. "The Local Dimensions of Global Reform." In *Global Futures: Shaping Globalization*. Edited by Jan Nederveen Pieterse. New York: Zed Books, 2000, pp. 119–32.
28. Rugendycke, Barbara. *NGOs as Advocates for Development in a Globalising World*. London: Routledge, 2007.
29. Meyers, Stephen. "Disabled persons associations at the crossroads of two organizational environments: Grassroots groups as part of an international movement and a local civil society." *Research in Social Science and Disability: Environmental Contexts and Disability* 8 (2014): 3–31.
30. Howell, Jude, and Jeremy Lind. "Manufacturing civil society and the limits of legitimacy: Aid, security and civil society after 9/11 in Afghanistan." *European Journal of Development Research* 21 (2009): 718–36. [CrossRef]
31. Ebrahim, Alnoor. *NGOs and Organizational Change: Discourse, Reporting, and Learning*. New York: Cambridge University Press, 2003.
32. Machetti, Raffaele, and Nathalie Tocci. *Civil Society, Conflicts, and the Politicization of Human Rights*. Tokyo: United Nations University Press, 2011.
33. Eschle, Catherine. "Globalizing Civil Society? Social movement and the challenge of global politics from below." In *Globalization and Social Movements*. Edited by Pierre Hamel, Henri Lustiger-Thaler, Jan Nederveen Pieterese and Sasha Roseneil. Basingstoke: Palgrave, 2001, pp. 61–85.
34. Biekart, Kees. *The Politics of Civil Society Building: European Private Aid Agencies and Democratic Transition in Central America*. Amsterdam: Utrecht International Books and the Transnational Institute, 1999.
35. Della Porta, Donatella, Massimiliano Andretta, Lorenzo Mosca, and Herbert Reiter. *Globalization from Below: Transnational Activists and Protest Networks*. Minneapolis: University of Minnesota Press, 2006.
36. Ghimire, Kleber. *Organizational Theory and Transnational Social Movements*. New York: Lexington Books, 2011.
37. Fisher, William. "Doing Good? The Politics and Antipolitics of NGO Practices." *Annual Review of Anthropology* 26 (1997): 439–64. [CrossRef]

38. Michels, Robert. *Political Parties: A Sociological Study of the Oligarchical Tendencies of Modern Democracy.* New York: Dover Publications, 1959.
39. Weber, Clare. "Women to Women: Dissident Citizen Diplomacy in Nicaragua." In *Women's Activism and Globalization: Linking Local Struggles and Transnational Politics.* Edited by Nancy Naples and Manisha Desai. New York: Routledge, 2002, pp. 45–63.
40. Thompson, Kirsten. "Women's Rights are Human Rights." In *Restructuring World Politics: Transnational Social Movements, Networks, and Norms.* Edited by Sanjeev Khagram, James V. Riker and Kathryn Sikkink. Minneapolis: University of Minnesota Press, 2002, pp. 96–122.
41. Masaki, Katsuhiko. "Recognition or Misrecognition? Pitfalls of Indigenous Peoples' Free, Prior, and Informed Consent." In *Rights-Based Approaches to Development: Exploring the Potentials and Pitfalls.* Edited by Sam Hicky and Diana Mitlin. Bloomfield: Kumarian Press, 2009, pp. 69–85.
42. Sikkink, Kathryn. "Restructuring World Politics: The Limits and Asymmetries of Soft Power." In *Restructuring World Politics: Transnational Social Movements, Networks, and Norms.* Edited by Sanjeev Khagram, James Riker and Kathryn Sikkink. Minneapolis: University of Minnesota Press, 2000, pp. 301–18.
43. Van Veen, Saskia, Barbara Regeer, and Joshe Bunders. "Meeting the Challenge of the Rights-based Approach to Disability: The Changing Role of Disability-Specific NGOs and DPOs." *Nordic Journal of Human Rights* 31 (2013): 359–80.
44. US Agency for International Development. "Uganda Request for Proposals." Available online: https://www.fundsforngos.org/usaid/usaid-expanding-participation-of-people-with-disability-and-strengthen-the-capacity-of-disabled-peoples-organization/ (accessed on 2 March 2016).
45. World Blind Union. "Third Round of Pacific Disabled Persons Organisation Fund." Available online: http://wbuap.org/index/funding/the-third-round-of-the-pacific-disabled-persons-organisation-fund-pacific-dpo-fund (accessed on 3 March 2016).
46. Disability Rights Fund. "Grantmaking." Available online: http://www.disabilityrightsfund.org/grantmaking (accessed on 15 July 2013).
47. ABILIS. "ABILIS Foundation Main Purpose." Available online: http://www.abilis.fi/index.php?option=com_content&view=article&id=9&Itemid=18&lang=en (accessed on 1 March 2016).
48. Open Society Foundation. "Disability Rights." Available online: https://www.opensocietyfoundations.org/topics/disability-rights (accessed on 3 March 2016).
49. Al Ju'beh, Kathy. "Disability and Inclusive Development Toolkit." *CBM*, 2015. Available online: http://www.cbm.org/article/downloads/54741/CBM-DID-TOOLKIT-accessible.pdf (accessed on 5 March 2016).
50. Geiser, Priscille, Stefanie Ziegler, and Ute Zurmuhl. "Support to Organisations Representative of Persons with Disabilities." Policy Paper 04, Technical Resources Division, Handicap International, Leon, France, July 2011. Available online: http://www.hiproweb.org/uploads/tx_hidrtdocs/SupportToDPO.pdf (accessed on 9 May 2016).
51. International Disability Alliance (IDA). *Guidance Document: Effective Use of International Human Rights Monitoring Mechanisms to Protect the Rights of Persons with Disabilities.* Geneva: IDA, 2010.
52. Derksen, Jim. "Editorial comment." *Challenger* 1 (1975): 1–2.
53. Disabled People International. "Dhaka Statement." Paper presented at World Council Meeting, Dhaka, Bangladesh, 28–30 June 2015.
54. Disabled People International. "About DPI." Available online: http://www.dpi.org/index.html (accessed on 1 March 2016).
55. Disabled People International. "Projects/Capacity Building Programme." Available online: http://www.internationaldisabilityalliance.org/en/capacity-building-programme (accessed on 1 March 2016).
56. Phillips, Sarah. "Civil Society and Disability Rights in Post-Soviet Ukraine: NGOs and Prospects for Change." *Indiana Journal of Global Legal Studies* 16 (2009): 275–91. [CrossRef]
57. Ncube, Jabulani. "Capacity build of disabled people's organisations in Mozambique." *Disability Knowledge and Research*, 2005. Available online: http://r4d.dfid.gov.uk/PDF/Outputs/Disability/PolicyProject_mozambique.pdf (accessed on 9 May 2016).

MDPI AG

St. Alban-Anlage 66

4052 Basel, Switzerland

Tel. +41 61 683 77 34

Fax +41 61 302 89 18

http://www.mdpi.com

Laws Editorial Office

E-mail: laws@mdpi.com

http://www.mdpi.com/journal/laws